William Washington, American Light Dragoon

William Washington, American Light Dragoon

* * *

A Continental Cavalry Leader in the War of Independence

* * *

DANIEL MURPHY

WESTHOLME
Yardley

This book is dedicated to my father,
First Mate Maurice F. Murphy,
U.S. Merchant Marine Fleet who served at sea from 1940-1947.

for Sadie

First Trade Paperback 2020

Westholme Publishing, LLC
904 Edgewood Road
Yardley, Pennsylvania 19067
Visit our Web site at www.westholmepublishing.com

ISBN: 978-1-59416-343-2
Also available as an eBook.

Printed in the United States of America.

CONTENTS

List of Maps

PROLOGUE

September 8, 1781
Eutaw Springs, South Carolina

The coral sun dawned hot and soon burned through the low-hanging fog that rolled across the indigo fields and thick low-country woodlands. First light found the American cavalry already on the move, horse hooves raising a cloud of dust from the baked clay road. The sounds of harnesses and arms jangled on the humid morning air.

Lieutenant Colonel William Washington of the 3d Continental Light Dragoons rode quietly at the head of his regiment. He was big for a light horseman–six feet tall with bearlike shoulders, a ruddy face, and clubbed brown hair. One of his commanding generals described him as the Hercules of his day, but a postwar portrait shows a common man sitting comfortably with no wig or hat, round honest features, plain face, and casual open stare.[1] By September 1781 he was twenty-nine years old, a six-year veteran of the conflict, and a medaled hero, having started the war as a junior infantry officer before earning a field command in the light dragoons.

Washington was born to a family of Virginia gentry and his distant cousin, George, was the commander-in-chief of all Continental forces. However, the younger William was far more comfortable in the saddle than in the formal parlors and drawing rooms frequented by his elder cousin. William's amusements were those most common among Americans of his day; he had a penchant for fast horses, cigars, and a good wager.[2] He was confident, good-humored, and friendly in disposition. But William was also known to be hot-tempered when his blood was up and always led from the front when he took his troops into battle.[3] This morning he had the honor to command the *Corps de Reserve.* Like everyone else on the march, he fully expected to see a stiff fight by day's end.

At the column's head rode Major-General Nathanael Greene, the commanding general of the Continental forces Southern Department. Greene was a master strategist and had proven his genius on more than one occasion. The general had been driving his men for several days, hoping to close with a British force their scouts had reported to be camped at nearby Eutaw Springs. All intelligence indicated the British had no idea Greene's force was anywhere in the vicinity.

First contact was made before the sun cleared the tall pines bordering the narrow road. A series of shots rang out ahead as the American van encountered a British scouting party. A sharp clash ensued and the British were driven back in a whirl of musket smoke, flashing broadswords, and charging horses. General Greene had found his quarry, and he now waved his men forward.

Drums rolled, colors unfurled, and the infantry bit open cartridges. Rammers scraped and sang against steel barrels to seat powder and shot while mumbled prayers ran through the ranks like a river's current. Officers barked commands, sergeants dressed ranks, and the first wave of troops stepped forward through fields of open Carolina timber.

British infantry deployed and muskets sputtered and crashed in growing volleys until a blazing fire ran from flank to flank. Artillery joined the mix, and sulfurous clouds of blue smoke billowed through the scattered trees as Washington and his light dragoons held their mounts in reserve. The fighting swayed back and forth as charge met countercharge. General Greene rode down the line yelling praises and calling for a final push to win the day. However, the right flank of the British line was anchored in a dense thicket of tight blackjack, and the cover it afforded was allowing the British foot soldiers to hold their ground and open an enfilading fire on the charging American ranks. Seeing victory ebb away, Greene now called for the reserve to clear the thicket of the British infantry.

The odds of cavalry charging a thicket of blackjack and carrying the position were extremely long, if not ridiculous or even suicidal. However, Washington brought his reserve forward, ordered his troopers to draw swords, and took his place at the head of the column. Spurs came back and horses rushed forward at a gallop. Swords flashed in the dappled sun and then a musket volley ripped through the charging light horsemen. Washington went down in a heap along with a third of his command and the British infantry rushed forward with bayonets at the ready. Trapped beneath his dying horse, Washington was nearly staked to the ground when a British officer intervened and took him prisoner. In less than a minute's time William Washington's role in the Revolution went from American hero to prisoner of war, and he soon penned the following letter to his commander:

> Eutaw. Sept. 8th, 1781
> Sir
> I have the Misfortune to be a Prisoner of war . . . I am not to be indulg'd with Parole on any Latitude. I have been treated politely by many of the British officers.
> I have the Honor to be yrs.
> Very H. Servt.,
> W. Washington[4]

The following pages will tell the story of William Washington's role in the war–how he rose to field command, what effect his troops had on multiple battlefields, and why a veteran of his experience and expertise attempted the impossible at the battle of Eutaw Springs.

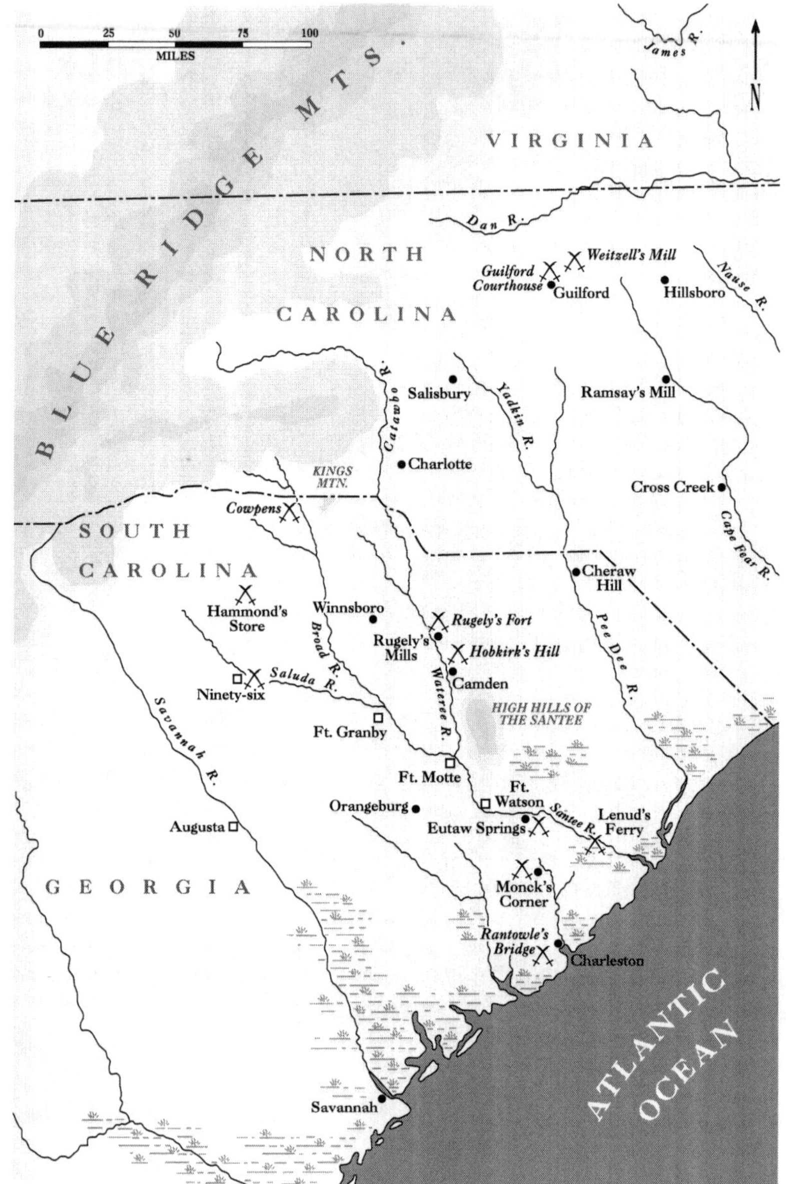

The Southern Theater during the American Revolution.

One

FORTUNE'S SON

"It is not now a time to talk of ought, but chains or conquest, liberty or death."–Joseph Addyson, Cato: A Tragedy, Act II, Scene IV

On February 28, 1752, Catherine Storke Washington gave birth to a son. Catherine's husband, Bailey Washington, named the newborn William, likely after Catherine's father, William Storke, the sheriff of Stafford County, Virginia. From his first breath William Washington belonged to the privileged class of colonial gentry spread throughout the American colonies. William's father, Bailey, was modestly wealthy and owned a 1200-acre plantation set in the bountiful eastern Virginia countryside beside Aquia Creek.[1] Unfortunately for young William, he was the second-born son of the family.

Despite not being heir to the estate, William grew up in a secure life of privilege, even though his father's holdings were decidedly middle-class compared to other landed families in the area. One example of this was William's second cousin, once removed, a Virginia planter and former militia officer named George Washington whose wealth and holdings fully eclipsed Bailey Washington's 1200 acres.[2] Nonetheless, William was still the son of a planter and a member of the colonial elite, albeit of modest standing. His father made a handsome profit off the 1200 acres, producing tobacco, corn, barley, and wheat while following the wildly successful English colonial model of using African slaves to work his land.

Southern cash crops of rice, indigo, and tobacco had lucrative export potential and differed greatly from the New England style of farming that was based more on cereal grains of wheat, barley, and rye. With rockier soil, shorter growing seasons, and limited export value, the profit margin of Northern crops was far narrower than that of the Southern cash crops.[3] This affected society in a number of ways. In the North, raw acreage held less value and there was less incentive to clear new farmland while communities looked to other interests. In the Southern colonies, landholders were inclined to invest in larger and larger tracts of land to yield higher profits and import more slaves to work the ever increasing tracts. Farmland was more valuable, and the distance between neighbors and towns grew exponentially.

This Southern sprawl had a direct effect on one aspect of eighteenth-century life in particular: horses. The greater distances resulting from cash crop farming required horses that could quickly travel over longer distances and not simply pull a plow like an ox. Horses and horse breeding became part of the Southern culture and horse racing became a favored pastime.[4] On Sundays and holidays all classes would gather elbow to elbow in Southern townships to watch and wager as local horses went sprinting down Main Street to the cheers of crowds that hoisted juleps and small beers. These short street races developed a breed known as a Quarter Miler, the foundation for today's American Quarter Horse.[5]

In addition, landed Southern gentry had their own more exclusive and rapidly growing past time, foxhunting. The first gentleman to have a pack of hunting dogs in the colonies was a well-to-do Londoner named Robert Brooke, who arrived in Prince Georges County, Maryland, on June 30, 1650. Brooke settled in with his wife, ten children, twenty-eight servants, and a pack of hounds.[6] By 1759, foxhunting was alive and well in Virginia and one of its greatest enthusiasts was William Washington's wealthy cousin, George Washington. The future general spent a great deal of his time breeding his own hounds and gave them such names as Musick, Mopsy, Sweetlips, and Truelove.[7]

Eighteenth-century foxhunting was the equivalent of today's extreme sports, in which enthusiasts wrestle whitewater, climb mountains, or parachute out of airplanes. Yet in the Southern colonies there was a secondary, social aspect, to foxhunting; it was what gentlemen did for sport, and most any landed Virginian's youth was spent learning horses and horse husbandry. We can only speculate that William Washington grew up like many boys in rural Virginia: swimming, hunting, and fishing, and then–once he entered his teens–riding in his first foxhunt.

Author Stephen Haller has documented much of William's early life in his prior biography, *William Washington: Cavalryman of the Revolution.* The young Washington attended the Aquia Episcopal Church and for formal education was tutored by the Reverend Doctor William Stewart, a rector of Saint Paul's Episcopal Parish in Stafford County, Virginia. Under the Reverend Stuart's supervision he received a typically liberal eighteenth-century education that leavened modern literature with a heavy emphasis on the ancient Greek and Latin classics in their native languages. After Washington completed his primary studies he decided to enter training for the ministry.[8]

The pulpit opened many avenues for young men from good families, especially second sons of wealthy estates. It may seem odd to modern readers that a future soldier of Washington's talents would first choose the pulpit, at least until one considers the time in which he lived. In colonial America, pulpits served as a point source of social commentary and leadership and many ministers were staunch advocates of justice and its secular pursuit.[9] By the 1770s the call for revolution rang throughout the colonies and William Washington's own tutor, the good Reverend Stuart of Saint Paul's Parish, was a leader to his congregation and a staunch public critic of George III and British policies.[10]

Virginia was an interesting social paradox in the years leading to the American Revolution. Virginia was the eldest, largest, and most populated colony prior to the revolution. She was one of the wealthiest among the colonies, and a true model of Mother England's colonial vision. Yet Virginia also gave birth to some of the most radical anti-English writers and orators of the period in George Mason, Thomas Jefferson, and Patrick Henry. All three of these rural revolutionaries were fervent members of the liberal Whig political party, which called for social change and a greater voice in Great Britain's political rule over the American colonies. Patrick Henry was one of the most outspoken critics early on and presented a series of resolutions in the Virginia House of Burgesses against the king's policies in 1765.[11] On the other hand, a large number of Virginians remained staunchly loyal to the king and were members of the politically conservative Tory party.

Prior to 1775, even ardent Whigs approached the growing crisis with Great Britain as disgruntled but essentially loyal subjects of George III. Their objections to the crown grew in the years after the French and Indian War, as the colonists began to chafe under the crown's arrogance toward the colonials' concerns and the ever-increasing series of tax increases imposed by the British Parliament, where American colonists had no vote. The Sugar Act (1764), the Stamp Act (1765), and the Townshend Acts (1767) all raised the ire of American colonists in turn.[12] William Washington's father and the Reverend Stuart both signed a formal protest of Stafford County freeholders that protested the British Parliament and "her attempts to enslave us."[13] Clearly this was no small event in William Washington's life as two of his closest role models went on public record opposing George III.

Matters finally came to a head in Massachusetts when angry citizens boarded three ships in protest and dumped several tons of tea into Boston Harbor. King George was deeply angered and the British Parliament imposed a series of harsh punishments for Massachusetts after the tea riot. The Port Act of 1774 shut down the Boston Harbor. Virginia and other sympathetic colonies sent aid to Massachusetts, which in turn strengthened internal ties between the colonies.[14] Deep feelings of animosity toward the crown were amplified across Virginia when other punitive measures were added for Massachusetts: all government positions would be appointed by the crown and no longer elected locally, town meetings were curtailed, and any royal official standing trial in the colonies would now be granted the right to have the trial moved across the Atlantic to the safety of England.[15]

American colonists were outraged by these new measures, and felt that if they occurred in one colony they could occur in all. Protests abounded in Virginia and the royal governor, Lord Dunmore, was soon so concerned with the anti-government sentiment that he retreated offshore to the safety of a British warship.[16]

Soon after Dunmore's retreat, the first Virginia Convention was convened and Thomas Jefferson's *A Summary View of the Rights of British Americans* was introduced. A second convention followed in March of 1775 where Patrick Henry called for his fellow Virginians to prepare the state militia to defend the colony against the crown. "The war is inevitable," boomed the famous speaker. "Let it come!"[17]

War was indeed coming. In the following month of April, shots were fired in Massachusetts and eight men were killed on Lexington Green. By day's end, forty-nine colonists lay dead along with seventy-three British soldiers. All knew there would be no turning back now, and the call to arms sounded across Virginia.

William Washington was engaged in his studies for the ministry when the first shots of the revolution were fired. Just how serious a divinity student he had ever been is hard to tell; he may have simply been an impassioned youth searching for something to follow. It is known that he answered the first call to arms in Stafford County, Virginia. On September 12, 1775, he was elected captain of his company.[18]

Two

HARLEM HEIGHTS

"No great dependence is to be placed on the eagerness of young soldiers for action, for the prospect of fighting is agreeable to those who are strangers to it."–Flavius Vegetius Renatus

AFTER HE RECEIVED HIS COMMISSION AS CAPTAIN, Washington's Stafford County Minute Men were amalgamated with other Virginian militias and designated the 3d Virginia Continental Regiment. Continental troops differed greatly from the militia. The militia was composed of citizen soldiers whose first calling was to their farms or trades and typically served in only a temporary capacity against local threats. Continentals, on the other hand, were congressionally sanctioned troops; a professional, standing force enlisted by the different states for long terms of service and trained in the same tactics and discipline as the professional armies of continental Europe.[1] Captain Washington and his eager regiment of fresh professionals were maneuvered about Virginia–marching, drilling, and marching some more without a glimpse of any combat whatsoever. It wasn't until the summer of 1776 that the 3d Virginia was ordered north to the front lines of the war.[2]

Meanwhile the main theatre of the war had drifted down from Massachusetts to New York, where a British force of some twenty thousand men landed on Staten Island in a bid to take the thriving port of New York in August of 1776. General Washington sat waiting for the British on Long Island with half that number and the veteran British troops swept the fledgling Continentals from the field in the first major battle of the war.[3] General Washington evacuated his remaining forces across the East River to the island of Manhattan and the British followed close behind where they landed a combined force of British and Hessian troops at Kip's Bay on the eastern shore of Manhattan. After a brief battle the British again routed the Continentals and captured the city of New York on September 15th. General Washington next retreated to the upper portion of Manhattan and deployed along high ground at Harlem Heights where he expected to be attacked yet again.[4]

The following morning found Captain William Washington and his fellow 3d Virginians at Harlem Heights waiting for orders. They had arrived too late to take part in the earlier fight for Kip's Bay, and that morning expected to be detailed to the work parties tasked with improving the entrenchments across Harlem Heights.[5] Before the Virginians started their work, a rolling skirmish erupted well forward of the lines. Continental drums rattled in reply, sergeants began to count files, ammunition was issued, and all picks and spades were set aside. The 3d Virginia was about to receive their baptism of fire.

Oddly enough it may have been a foxhunting call that first brought William Washington into combat. Before dawn Lieutenant Colonel Thomas Knowlton's New England Rangers were sent out to probe the British lines and a skirmish soon began between Knowlton's Rangers and some British light infantry. The fighting escalated, and when Knowlton realized he was outnumbered, he ordered a retreat with the British lights in close pursuit. The pursuing British began to blow "Gone Away" on their signal horns, the universal foxhunting call for a fox in full flight when the hounds were tight on his tail, and the British had clearly sounded the call as a direct insult against General Washington's Continentals.[6]

After he heard the call, Colonel Joseph Reed rode back to report the insult to General Washington. The insult grated on

Washington's honor and he decided to lay a trap for the cocksure British lights. He gave orders to make a small advance in the direction of the enemy so as to draw them down into a sunken lane while he ordered a second force to try and circle behind the British and cut off their retreat.[7]

Lieutenant Colonel Crary's Rhode Island Continentals formed the baiting force and the 3d Virginia's three rifle companies stepped off under Major Andrew Leitch with Knowlton's Rangers as the flanking force. Captain William Washington and the remaining musket companies of the 3d were held in reserve with their regimental commander, Colonel George Weedon.[8] Crary's men advanced toward the British lights and true to form the lights quickly deployed along with the 42d Highlanders, charging down the hill and taking possession of a fence row where they began firing on Crary's command. General Washington quickly supported the Rhode Islanders and committed the rest of General Nixon's brigade and the remains of Weedon's 3d Virginia, including Captain Washington's musket company.[9]

A smoothbore musket had an effective range of eighty yards on a man-sized target, and companies of infantry were used much like mobile artillery batteries; men were usually formed in solid blocks two ranks deep and marched by drum to within range of the enemy and then given the order to fire. With the troops massed together to fire disciplined volleys, the range was slightly extended. Infantry officers directed their men's fire at areas rather than individuals, and effectively launched land-borne broadsides of lead balls at the enemy. Reloading speed was critical in these brutal exchanges, and a trained infantryman was expected to fire three rounds a minute during combat in a strictly organized series of movements that was drilled by rote into every man in the ranks to ensure a high rate of fire. The two sides would typically trade volleys at maximum range until one side developed an advantage over the other through timing, terrain, or maneuver. The disadvantaged then generally gave way or risked suffering a bayonet charge.[10]

This was exactly the sort of combat William Washington had trained for and the first he took part in as his company advanced and fired at the British in a bid to pin the enemy in place and keep them occupied on their front.[11] The firing escalated rapidly as Leitch and Knowlton's riflemen maneuvered unseen through a rocky stand of timber to try and gain the British lights' right rear, but they came up short and instead fired into the British flank without sealing the rearward escape route. A close-range firefight now erupted on the British flank, and both Leitch and Knowlton were shot down as the British gave ground and retreated back up the hill under heavy fire from Weedon's and Nixon's pursuing musket companies. The British soon redeployed in a wheat field and urgently called for reinforcement from Hessian Jaegers and the main British reserve.[12]

The Continentals responded in kind and began pouring volleys into the British ranks. British artillery arrived on scene but still the American troops continued to press ahead. Colonel Reed and General Israel Putnam rode through the ranks and urged the Continentals forward in a bid to keep the momentum in Continental hands. Both sides fed still more men into the fight until the American line numbered 1,800 men, and by day's end the British had nearly 5,000 men engaged.[13]

The British then fell back from the wheat field and were pursued through an orchard until General Washington decided to halt the chase and claim victory. After being soundly defeated at Long Island and Kip's Bay, the Continentals could rightly claim a victory here among the hills of Harlem. British casualties were around 170 killed and wounded, and the Continentals suffered slightly less at 130 despite having been on the offensive throughout. Praise was passed all around. General Washington said the "troops charged the enemy with great intrepidity" and added the affair "seems to have greatly inspirited the whole of our troops."[14]

The fight for Harlem Heights was William Washington's first look at combat; casualties had been blessedly low among the musket companies of the 3d Virginia, and William had been lucky enough to enjoy a victory in his first fight. Luck wouldn't follow the younger Washington on every field, but it certainly had on his first.

Three

AN AMERICAN CRISIS

"Our All is at stake."
–George Mason to George Washington

THERE WAS LITTLE FIGHTING OVER THE FOLLOWING WEEKS, and General Washington was content to work on his defenses at Harlem Heights as the British busied themselves with their occupation of the city of New York and their efforts to quell the population within. Once settled, the British used their naval superiority to bypass the Continental line along Harlem Heights and leapfrogged a series of amphibious assaults that flanked the American position.[1] A string of sharp skirmishes took place at Throg's Neck and Pell's Point in October as General Washington retreated north from Manhattan to high ground on the mainland.[2] At White Plains he built a strong defensive line and waited for the combined British and Hessian force to attack. Posted on the far right were William Washington and his fellow 3d Virginians, who watched as Hessian artillery deployed and opened fire on the American line. The British 17th Light Dragoons then made a brilliant charge, which routed the American militia and drove them back in an utter panic.[3] In an effort to emulate their mounted comrades' success, the Hessian and British infantry charged forward at the main American line. The Continentals fired withering volleys into the advancing British and Hessian ranks. Casualties soared, but these professional Europeans endured the fire and kept coming ahead. Eventually they flanked the American left and forced the Continentals back in an orderly withdrawal.[4] Aside from the rout of the militia by British cavalry, the Americans had shown a marked improvement in their craft and fought well at White Plains. A Hessian lieutenant wrote that the Continentals "maintained their posts with extraordinary tenacity."[5]

Still, White Plains was yet another defeat for Washington's army in a growing list of reversals. The next American position to fall was General Washington's namesake, Ft. Washington, which capitulated on November 16 with three thousand men and over thirty pieces of artillery.[6] The devastating loss of the fort again forced General Washington to give ground, and his army began a ragged retreat across New Jersey for Pennsylvania and the fledgling nation's capital at Philadelphia.

The year of 1776 had opened with immense promise for America, with victories to the north when the British evacuated Boston, Massachusetts, and to the south when a British assault failed on Charleston, South Carolina. Now, as the year was coming to a close, providence had seemingly abandoned the cause of independence and with it the ranks of the Continentals. The once jaunty volunteers were now wrapped in rags and walked with bowed heads bent to the cold autumn wind. Their rations were running low, no one had been paid in months, and many were now walking barefoot as they made their way across New Jersey. Deserters left the army in droves, sickness plagued those who remained, and thousands more left as their one-year enlistments ran out.[7]

By now Captain William Washington and his 3d Virginia were attached to General William Alexander, Lord Stirling's Brigade, and posted as the rear guard for parts of the New Jersey retreat, where they fought repeated skirmishes with the pursuing British infantry, Hessian Jaegers and British Light Dragoons. This was a different sort of warfare than the young captain had trained for; the goal here wasn't to take ground or even hold it but rather to bleed the enemy with Fabian skirmishes and frontier-style ambuscades whenever an opportunity arose. Cold, tired, and growing disheartened, the Virginians did their best to make the British pay for every mile gained in the frost-ridden farms and thick wood lots of rural New Jersey.[8]

Despite the plummeting temperatures, the Virginians were still dressed in the lightweight hunting frocks they'd been issued in the heat of Virginia's summer.[9] After months of hard campaigning, these linen frocks and breeches were but rags and the Virginia troops were starting to suffer from the Continental Army's woefully inadequate supply system. Harsh weather, poor clothing, and scant food took its toll throughout the month, and by mid-December the 3d Virginia was down to just 140 men.[10] Nor was the 3d Virginia the only regiment in such a sad state. General Washington summed up the desperate state of the Continental Army as he described the 3d Virginia: "Weedon's, which was the strongest, not having more than one hundred and forty men fit for duty, the rest being in the hospitals."[11]

Unfortunately we have no record of Captain Washington's thoughts at this time. No memoir of his has ever been found, and what remains in his hand are only scant letters and dispatches. The record only shows that he was one of the remaining men fit for duty in his regiment. If William did write any letters home, it's doubtful they were very positive as the Continentals retreated west across the Delaware River and into Pennsylvania. The capital city of Philadelphia was now in a state of fundamental panic as citizens fled into the snow-swept countryside and the Continental Congress evacuated the capital and moved to Baltimore in expectation of the inevitable.[12]

On the eastern side of the river, the British commander General William "Billy" Howe watched the Americans limp into Pennsylvania and felt no sense of urgency to pursue them. In his eyes, the campaign for New York had gone swimmingly well. Ice floes had now started to drift down the Delaware River and Howe deemed it unwise to cross such a dangerous river, as boats could easily be crushed in the drifting ice and all aboard drowned in the freezing currents. Howe thought it far more prudent to cross the river in the dead of winter, when it was frozen solid and could bear the weight of his wagons and his army could simply walk across, or better yet, wait until spring–when, by most all predictions, Washington's rebel army would fall apart on its own without another shot fired.[13]

Howe decided on the prudent course. His army had seen steadily mounting casualties of late and his supply lines were growing longer and harder to maintain. Howe chose to let the winter's cold whittle away at Washington's amateur Continentals while his own professionals caught their breath, restocked their stores from local farmers, and found garrisons in western New Jersey. Howe's goal all along had been for American Loyalists to take control of their own affairs, and the time now seemed perfect in Howe's mind for the Tories to rise against the crippled American Whigs. With the winter holidays in sight, Howe turned his back on the Delaware River and faced toward the eager arms of his waiting mistress, the beautiful and alluring Mrs. Elizabeth Loring.[14]

Luckily for General Washington and his Continentals, the people of the surrounding farms and townships were a long way from surrendering. When needed most, local Whig militias rose against the occupying British and Hessian garrisons on their own accord. Bands of rebel patriots roamed the western New Jersey roads and shot down British and Hessian couriers whenever the opportunity arose. The Hessian troops General Howe had garrisoned along the Delaware River were excellent soldiers. In particular those stationed at Trenton under Colonel Johann Rall were the very same veterans who had stormed the Continental battle line at White Plains just two months prior, yet these sporadic attacks by local Whigs gave the Hessians little to no rest at all as the winter woods erupted in sporadic gunfire. The body count rose alarmingly and local resistance grew so extreme that Colonel Rall was forced to send 100-man escorts with couriers traveling the countryside.[15]

Meanwhile, on the far side of the Delaware, General Washington was trying to divine the proper course of action. By late December his adjutant Joseph Reed was being flooded with reports of the success the militias were having against the enemy in New Jersey. Reed in turn was urging General Washington to make some sort of demonstration against one of the enemy garrisons, and the garrison at Trenton was being reported as the most vulnerable.[16]

George Washington had been looking for an opportunity to strike a blow against Howe's troops since losing New York and he knew that his Continentals were in need of a victory to survive. Still, Washington feared that if he risked an attack and failed, all would surely be lost and he would very likely hang for treason along with many of his men. He also knew if he did nothing but wait for a miracle, then he could expect to face the same appointment with the gallows come spring. Something had to be done or all would be lost, so Washington called a meeting of his staff officers and put the idea before them.[17] It was quickly agreed that the Continental Army would cross the Delaware on Christmas night and attack the Hessian garrison at Trenton. They had but two days to prepare for the first general attack in the history of the Continental Army.

The Continentals formed in the afternoon on Christmas Day. The ground was flocked with snow and the high thin clouds drifting overhead warned of another nasty storm in the making.[18] Every man had three day's rations in his haversack, fresh flints for his musket, and sixty paper cartridges containing powder and ball. Columns were formed and drums beat the advance as the men began the march down to the banks of the Delaware.[19] Few knew where they were going, but most all believed that any change would be for the best.

Prior to Christmas a new pamphlet had circulated through the Continental camp by the author Thomas Paine. General Washington was so impressed with the work, he ordered the pamphlet to be read aloud as the men waited to move out.[20] Given the times it was aptly titled *The American Crisis,* and the brilliant prose Paine penned in the opening paragraph remains part of the American fabric to this day:

> These are the times that try men's souls: The summer soldier and the sunshine patriot will, in this crisis, shrink from the serv-

> ice of their country; but he that stands it now, deserves the love and thanks of man and woman. Tyranny, like hell, is not easily conquered; yet we have this consolation with us, that the harder the conflict, the more glorious the triumph.[21]

And the task assigned the Continentals that Christmas night would indeed be difficult. They would have to cross a river jammed with ice floes, split into multiple columns, make a ten-mile night march in the snow through enemy territory, and then make a near-simultaneous surprise attack on the enemy at dawn. Security on the march would be crucial to maintain order and allow for a surprise attack, and vanguards were selected to secure critical points ahead. One of the vanguards was put under the command of none other than Captain William Washington of the 3d Virginia. The young Washington's second-in-command was Lieutenant James Monroe, the future fifth president of the United States:

> The command of the vanguard, consisting of fifty men, was given to Captain William Washington, of the Third Virginia Regiment, an officer whose good conduct had already been noticed.[22]

Why William Washington was picked for this important post is still a bit of a mystery. He was relatively new to the front, but his conduct to date had apparently drawn the attention of his commanding officers. Monroe's use of the term "given" may imply that William volunteered for the assignment or that he may have been awarded the posting. Either way, General Washington was likely glad to have a relative he could trust up ahead securing the march.

William and his vanguard were some of the first troops across the river. They quickly assembled in the dark and marched inland to form their checkpoint at a crossroads en route to Trenton. A nasty, freezing mixture of sleet and snow began pouring from the sky as an especially bitter storm descended over New Jersey.[23] The vanguard quickly halted, secured rags about the locks of their muskets to keep them in firing order, and pushed on through the storm to their checkpoint.

> Captain Washington executed his orders faithfully. He soon took possession of the point to which he was ordered and, holding it throughout the night, intercepted and made prisoners of many who were passing through Trenton.[24]

A man named Riker from a nearby house approached; he cursed Lieutenant Monroe and tried to order the vanguard off. Monroe was about to have the quarrelsome man arrested, but Riker changed his tune when he realized the ragged-looking party forming the checkpoint was made up of American soldiers and not British or Hessians. Riker quickly brought them food and joined the expedition on the spot, announcing that he was a doctor and might be of use to them.[25]

Hours passed as the vanguard held their post while the crossing at the river continued slowly but steadily. General Washington sat on a crate through most of it, pelted with sleet and snow and watching the slow progress in patient agony as the tedious operation took much longer than expected. Colonel Knox's guns and artillery horses were the last to cross, and it was only through an extraordinary effort of boatmen and gunners that the deed was accomplished over the ice-swept river. Finally all were across and moving for Trenton with General Nathanael Greene's brigades taking the northern course and General John Sullivan's the southern. Both had orders to attack Trenton, force the outer guards, and push directly into the town center to keep the enemy from forming.[26]

Greene's column eventually linked up with Captain Washington's vanguard and struck out for the final approach to Trenton. Sunrise came and went, but the swirling snow and sleet was so thick it went largely unnoticed. Many marching in the main column were without shoes and the rags they had wrapped their feet with the evening before were now nothing but tatters. Officers reported seeing scores of blood-stained footprints in the freezing snow.

Despite the vanguard's best efforts the Hessians' post at Trenton had plenty of warning of the coming attack. A spy from Washington's headquarters had warned the British of the impending attack and Colonel Johann Rall, the Trenton post commander, had been warned Christmas evening of the Continental plans. In addition, a separate local force of militia who were unaware of General Washington's attack had earlier advanced toward Trenton as darkness fell and fired on Hessian pickets. Six Hessians were wounded in the assault, which threatened to ruin the Continentals' entire operation. An alarm was raised and the Hessians turned out two companies to search the roads and woods on the outskirts of Trenton, but the search yielded no result.[27] As previously mentioned, the Hessian garrison had endured weeks of sniping and ambush at the hands of the local militia and, contrary to legend, there had been no heavy drinking in the garrison to celebrate Christmas.[28] In addition, Colonel Rall had given strict orders that all his men sleep in their uniforms so they might respond to an alarm at a moment's notice. Luckily for the Continentals, the Hessians associated the militia attack with the earlier warnings.

Greene's column was an hour late when it finally halted at the edge of a field bordering the Pennington Road. Before them stretched a long open field, and scouts reported back that the first Hessian guard house sat perched on the far side of the field in a cooper's shop with separate pickets to either side.

General Washington quickly arrayed Greene's brigades into three separate columns: New England regiments on the right, Delaware and Virginians in the center, and Pennsylvanians on the left. On one command, the columns of rag-wrapped Continentals stepped out of the woods and trotted across the snow-swept field in the morning light. There were no trumpets, drums, or martial fanfare as the Americans quick-timed their way across the stark white field–only the sound of jostling cartridge boxes and feet crunching snow as General Washington rode forward before all. The Americans were halfway across the field before the Hessian pickets raised a shout and muskets cracked in the early morning air.[29]

Outnumbered, the Hessian pickets fell back toward town and raised the alarm just as the sound of musketry was heard coming from Trenton on the lower River Road. The booming of guns served as music to the ears of Generals Washington and Greene, for it meant Sullivan's southern column had arrived on the far side of town at nearly the same instant as the northern column's attack.[30] German kettledrums now spread the alarm and Hessian soldiers ran from their quarters and into the streets as American soldiers sprinted ahead to gain the town. The Hessian pickets fell back to the outskirts of Trenton and then rallied on a point of high ground to make a stand.[31] Lieutenant Monroe wrote: "Captain Washington moved forward with the vanguard in front, attacked the enemy's picket, shot down the commanding officer, and drove it before him."[32]

Continentals now surged through Trenton and opened a scattering fire on the Hessians as they attempted to form their ranks. Many Americans broke down doors and ran into houses to keep their weapons dry as they started firing from windows, doors, and porches. Unfazed, Colonel Rall remained calm under the growing onslaught of American musketry as he formed his men and pressed north along King and Queen streets, square into the maw of the American attack.

Artillery now joined the mix as the Hessians quickly deployed two guns along King Street and opened fire on the still-forming Continental gunners.[33] The crack Hessians fired twelve quick rounds at close range before the Continental gunners returned fire in a frenzied contest of flying grape and bouncing roundshot. The Continental guns outnumbered the Hessians, and they soon gained the upper hand with a greater concentration of firepower, driving the Hessians from the street. However, Hessian grenadiers quickly mounted a counterattack, and stormed back with drums beating and colors flying to retake the guns as the fighting surged up and down the narrow street.[34]

At this point William Washington led a charge against the enemy grenadiers holding the Hessian battery. Following behind were a mixed force of New England gunners whose cannon had just been dismounted by the Hessian's fire.[35] Washington's vanguard swept over the enemy battery and a stiff hand-to-hand fight followed as the Hessian Grenadiers refused to give up the guns. Men fell on both sides in a sudden brawl of bayonets, swords, and musket butts. A New England gunner who joined

Captain Washington's charge wrote: "My blood chill'd to see such horror and distress, blood mingling together, the dying groans, and garments rolled in blood."[36]

Washington was wounded in both hands during the fray, and the Hessian Grenadiers were finally driven off in a final push by the Continentals. Lieutenant Monroe then fell to a musket ball and was carried from the field spurting blood; the future president was later saved by the quick actions of none other than Dr. Riker, the belligerent man on the road who had cursed Monroe earlier that night.[37]

With the battery secured, the tide of the fight again shifted in favor to the Continentals. They rushed forward in clouds of musketry fired from streets, alleys, and houses, and drove the Hessians at all points. Colonel Rall attempted to rally his fleeing men and was shot from his horse in the process.[38] When the Hessians saw their commander carried from the field, the remaining 900 struck their colors and surrendered.

The entire battle lasted only half an hour. However, that single half-hour did more for the cause of American independence than any thirty minutes of combat before or since. General Washington and his men had turned certain defeat on the west bank of the Delaware to forbearance, resolve, and jubilation on the east. The victory at Trenton saved the war and forged the belief in the American people that they could, in fact, defeat King George and triumph in their cause.

William Washington had played no small part in the victory, and General James Wilkinson later wrote of the young captain's charge on the Hessian battery:

> These particular acts of gallantry have never been noticed, and yet could not have been too highly appreciated, for if the enemy had got his artillery into operation in [that] narrow street, it might have checked our movement and given him time to reflect and reform.[39]

In just four months at the front, William Washington had gone from a tidewater amateur to a noted officer of merit.

Four

CREATING THE CONTINENTAL LIGHT DRAGOONS

"An Army might be considered as a machine . . . it is not only necessary to have good material, but to know how to form and put them in motion."–Emanuel von Warnery, Remarks on Cavalry

At the start of the war there were few on the American side who foresaw a need for cavalry. Instead the emphasis was placed on infantry and artillery, as everyone knew a mounted arm would be massively expensive to build.[1] Even those few early proponents of a horse corps were forced to wrestle with the idea that no one expected the war to last long enough to justify the time and expense.

The British, on the other hand, began the New York campaign with two cavalry regiments that quickly proved their worth in scouting out Continental forces and screening British maneuvers from American eyes. The British horse also made two brilliant charges at the battles of White Plains and Indian Fields and broke American infantry on each occasion.[2]

By now, General Washington realized that the war was going to be anything but a quick run affair. He also knew a trained cavalry force would be needed if the Continentals expected to win the war, and so penned the following lines to Congress:

> From the experience I have had in this campaign, of the utility of horse, I am convinced there is no carrying on the war without them and I would therefore recommend the establishment of one or more corps.[3]

In January of 1777, the Continental Congress granted Washington's wish and authorized four regiments of Continental Light Dragoons. Each regiment was to be commanded by a full colonel with two additional field officers, a lieutenant colonel and a major, and six full troops of light dragoons composed of officers, non-commissioned officers, and thirty-two privates each. The 1st Regiment went to Theodoric Bland, the 2d to Elisha Sheldon, the 3d to George Baylor, and the 4th to Stephen Moylan. As commander-in-chief, General Washington reserved the right to appoint all field officers in the newly formed horse corps and when it came time to select field posts for Colonel Moylan's 4th regiment General Washington selected a young up and coming officer of proven loyalty, ability, and bravery. William Washington was still recovering from the wounds he received at Trenton when he was commissioned a major in the newly formed 4th Light Dragoons.[4]

Cavalry had progressed a great deal by the time of the American Revolution. Since the invention of stirrups in the 4th century, the horse soldier had seen a steady progression of arms, armor, and animal husbandry. Medieval knights had first mastered European shock tactics upon heavy, big boned horses and couched steel tipped lances under their arms to pierce enemy formations like mobile battering rams. At slower speeds these larger animals still gave every advantage to their riders in both leverage and momentum.[5] When it came to the medieval warhorse, bigger and slower was better for centuries running.[6]

However, the advent of gunpowder changed everything. The matchlock gave way to the flintlock and armor became a heavy nuisance. Tactics evolved, as well, and the next dominant cavalry weapon was thought by many to be the firelock over the lance or sword. Circular, *caracole* charges were designed whereby pistol wielding troopers rode up to the enemy and fired in a repeating merry-go-round of wheeling pistol fire. All shock value was lost and the results were mediocre at best.[7] The smoothbore pistols were woefully inaccurate beyond thirty paces and the range was even worse from the back of an excited horse in a battle line. Longer length carbines increased the range but required two hands to aim and fire and that simply wasn't practical when a horseman engaged an enemy at close quarters. Opponents countered by drawing swords, clapping spurs, and charging full bore through the weak gunfire to bowl over the mounted musketeers and cut them to the ground.[8] Frederick the Great once wrote of his cavalry:

> They were besotted with the idea of firing off their pistols. I finally had to make some straw dummies and I was able to show them that all their pistol shots missed, whereas they cut down every single figure with their swords.[9]

Cavalry had come full circle and the shock of the horse charge reigned once again.

European cavalry next evolved into two basic types: heavy and light. Heavy units of cavalry known as dragoons, guards, or cuirassiers, were mounted on larger, heavier horses and rode in the "high Spanish school" style of straight legs and long stirrups.[10] They specialized in making massed charges designed for breaking enemy infantry formations and carried straight-bladed thrusting swords, as the thrust was generally regarded as the best technique to use against enemy infantry. Heavy cavalry attacks were much like accelerated bayonet charges, where speed wasn't quite as important as compact, uniformed ranks to deliver the weight of the charge on large "heavy" horses.[11]

Light cavalry were mounted on smaller, lighter-bodied horses that were capable of both speed and stamina. Highly versatile, these new "light horsemen" relied on the speed of their horses rather than sheer mass to deliver the shock of the charge.[12] This new light cavalry was based on Hungarian militiamen known as Hussars who had fought against Turkish incursions in Eastern Europe for generations and whose eastern influences had taught them to use a curved sword, or *sabre.* The curved blades cut better than a straight-edged blade, and were also easier for a horseman to wield about his body and his mount's head, neck, and shoulders in the heat of a melee.[13] Hussars also rode with shortened stirrups to allow them to raise a hand's width above their saddles and generate more powerful cuts with their sabres.[14] These Hungarian horsemen excelled at reconnaissance and skirmishing and were typically detached on distant flanks and fronts to shield a movement from the enemy, lead the advance, or, in one of their most noted roles, sent in pursuit of a retreating or crumbling enemy line to create a rout.[15]

> A pursuing army is always impeded by the effort that is necessary to maintain its own order; whether from terror, for safety, or for rallying, the speed of the fugitive, is unrestrained. Hence, Cavalry are the military means for rendering disorder irretrievable.[16]

Frederick the Great's cavalry commanders, particularly General Hans von Zieten, then combined the hussars' scouting and skirmishing abilities with the legendary line discipline of the Prussian Army. By the mid-eighteenth-century, these newborn hussars were the epitome of light horsemen and were known throughout Europe as elite troops who could not only screen and pursue the enemy but also meet him in head-to-head battle with swirling sabre charges at the gallop.[17] Hussars wore extravagant uniforms consisting of an outer fur-trimmed jacket called a pelisse. Originally, the (pelz) was a wolf skin worn loose on the off-hand shoulder to snare and slow down enemy sabre cuts.[18] By the time of Frederick the Great the pelisse was an ornate jacket bestrewn with gleaming rows of buttons, lace, and fur but still worn slung casually on the off side of the hussar. An underjacket or dolman of equally resplendent lace and buttons was worn beneath.[19]

From head to toe, no expense was spared when it came to a hussar's uniform, and the courts of Europe soon decided that while the service of these specialized horsemen was necessary for every modern army, the flamboyant uniforms were not.[20] England also decided to limit the number of its hussar troops and soon developed their own form of light horsemen, which would perform the same duties of hussars but do so with simpler, less expensive uniforms. England named these new troops Light Dragoons, and the tactics they used in battle were based on the combat-proven trinity of a light horse charge: speed, surprise, and momentum.[21]

Speed

Any cavalry charge was a gamble. To improve the odds, mounted charges were not headlong gallops from start to finish. Charges typically began at a trot, progressed to a canter, and a gallop wasn't called for until the final one or two hundred yards. In this way the horses were not exhausted upon reaching the enemy and the troopers were able to maintain their formation and strike the enemy en masse to deliver their full shock potential. Attacking formations varied in frontage between columns, long deep formations with narrow fronts, and lines, wide platoon style fronts either two or three ranks deep. Emanuel von Warnery, a Prussian Hussar officer of the Seven Years War, recommended charging in a line three ranks deep. "A squadron formed in two ranks is very subject to waving, and much easier broken than one of three, which also must naturally have a greater weight in the shock, and be much more difficult for an enemy to penetrate."[22]

Surprise

A cavalry charge directed against formed infantry, poised artillery, or alert enemy cavalry was a dire proposition at best and rarely succeeded unless supported by some other martial arm or turn of event. Mounted ambushes, though incredibly effective, were difficult to execute. Cavalry commanders were more often presented with the opportunity of generating a surprise attack by striking an enemy force while that enemy was engaged and focused elsewhere. This way the enemy couldn't easily disengage from the first opponent and face up to the second threat of an incoming charge, which allowed the attacking force a better opportunity to take the enemy in the flank. Above all, timing was crucial and the window of opportunity was extremely narrow. A keen light horseman needed to have a sixth sense about him to know when to risk a charge; his patience, nerve, and perception in observing the enemy and seizing just the right moment to launch an attack were paramount. If surprise was effected it nearly guaranteed success.

Momentum

Beyond any weapon a trooper carried it was the horses' physical mass, coupled with speed, that consistently produced results in battle. With trooper, weapons, and kit aboard, each animal became a thousand pound missile that closed at over thirty miles an hour, drove through the opposing ranks, and broke the enemy apart.

The goal of a cavalry charge wasn't so much to kill the opposing troops but rather break their formation and destroy their discipline. Once the rout was on, a cavalry sword was at its most effective. However, sword work was just the latter part of cavalry combat. In most cases the issue was settled with the shock of the horses before the first sword blow ever landed. It was the directed mass of horses bowling through the enemy that broke the opposing ranks and created the rout. The attending sword blows, though brutal and potentially deadly, were secondary.[23]

British Light Dragoons excelled at this trinity of speed, surprise, and momentum, and quickly earned a reputation for charging through their enemies during the Seven Years War. They went on to capture the public eye at the Battle of Emsdorf in 1760 where they made a brilliant series of galloping charges and captured over a dozen enemy colors.[24] Sixteen years later, the British 17th Light Dragoons stampeded the American militia at the Battle of White Plains to prove the British hadn't lost a step by switching continents. Any American soldier of merit knew it would be a true challenge to raise a force of Continentals capable of going spur to spur with the British Light Dragoons.

Major William Washington reported for duty in February of 1777. His new commander was Colonel Stephen Moylan, an Irish-born Roman Catholic fifteen years William's senior. Moylan had been born to wealthy parents and was educated in Paris. He was engaged in the shipping business with his family at an early age, first in Spain, then in Philadelphia. His jovial nature and zealous anti-English politics won him many friends among Pennsylvania merchants.[25]

Moylan had joined the war effort early on, and quickly impressed General Washington, who appointed Moylan Muster-Master of the army in 1775. He next tasked Moylan and Colonel John Glover to secure and equip two armed vessels to harass British shipping interests. Moylan and Glover were successful in their task, and instead of two vessels General Washington soon had seven privateering rigs at his disposal.[26] Washington was so pleased with Moylan's character and performance that he briefly appointed him his aide de camp and then made him quartermaster general in June 1776. Unfortunately for Moylan, this came on the eve of the New York campaign and his two main supply lines, the Hudson and East rivers, quickly fell to British control despite Moylan's efforts at placing submersible *chevaux de friese* in the rivers to force English ships in range of Continental shore batteries.[27] This quixotic exercise was a patent failure, and the Continental Congress called for an investigation.

Moylan handled the affair with great composure and willingly resigned his position as quartermaster. Many men would have retired from the war altogether under such circumstances, but Moylan proved he was a better man than most by continuing to serve the cause as a mere volunteer with no pay or official commission. He fought at the battle of Princeton and served on Washington's staff until given command of the 4th Light Dragoons.

Moylan's second-in-command was Lieutenant Colonel Anthony Walton White. White came from an extremely wealthy family in New Jersey and attempted to gain a slot on General Washington's staff as his aide-de-camp. Washington felt White's personality and demeanor weren't up to the task, however, and dismissed him. White lingered around the outskirts of Washington's headquarters for several months in the hope that the commander in chief would change his mind. When that didn't happen, he used his father's influence to attain a field commission in the 3d New Jersey Infantry and, once there, was soon embroiled in a controversy of reported theft. White was arrested along with other officers, but after a lengthy trial over the course of several months White was acquitted of the charges.[28] White was still incensed over the affair a week later, and when he learned that a fellow officer might have been the cause of the charges, he burst into the man's quarters with his sword drawn and attacked the unarmed officer who quickly ran for cover. White then fled the scene and was later found in the woods with a small arsenal and claimed he was waiting to fight a duel with the officer he'd just attacked. White avoided a second trial when several influential friends intervened on his behalf.[29]

Why General Washington selected White for the post in the 4th Light Dragoons is unknown, but the commander-in-chief was not above playing politics; White's appointment may have had something to do with his family's immense wealth and influential connections. It is clear, though, that General Washington planned to keep an eye on the volatile young officer. He wrote a stern letter reprimanding White's recent actions and loose manner of talking, which often brought his "own veracity in question and trouble upon others."[30]

Finally, the major's commission in the 4th Light Dragoons went to William Washington. Colonel George Weedon, William Washington's infantry commander in the 3d Virginia, had recommend William be commissioned the Lieutenant Colonel of the 4th Light Dragoons over Anthony White but General Washington had declined on the grounds that such an advancement might be viewed as nepotism despite William's heroic actions at Trenton.[31] It's highly doubtful William Washington cared one way or the other; having grown up in the saddle he was no doubt thrilled to be awarded any commission in the light dragoons.

Yet the challenges of raising a light horse regiment in the cash strapped days of the revolution quickly became apparent.

Thomas Paine's *American Crisis* brought a wave of recruits to the ranks and, while there was no shortage of volunteers who wanted to join the cavalry, the initial drafts issued for the purchasing of horses proved woefully inadequate.[32] Not only were mounts hard to come by, so were uniforms, military horse furniture, and the specialized arms required of mounted troops: pistols, carbines, and proper horsemen's swords. The latter proved practically nonexistent in a country whose martial focus had been one of frontier defense in the dense woodlands of eastern America. In addition to lacking equipment, trained mounts, and weaponry, there were no experienced cavalry officers in the Continental ranks to drill the new recruits.[33] Growing up on horseback was one thing; knowing the multitude of logistical and tactical tasks in building and training a mounted regiment, leading them on the march, collecting intelligence, and engaging the enemy as a cohesive force was another altogether.

To fill this vacuum General Washington recommended Augustin Mottin de la Balme to the Continental Congress. De la Balme was a former French cavalry officer who had written two treatises on cavalry, and Congress named de la Balme inspector general of the cavalry in July 1777.[34] Since the four regiments of light dragoons were spread across Virginia, Pennsylvania, and Maryland, de la Balme hardly had a chance to make an impression on the distant commands. This was especially true regarding Moylan's 4th Light Dragoons, who took to the field before de la Balme's appointment was approved by Congress. In fact, there was such a need for cavalry, and Colonel Moylan was in such a rush to take the field against the British, that his men first appeared in the field in captured British uniforms of Madder red! After a nearly disastrous friendly fire incident, General Washington ordered the captured red uniforms be dyed a safer color.[35]

With the start of the new campaign, British General Howe decided against a direct crossing of the Delaware River and instead opted for an amphibious assault on Philadelphia from the southward through the Chesapeake Bay. General Washington moved south to defend Philadelphia with his new light dragoons posted forward of the army in two wings; Moylan's 4th and

Sheldon's 2d on the left, and Bland's 1st and Baylor's 3d on the right.[36]

This was the start of William Washington's active service as a light dragoon, and Moylan and Sheldon's regiments were the first to make contact with General Howe's advancing army in early September. They even forced the British van to briefly retire.[37] Overall, however, General Washington continued to give ground before the British and soon began preparing a defensive line south of Philadelphia along Brandywine Creek.[38] Howe's Army attacked on September 11 and again swept Washington's force before him. Despite the fact that all four regiments of Continental Light Dragoons were present, their reconnaissance potential went largely unused due to inexperience and lack of direction. Colonel Bland of the 1st Light Dragoons discovered the British turning movement but the intelligence wasn't processed effectively, and an hour was lost before the information passed to command level.[39] As a result, the British were able to execute a brilliant turning maneuver on General Washington's flank and drive the Continentals from the field.[40] The British then marched unopposed into Philadelphia and captured the capital.

The only bright spot for the Continental horse at Brandywine occurred when a foreign-speaking officer named Casimir Pulaski collected General Washington's mounted escort and led them in a charge against the British advance. The galloping charge temporarily stalled the British attack in a small section of the field and aided the American retreat.[41] Though Pulaski's attack hadn't changed the course of the battle, Washington had been duly impressed with the bold charge on the British. By this point General Washington had met a number of foreign officers with long lists of glowing recommendations, but few had lived up to their promise. However, Pulaski was a combat veteran, and seemed different. He was a Polish nobleman who had been fighting to free his own country from Russian domination, and despite a language barrier (Washington and Pulaski conversed in broken French) Washington found a sense of common ground with the man.

General Washington wrote to Congress that Pulaski "has been like us, engaged in defending the liberty and independence of his Country" and he recommended the foreign count be appointed a brigadier general of cavalry where "a man of real capacity, experience and knowledge" would be "extremely useful."[42] On September 21, 1777, the Continental Congress appointed Pulaski a brigadier general and he assumed command of all Continental Light Dragoons.

Just two weeks later, General Washington decided to make a surprise attack on British troops deployed at the village of Germantown outside of Philadelphia. The American army marched at dusk on September 3 and covered 16 miles overnight to attack the British at dawn in four separate columns.[43] The roads used for the advance were seven miles apart, and though Pulaski's brigade tried their best, it was nearly impossible to keep the different columns coordinated as they moved down pitch-dark roads on strange ground so close to the enemy.

A heavy fog descended on the march and slashed what precious little visibility there was to begin with, which made the mission even more difficult. As a result, General Washington's separate columns were unable to synchronize their efforts. Regardless, some of the columns enjoyed success in their initial attacks. A British officer later wrote: "Had their Light horse charged us . . . we must have been cut to pieces."[44] Yet that wasn't the case, as Pulaski failed to wield his two-week-old brigade with much skill. Washington's columns soon lost their initial momentum and a hard fight before a stone house blunted the advance of one of the columns for a half hour.[45] Elsewhere the ghosting fog prompted rumors to spread through the American ranks; unseen flanks were turned, and men came back on the run with news that the British had gained the American rear.[46] These rumors, some founded and some not, stifled the American advance and with it any ongoing success. The separate American columns were defeated in turn and forced to fall back one by one. Moylan's 4th helped cover the retreat, but overall the Continental horse was largely ineffective in the thick cloying fog that robbed them of their potential.

After the loss at Germantown, General Washington pulled his army back out of range of Philadelphia and he and General Howe skirmished with one another from various outposts ringing the former Continental capital. The following account relates a typical cavalry encounter fought between the lines by the two opposing armies:

> General Polasky [sic] (the commander of all our Light Dragoons) with a body of his troops attacked a body of the Enemy's Light horse . . . He sets no store by carbines or pistols, but rushes on with their swords . . . They had severe cutting and slashing; the enemy had 5 killed and two taken prisoners besides a number wounded. We lost one killed and two taken prisoners.[47]

As the armies settled into winter quarters, Pulaski began attempting to build his cavalry corps into a more organized force. Pulaski felt the Continental Light Dragoons were woefully deficient in trained officers and were being mishandled and distracted when in the field by requests from other officers outside the dragoons. The new brigadier wisely wanted to leave courier and orderly duties to militia horsemen and keep his corps of light dragoons available as a mobile strike force in the European tradition.[48] He ordered all regiments of light dragoons to adopt a Prussian-styled drill after that of the renowned Frederick the Great's cavalry, appointed a riding master to oversee the training, and ordered all regiments into quarters at Trenton over the winter so they could drill as one brigade.[49]

These were all astute, necessary changes that had to be made if the Continental Light Dragoons were ever to become an effective combat force–particularly the rejecting of outside courier duties and standardizing the drill.[50] However, Pulaski's royal bearing and aristocratic manner–learned in European courts–didn't sit well with most Continental officers, who were typically independent-minded and bristled at any breach of social equality. That, coupled with Pulaski's limited grasp of English, created an uneasy gulf between the Polish patriot and most of his American officers.

This was particularly manifested in Pulaski's quarrelsome relationship with Colonel Stephen Moylan, William Washington's commanding officer. Strangely enough, Moylan had been born abroad and educated in France, and of all the American Light Dragoon officers, would seem to have had the closest common ties with the European-born Pulaski and his foreign staff. Yet the opposite proved true, and the tension came to a head when one of Pulaski's officers, Jan Zielinski, took umbrage at an off-hand remark uttered by Moylan. Zielinski replied by insulting Moylan, who responded by striking Zielinski. Moylan was arrested, brought up on charges and cleared.[51] Tensions continued to escalate and Moylan was later unhorsed by one of Pulaski's lancers on the drill field.[52] Exactly what role if any William Washington played in this series of events is not known, but he most assuredly sided with his commanding officer, and, following the strict civil etiquette his elder cousin and commander-in-chief lived by, knew to keep his mouth shut as much as possible!

There was certainly plenty of work to be done elsewhere that winter as General Washington arrayed his troops in a broad arc that stretched from Valley Forge across New Jersey to New York, and the Continental Light Dragoons were constantly engaged in gathering food and forage and had frequent skirmishes with the enemy.

Meanwhile, circumstances and personalities continued to frustrate Pulaski's efforts to build a cohesive brigade of light dragoons. Even quartering the different regiments close by for combined drill was proving impossible as there wasn't an available location offering enough space, forage, and shelter for all four regiments and their horses. As winter came to a close the disheartened Pulaski decided to resign his post and form his own legion of lancers and light infantry. General Washington accepted his resignation and wrote Congress explaining that Pulaski "labored as a stranger not well acquainted with the Language, Genius and Manners of this Country."[53] Washington went on to recommend Pulaski for the appointment of forming his own legion, and Congress duly approved the measure.

Had Pulaski been able to coordinate the differing light dragoon regiments into a single cohesive force, there is no doubt the benefit would have been substantial–but the timing simply wasn't right, and resources were particularly hard to come by during the winter of Valley Forge. Colonel Stephen Moylan was named Pulaski's successor as corps commander, and, perhaps in a mild rebuke, Moylan was not promoted to brigadier general but rather brigade-major of the Light Dragoons.

By the start of the 1778 campaign, Major William Washington had served for one year as a field officer in the Light Dragoons and, with Moylan's promotion to brigade command, his duties were about to increase. This proved to be a threefold increase as Lieutenant Colonel Anthony White left the 4th Light Dragoons on detached service with Generals Dickinson and Scott, and Major Washington effectively became the 4th's day-in, day-out commander from spring through summer.[54]

The campaign opened with a new British commander, General Sir Henry Clinton, who decided to retreat from the more remote Philadelphia and pull back to the city of New York with its larger harbor and greater logistical base. The opportunity to strike the retreating British was apparent to both sides and as the British began their march Moylan sent his light dragoons into the field to scout and harass the British column on their route across New Jersey. A deadly game of hide and seek developed as Moylan's regiments tried to pry and dodge their way past the British cavalry screen and keep General Washington apprised of British troop locations and lanes of march, especially in regard to the British wagon train and rear guard.[55] The excellent flow of information provided by Moylan's horsemen prompted General Washington to act and he soon had the Continental Army poised to deliver a crushing blow on the British rear guard at Monmouth Courthouse, New Jersey. The light dragoons had proved their worth, and all the pieces were in place on the morning of June 28 as General Washington ordered the American advance to attack the British rear guard. The advance would be led by General Charles Lee while General Washington moved the rest of the Continentals forward for the fight. Lee's advance struggled through rough terrain and Lee dawdled in his approach. The British, responding to information from an American deserter, turned and attacked first. When Lee saw the British columns of horse and foot, he ordered a retreat with hardly a shot fired.[56]

General Washington was with his main column when he heard that Lee's advance guard was in full retreat, and he promptly spurred to the front and confronted General Lee in front of the troops. Washington, in a loud fury over what he saw as a squandered opportunity, dismissed General Lee and then tried to salvage the American attack.[57] The result was the disjointed battle of Monmouth Courthouse, and casualties quickly mounted as the two sides fought toe to toe for several hours in the sweltering summer heat. American fire turned back a British cavalry charge and several infantry attacks, and in the end General Washington's Continentals succeeded in holding the field despite the best efforts of the British to break the American line. Technically it was a draw, but the bruised and bloodied British limped away at day's end, and the morale of Washington's army soared as they stood and watched the British retreat from the field.

The following day Moylan's 4th struck the retreating British in classic light-horse fashion, and the 4th captured "one Captain, and one Ensign with two privates prisoners and killed a few more."[58]

The rest of the year saw the two armies square off against each other in a standoff. The British occupied Manhattan and the lower Hudson River while the Continentals fortified the surrounding counties across New York and New Jersey. Feints, raids, and small-scale attacks were made against each other, but neither side gained any real advantage of note, though the cavalry and light infantry were constantly employed in sharp skirmishes between the lines.[59]

One incident in particular had a watershed effect on William Washington's career. In the early morning hours of September 28, Colonel George Baylor's 3d Light Dragoons were attacked in a devastating night raid led by British General Charles "No-Flint" Grey. Grey had earlier earned his moniker at the battle of Paoli in September of 1777, when his forces led a surprise night attack on General Anthony Wayne's camp of Continentals. Grey had his men remove the flints from their muskets on the approach march to ensure against any accidental or unordered shooting that would give away their approach. Grey's men attacked with their bayonets when they came in range and devastated the American camp with a surprise bayonet charge in the dead of night. Just a year later, Grey employed similar tactics against Colonel Baylor's command and was equally successful. The naive Baylor had allowed his men to be lulled into complacency with false assurances and liberal doses of applejack brandy from a Tory farmer and his pretty daughters, who posed as Whigs even as they sent word to the British. As Baylor's men slept, Grey and his men stole forward in the dark of night and made their attack on the sleeping Light Dragoons. Roughly half of Baylor's command were bayonetted in their bedrolls. Others were killed as they grabbed for their swords or pistols, and Colonel Baylor was wounded and captured.[60] It was a devastating blow to the Continental Light Dragoons, and altogether Baylor lost two thirds of his command–along with his executive officer Major Alexander Clough, who was killed in the attack.

George Baylor was a personal friend of General Washington, and the commander-in-chief was stunned by this devastating blow to his Continentals. Still, Washington realized a new commander would be needed to collect, reform, and lead the remains of the 3d Light Dragoons. The 3d was also a Virginia-based regiment, and the commander-in-chief quickly recommended a fellow Virginian to the post. He selected his cousin, William Washington.

Five

FIELD COMMAND

"The officers must acquire an absolute authority over their men, and never suffer them to attack the enemy, or to break, under any pretense whatsoever, before they receive orders for it."
–Regulations for the Prussian Cavalry

William Washington traveled to Maryland and assumed command of the 3d Light Dragoons in November of 1778. Newly promoted to Lieutenant Colonel, he took the reins in the shadow of the very popular Colonel Baylor, and the regiment was often referred to as Baylor's horse throughout the war.[1] Washington inherited a shattered regiment with morale at an all-time low, and he spent the winter months on the drill field with his remaining troops as he rebuilt the regiment and selected new officers and recruits.

The perfect light dragoon candidate was young, in his late teens or early twenties, had grown up in the saddle, and was either lean in build or small in stature. No commander wanted his mounts to carry more than they had to, and the more a rider weighed the more wear and tear he placed on his mount. A typical recruit for the 3d joined through their headquarters in Virginia where he would be sworn in and turned over to a sergeant. Recruits were first taught to march in ranks and then instructed in the use of the broadsword, which began with learning the proper balance and footwork on the ground. Broadsword fencing was mostly about the cut and this technique applied to all horsemen's blades at the time. In the eighteenth-century the terms broadsword and horsemen's sword were practically interchangeable. The term applied to true broadswords with straight double edged blades, the more common horseman's backsword with straight single-edged blades, and curved sabres in the style of the European hussars. All these weapons were capable of both thrusts and cuts, but the extra forward balance and flat cross section of these "broad" blades made them better suited for cutting and slashing than lighter thrusting blades built with diamond-styled cross sections more commonly known as small swords, rapiers, or epees.[2]

Once the recruit had learned his footwork, he moved on to learning the system of basic, hanging, and compassing broadsword guards. He was next taught the basic cuts and the lunge, or thrust.[3] As recruits learned these ground skills they were also taught mounted drill, the military way to pack and load a saddle, how to care for their mounts on campaign, and the system of myriad commands and trumpet calls used for marching in the ranks and shifting fronts from column into line, all of which needed to come as second nature by the time they took the field. This time also served as a weeding-out period for both men and mounts alike, and those who didn't possess the proper stamina and temperament were shuttled elsewhere.

After the recruits had demonstrated a working knowledge of both fencing and mounted drill, they were taught to wield their swords from the saddle, and they trained by striking head-sized targets as they galloped past and sparring with wooden sticks. Fighting with a broadsword on the ground was largely about one's footwork and the better riders quickly proved to be the better swordsmen when in the saddle.

Continental Light Dragoons also carried pistols but they had proved to be secondary weapons in combat and better served for use as a warning device when on guard or vedette duty. Much like the earlier European experiments with the *caracole,* the

Continentals had learned to resist the temptation to shoot at their enemies and instead charge home with broadswords aloft.

> Fire arms are seldom of any great utility to cavalry during an engagement . . . Indeed there is little hope of success from any who begin their attack with the fire of carbines or pistols . . . It is by the right use of the sword they are to expect victory.[4]

Having a sword as their principle arm separated light dragoons from other soldiers of the day; artillerists killed from long distance, riflemen worked as snipers from one to two hundred yards out, and infantry would occasionally use the bayonet–though their principal arm was the smoothbore musket, with an optimal range of fifty yards. It was only the light dragoon who expected to meet his enemy in hand-to-hand combat every time he was engaged. Therefore, a light dragoon had to believe he was good enough to charge through his enemy, sword in hand, and come out the other side in one piece. Other military arms certainly inflicted greater casualties, but when light dragoons closed they were expecting a knife fight every time. It was no easy task to take aim and kill a man by pulling a trigger from fifty yards, but another thing entirely to rise up in the stirrups and cut the enemy to the ground from three feet away: close enough to read the fear on his enemies' face and feel his blood spatter back when landing a blow.[5] Light dragoons may have been typically small in stature but they had to possess hearts as big as their horses to repeatedly enter combat with such intent.

At the same time a light dragoon had to exhibit enough control and self-discipline to not go tearing off on his own like a murdering banshee; sabre charges were still disciplined attacks, not the wild rushes of Norse Beserkers. If the charging force frayed before hitting the enemy the shock of the charge could be lost altogether, and therefore discipline was paramount.[6] Upon impact the attacking ranks would nearly always break apart and lose their order as they passed through or collided with the enemy, and it was crucial that troopers continued to listen to the trumpets, heed commands, and continue to fight as a unit even as they worked at cutting down the enemy. A squadron could be broken and scattered only to ride clear, reform, and charge back again in a series of reversals and countercharges until attrition, frontage, or surrounding events ended the melee. Self-control was crucial; if the recall was sounded on the trumpet, all troopers had to break off whatever combat they were engaged in and rally back immediately to reform the ranks, or risk being cut off from their troop and surrounded by the enemy. Such attributes were difficult to teach and good recruits were hard to come by.

As he trained his new command, William Washington attempted to procure horses and equipment from the Continental Congress. Now removed from the front lines, the adrenaline-driven Washington must have been irritated at the endless blizzard of warrants and requisitions required to refit his regiment and his recent experience as the 4th's executive officer surely served him well in his new post. Yet as he toiled indoors with quill and ink the war began to take on a new aspect that was to have far reaching effects.

Back in New York, General Sir Henry Clinton was exploring a different strategy. To date the British had taken both New York and Philadelphia; however, the Americans had merely shifted their capital and continued to resist. After the British retreated from Philadelphia, the war stalled outside Manhattan, and Sir Henry was now looking south in a bid to cripple the lucrative exports of Georgia, the Carolinas, and Virginia to sink the American economy, which continued to fuel the American war effort.[7] Clinton's new plan was to first invade Georgia and gain control of the lucrative rice trade ruled by the patriot planters. Known as rice kings, these wealthy planters inhabited the southern seaboard and tended to be staunch Whigs in open opposition to the crown. Clinton planned to first cripple the rice kings of Savannah, and then move on toward Charleston, South Carolina, where an even larger base of patriot wealth resided. With the powerful rice king's subjugation, Clinton was hoping to incite an insurrection among the reported thousands of yeomen Tory loyalists in Georgia and South Carolina, who were said to be hiding in plain sight and keeping their heads down under the present patriot Whig administration.[8] With local Tory support British troops would then move up the rice coast to capture the tobacco and indigo fields of North Carolina and Virginia, wrecking the fledgling Americans' ability to raise capital, and bringing an end to the war.

Following this planned course, Clinton sent an expeditionary force under Archibald Campbell to the Georgia coast, and Savannah fell to the British in December 1778. The British under Campbell then moved inland and began to explore overland routes for an attack on Charleston.

Aware of this developing shift in the war, William Washington quickly tried to have his new regiment posted southward where more funds would naturally be directed. General Washington replied, "I see no prospect at present of any other troops going to South Carolina besides Polaski's [sic] Legion."[9] However time would tell a different story as the British continued to step up the pressure on Charleston. General Benjamin Lincoln, the Southern Department's Continental commander, alerted Congress to the dire situation at hand and in late May William Washington received orders to move his 3d Light Dragoons to South Carolina.[10]

It was one thing to order the 3d to depart for the southern front, but they were still badly in need of horses after the "Tappan Massacre" in September, where they lost a large number of men and mounts in northern New Jersey to a British night time suprise attack, and were therefore unable to take the field without the funds to procure replacements. As a result, Washington was only able to send a single troop south under Captain John Smith, while the rest of his regiment remained with him in the north awaiting money to purchase more mounts. Both the elder and younger Washington were frustrated by the lack of resources, and General Washington wrote the Continental Board of War:

> With respect to Baylor's regiment [the 3d Light Dragoons] I am at a loss to know what to say. If the dragoons were available their services might be very essential; but as this is not the case, I can not tell how to advise the unassured.[11]

Even the commander-in-chief's prodding of Congress failed to produce additional funding. Suitable mounts were scarce throughout the war and therefore expensive, which caused Washington and the rest of the 3d to cool their heels with a small collection of horses that allowed them to train and perform small escort duties but little else. William was even having trouble with his own personal mounts. As a field officer he kept three, and of those one was lame and another with foal, prompting William to write Colonel Alexander Spotswood in Fredericksburg, Virginia, to purchase another sturdy mount for him and confine the color to a "good bay."[12]

The two Washingtons traded a number of letters over this period, and in reading them one can sense the cousins were not all that close. George's letters to William are very straightforward and to the point, lacking the warmth seen in letters he wrote to another cousin, Lund Washington, or to his friends such as Stephen Moylan and the captured George Baylor. Some of this may have been due to age and circumstance. George was twenty years older than William, and unlike William, George had lost his father at an early age. He afterward followed a rigid personal, social, and civil code to lift himself in society and maintained that code throughout his life. In personality George was stoic, deliberate, and measured, and though not necessarily cold to others, John Adams said he "enjoyed the gift of silence."[13]

The younger William, on the other hand, was cut of a different cloth. He had a far less stressful childhood than his cousin and was described as "lively" and "upright." William was the sort who would rest his hand on a friend's shoulder as he walked through camp telling a funny story, and even became close friends with some of his non-commissioned officers–a crossing of social and military boundaries the elder George would have never sanctioned.[14] Both George and William were brave before the enemy, possessed explosive tempers, and were magnetic leaders.[15] However, each did it in his own way, with George acting the reserved, old-world patriarch, and William affecting the rough confidence and casual traits of a landed country squire.

Months passed as William drilled his troops, waited for funding, and continued his recruiting efforts. In the meantime a combined French and American force set out to recapture Savannah and secure the American southern flank in September of 1779.

Despite a gallant effort to breech the British lines, the attack failed, and the allied force sailed away after suffering heavy losses.[16] Among those killed was Brigadier General Casimir Pulaski, who fell to cannon fire during the failed assault.

The drafts for new mounts were finally allocated in December 1779 and the 3d promptly moved south to join with Captain Smith's prior troop.[17] Washington left for the Carolinas with 120 troopers, kitted in the regiment's French white dragoon coats with blue facings, broadswords, and black leather helmets with white horsehair crests. Snow, rain, poor winter roads, and tardy forage drops delayed their progress and it wasn't until February 1780 that Washington's 3d Light Dragoons rode into Charleston, South Carolina.[18]

Six

INTO THE LOW COUNTRY

"In an open country, an active, brave, and well disciplined cavalry, will frequently decide the fate of a battle."
–Emanuel von Warnery, Remarks on Cavalry

By 1780 the low country of South Carolina was the richest region in America, and the landscape was far different from the Jersey wood lots and tidy, rock-walled Hudson valley farms Washington and his men had grown accustomed to. Here palmetto palms, salt grass, and cattails filled tide pools and marsh while massive oaks towered overhead and strings of Spanish moss drifted down like giant horsetails. Rivers and maritime forests teemed with fish, oysters, deer, turkey, whooping cranes, alligators, and brightly plumed parakeets, and the countryside was dotted with the grandest plantation homes seen anywhere in America: giant columned structures with wrought iron gates, slate roofs, paved carriage circles, and private gardens larger than the village greens of many New England towns. If not for the clouds of summer mosquitoes and outbreaks of yellow fever, the low country of South Carolina would have been the most inhabited portion of North America.

The region's fortune centered on rice, rum, and slaves–the triangle built upon Mother England's African slave trade–and

Charleston was the social, cultural, and capital center of that wealth. The city itself sat at the southern tip of a peninsula surrounded by a vast inland harbor that shielded Charleston from the unpredictable ravages of the Atlantic. At first glance Charleston was a bustling collection of tall sails bobbing in the harbor, elegant townhomes gracing cobblestoned streets, and whitewashed church spires stretching toward the sky. Charleston was trade, riches, and sheer New World magnificence.[1]

At the time of William Washington's arrival it was also a city preparing for war with soldiers and slaves working side by side at forming siege walls and shoring up artillery batteries. The streets were an awkward jumble of carts, artillery caissons, and fine carriages as wealthy civilians dressed in the height of fashion strolled past muddy, swearing soldiers that dragged cannons into place and marched in rote step down tree-lined streets of elegant townhouses. Charleston's wealth was unmatched on the continent, its displays were surreal by all accounts, and yet the looming threat of invasion was gaining strength with every passing day.

Sir Henry Clinton had tried taking Charleston earlier in the war in 1776. The first attempt had been a two-pronged attack as the Royal Navy boldly sailed into the harbor with cannons ablaze to land an assault force.[2] The British ships were savaged by shore batteries, and the assaulting infantry raked with American musketry and grapeshot. His Majesty's ships soon sailed away in defeat, and the Americans counted it as one of the great victories of the war. Now on his second attempt, Sir Henry was taking a far more conservative approach. This time he opted to place some 11,000 men on the chain of coastal barrier islands south of Charleston and work his way across the maze of rivers, marshes, forests, and rice dykes in a slow, methodical land assault upon Charleston. As Clinton's infantry worked its way inland, the British fleet would block the Charleston harbor and cut off any American support from the Atlantic.[3]

Tasked with defending Charleston and its wealth was Major General Benjamin Lincoln of Hingham, Massachusetts. Lincoln had only 4,000 men to defend the city and its approaches against

Clinton's army of 11,000, but he did have one advantage in the horse-rich American south: cavalry.[4] As Clinton landed, Lincoln ordered Colonel Daniel Horry (pronounced *Or-ee*) to keep a constant force of dragoons in the field observing and harassing the British advance, which, due to the multitude of marshes, rivers, and tide pools was largely restricted to the established roads, causeways, and foot trails of the low country. Horry didn't disappoint, and kept a rolling reconnaissance of these routes with Majors John Jameson's 1st Light Dragoons, Hezekiah Maham's South Carolina Horse, and Paul Vernier's (pronounced *Vern-yae*) American Legion Lancers. Totaling only two hundred men, these fleet horsemen rendered excellent service and made a series of swift, debilitating attacks on British patrols and foraging parties.[5] By the time Washington arrived with his 3d Light Dragoons, the British already had a healthy respect for the American cavalry in the area.

Washington was familiar with many of the men in Colonel Horry's camp. Major John Jameson was a veteran of the 1st Light Dragoons and had been in temporary command of the regiment since Colonel Theodoric Bland resigned in December 1779.[6] Washington may have also been familiar with Major Pierre-Francois Vernier, who commanded the remaining troops from General Pulaski's American Legion. Pulaski and his legion of lancers and light infantry had been some of the first troops to come south and defend the new southern front opened by the British when they took Savannah, and Pulaski had been killed during the failed French and American attempt to retake Savannah by storm.[7] Vernier had since assumed command of these foreign-born patriots and their unique pole arms, which harkened back to the days of medieval lancers.

In the hands of a trained lancer, the eighteenth-century lance was an incredibly effective thrusting weapon with a much longer reach than any sabre or broadsword. Fought one-on-one, and in open space with room to maneuver, a well-trained lancer was nearly always the victor over a swordsman–as Colonel Stephen Moylan had discovered one day at drill with General Pulaski's lancers.[8] These six-foot lances were also superior to the sword when fighting against infantry as the longer reach eclipsed that of a bayonet in the initial charge. In addition veteran European infantry had learned that one of the best survival tricks to employ when ridden down by sword-bearing cavalry was to simply lie down on the ground; by their nature horses will rarely ever step on a prone body and a broadsword, swung or pointed at the ground from the saddle is at the very outer limit of the weapons' range. A lance, on the other hand, was brutally effective against anyone foolish enough to play dead before the weapon.[9] Finally, a lance offered yet another advantage. Where the wooden shaft joined the steel tip was the pennon, a series of tassels and bright ribbons. Lancers used these fluttering pennons to distract opposing horses; if horses weren't trained to ignore the flapping ribbons, they could be unnerved at the sight and sound of them and refuse to close.[10]

Why, then, didn't the Continental Light Dragoons adopt the lance as Pulaski had with his legion?[11] First and foremost was the fact that most Americans just didn't like the lance–or Pulaski! Another was that the lance was only as good as the lancer and mastering the lengthy weapon was difficult and took years of practice, but most of all it came down to the nature of a cavalry fight. Melees were rarely one-on-one combats in open fields but rather more like small riots, with dragoons fighting in packs like wolves–slashing, ramming, and careening off one another at speed. In these crushes of men and mounts the lance was often too long and proved cumbersome. Sword-bearing cavalry had learned to deal with lancers by charging in close with sufficient numbers to jam the field, parry the first thrust of the lance, and spur up inside the lance's longer range, where a sword was faster and more effective.[12]

The lance was also a pointing weapon, and both British and American troopers seemed to prefer the edge over the point. While it was faster to deliver the point of a sword, there was always the chance a thrust blade would become embedded within the opponent's body, or caught within the enemy's kit or saddle furniture, and in the twisting, tussling speed of a mounted fight a pointed sword might not be able to be withdrawn from an enemy without breaking the sword or unhorsing the owner due to the sword knot about his wrist.

Instead light dragoons preferred to cut and slash with the edge of a proper horseman's blade, which offered far greater knock-down power, instant results, and less risk of a snag. Troopers' swords of the eighteenth century were not kept razor-sharp but were honed more like a butcher's cleaver, so that a trooper could hang the sword from his wrist by the sword knot and switch back and forth between pistol and sword with a quick flick of the wrist and not cut himself or his mount to ribbons as the sword dangled at his side.[13] This meant horsemen's swords acted more like steel whips than scalpels. Even with a curtailed edge, a well-compassed cutting stroke made from the back of a speeding horse delivered vicious concussive blows that cracked skulls and elbows, cleaved muscle and bone, and flayed faces wide open.[14]

Though instantly debilitating, these cutting wounds weren't usually lethal, but in the fast, fluid nature of mounted combat, killing an opponent wasn't nearly as important as knocking him out of the fight–quickly. There's no doubt a thrust point was faster to deliver as the point followed a straight line to the target, where a cut edge came in a compassing arc to make contact. The point was also deadlier in the days of eighteenth-century medical practice but the effect of a thrust to the body wasn't always as instantaneous as the concussive power of the sword's edge whipping down on a target, and period accounts lean heavily toward describing the use of the edge in the American Revolution. When asked which he preferred his light horsemen to use, the point or the edge, Frederick the Great replied, "Kill your enemy with one or the other, I will never bring you to an account with which you did it."[15]

Regardless, many of Vernier's European troopers had been raised with the lance and proved they were very capable with the weapon. On February 22, Vernier's men had run down and routed a British foraging party and the timely arrival of Hessian Jaegers was the only thing that had saved the entire British party from being staked to the ground.[16] Despite Pulaski's and Moylan's internecine feuding over the winter of Valley Forge, Washington and Vernier seem to have avoided any potentially lingering issues their former commanders held for one another, and worked together without any recorded issues.

Washington and his men also seemed to fit into their new surroundings with ease. Lieutenant Baylor Hill of the 1st Light Dragoons kept a journal in which he recounted parties, card games, and all manner of amusements at the plantation homes of the low country rice kings. This section of Baylor's journal reads more like a social calendar than a war diary with the officers breakfasting, supping, dancing, hunting, and playing cards at a myriad of homes along with several references to drinking "excellent punch." Hill recalled one night in particular when, after drinking "a plenty of punch," he was "dradg'd up neck & heals" by Major Call of the 3d Light Dragoons and proceeded to tear out his sleeve in the resulting fray of drunken officers.[17]

Unfortunately for Lieutenant Hill and the rest, there was a war going on and the enemy was slowly edging closer and closer. Leading that advance was British cavalry commander Lieutenant Colonel Banastre Tarleton. Born in 1754, Tarleton was a native of Liverpool, England. His father, John, was a wealthy trader who had profited greatly off slaves and sugar, two chief staples of English colonialism. At his father's death, the young Tarleton inherited 5,000 pounds and promptly gambled it away in London. Penniless, he begged his mother to buy him a commission in the King's Dragoon Guards.[18] She acquiesced, and Tarleton landed in America in May 1776. Once there he was assigned to the 16th Light Dragoons and quickly drew the attention of his superiors by playing a key role in the capture of an American general officer at White's Tavern, New Jersey.[19] The young and audacious Tarleton had clearly found his calling, and he advanced in rank at a meteoric pace.

By the age of twenty-four, he was promoted to Lieutenant Colonel and given field command of Cathcart's legion of cavalry and light infantry, which became known as the British Legion. Recruits were American-born Tory volunteers, hailing mostly from Bucks County, Pennsylvania, and the surrounding counties about Philadelphia. The horsemen of the legion were outfitted as light dragoons and wore short green coats with black cuffs and collars and black leather helmets crested in bearskin.[20] Tarleton had also been given an outstanding troop of mounted British regulars, the 17th Light Dragoons, who wore the typical madder red coats of British service along with brass helmets and a death's-head emblem embossed on the front shield with the motto "Death or Glory."[21]

Together these forces and their mounts boarded ships bound for the new southern front in South Carolina. Sea voyages have always been notoriously hard on horses, and when the fleet encountered a violent series of storms the seams began to leak on the ship carrying the cavalry mounts. Water began to pour into the ship's hold and despite all hands on station more water was coming in than the ship's pumps could handle. Many of the horses were thrown overboard to lighten the ship's load, and the vessel only made it to Charleston by the constant work of the crew at the pumps.[22] When Tarleton's force landed on the Carolina barrier islands only a few horses had survived the drastic measures. Luckily for Tarleton, he'd landed in the wealthiest countryside in America and quickly went about stealing as many horses as he could manage from the surrounding plantations.

William Washington wrote General Lincoln regarding Tarleton's thievery: "There were many fine horses in the area . . . the enemy lose no time in collecting all the Horses they can in order to mount Dragoons."[23]

Washington went on to recommend that these plantation horses be removed somehow, but there was really little he could do. Lincoln continued to use his cavalry to buy time and delay the British advance and had no plans for coming out of his Charleston defenses and striking the enemy a blow. Instead Lincoln held to the belief that it was better to prepare his defenses in a city at the base of a peninsula, which offered little chance of escape, rather than sallying forth and attacking a portion of his still-forming enemy. This had to be incredibly frustrating for Washington, as he inevitably gave a little ground each day and saw this valuable resource slip into the enemy's hands and strengthen his adversary. On the other hand, Washington couldn't very well impress the horses himself since they belonged to

Whig rice barons who regularly passed him information on the enemy's whereabouts and often fed and quartered his men in the face of the British advance.

By March both British and American troops were hard at the *petit guerre,* or little war, where each side shadowed the other between the lines with scouts, screens, and ambushes.[24] On March 26, Washington decided to set a trap for Tarleton and went about staging Vernier's Lancers, Jameson's 1st, and his own 3d Light Dragoons out of sight but in position for a charge from ambush. He next sent out a few volunteers dressed in civilian clothes and mounted on fine-blooded horses and had them ride in sight of some of Tarleton's green-clad dragoons on patrol along Rantowle's Creek.[25]

Tarleton apparently smelled a trap, declined the bait, and moved on. Washington then left Jameson and the 1st Light Dragoons in place and took the 3d back to check on the nearby abandoned Governor's mansion of John Rutledge, who had left his estate in the face of the British advance. While en route Washington perceived a redcoat in the distance, and he and the advance gave chase and captured a British surgeon named Smith as well as Colonel John Hamilton of Halifax, North Carolina, a well-known Tory militia commander.

Washington now reversed his order of march and ordered Jameson's 1st Light Dragoons still at the ambush site to begin the advance, followed by Vernier's Lancers as Washington and the 3d Light Dragoons covered the rear. The column had gone but a mile and a half when scouts reported that some three hundred of Tarleton's dragoons had looped behind them and were about to close on the column's rear.[26] Washington ordered his rear guard to draw swords, turned them about, and flew down the road to charge headlong into Tarleton's advance in a sudden blurring clash of horses and broadswords.

The British van crumbled under the onslaught and fled back down the causeway to join the remainder of their unit with Washington hard on their heels and Vernier's lancers coming on in close support. Washington sent word for Jameson's 1st to hold and form a reserve, and then closed on the fleeing enemy who were now bottlenecked and stacking up at a narrow choke point on the causeway leading to Rantowle's Creek.[27] The 3d spurred home and jammed the British in tight where some twenty of Tarleton's dragoons were cut from the saddle before the rest could ride clear and escape. A British officer wrote that "several dragoons of the Legion were wounded [and that] Quarter-Master Sergeant Mcintosh . . . was badly wounded in the face by a broadsword."[28]

This was Washington's first real engagement as the leader of the 3d Light Dragoons, and his men clearly won the contest as they suffered but three troopers wounded before they marched off with several British Legion Dragoons towed behind as prisoners.[29]

The event made Washington a local hero to the surrounding rice kings, but in the bigger picture Washington's victory was only a minor skirmish and the British continued to grind their way forward despite the Continentals' harassing attacks. The *petit guerre* continued unabated with Washington and Tarleton jabbing at one another across some of the wealthiest estates in the nation; Drayton Hall, Middleton Place, Runnymeade, and the Rutledge's Stono River Plantation.

One residence at which Washington made more than one appearance was the Sandy Hill Plantation, owned by Charles Elliot. Elliot was an ardent Whig and South Carolina Assemblyman who'd amassed a small fortune in the rice trade and owned several thousand acres and hundreds of slaves. He also had an alluring seventeen year old daughter named Jane–the sole heir to the Elliot fortune–who apparently fell for Washington during his visits to the estate. Washington seems to have been smitten in kind and snuck back to the plantation to see her as often as possible.[30] The tempting young Jane was apparently quite the catch and no doubt had a number of suitors, but by all accounts William was outgoing and athletic and had just trounced the enemy a few scant miles from Jane's own home. The legend has all the passion of a Hollywood romance with Washington risking British patrols and galloping back on moonlit nights just to see Jane for a few fleeting minutes. During one of William's visits Jane purportedly learned William had no guidon to ride under. Jane grabbed a window valance of rich damask crimson and gave it to Washington saying, "Let this be your flag." Known as the Eutaw Flag, the silk talisman was said to have flown in every action of the 3d Light Dragoons for the rest of the war.[31]

However, there was precious little time for romance as the British noose continued to tighten around Charleston. British warships soon gained the harbor and Sir Henry Clinton's infantry fought their way down the peninsula to within a thousand yards of Charleston's defensive works. With Charleston besieged, the Cooper and Wando river corridors now became important inland routes for supplies and reinforcements, as evidenced by a brigade of Virginia Infantry that was able to sail down the river and reinforce Lincoln's forces on April 7th.[32] To keep this vital route open Lincoln ordered Brigadier General Isaac Huger (pronounced *U-gee*) to take the Continental cavalry and whatever militia infantry was at hand and guard the upper Cooper at Mock's Corner, also known as Biggin's Bridge.[33] Cavalry would have a hard time holding such a post but Huger duly collected the varying commands of Horry, Washington, Vernier, and Jameson and posted them on one bank of the Cooper River and then inexplicably posted the militia infantry across the bridge on the far side of the river.[34]

General Sir Henry Clinton also realized the vital importance of the upper Cooper and sent Colonel James Webster into the area with two regiments of infantry, along with Tarleton's British Legion and the 17th Light Dragoons. Tarleton was no doubt still smarting from his defeat along Rantowle's Creek and took out on the evening of April 13th for Monck's Corner with orders to, "make a surprise on the Americans encamped at that place."[35] In a stroke of blind luck, Tarleton's advance guard rode down a slave on the road and found he was carrying a message from Brigadier Huger to General Lincoln in Charleston. Tarleton assured the slave he would come to no harm and even paid him a few pounds, which bought Tarleton a complete description of the layout of Huger's camp.[36]

Tarleton struck at 3:00 in the morning. His men charged down the one road into Huger's camp, bowled over the picket, and galloped into the Continental horse camp with swords aloft. The Americans were in the process of breaking camp and rushed to their horses to try to bridle and mount, but there was simply no chance of completing the task in the dark as Tarleton's dragoons stormed over the camp in a wave that hacked down everything in their path. On foot and without carbines, there was little the light dragoons could do as Tarleton's troopers drove strings of stampeding horses through the camp. The surprise was complete and the victory total. Washington was briefly captured at the start and then escaped in the plunging confusion. Major Vernier tried fighting back but was cut down with a blow to the head; he surrendered and appealed for quarter only to be struck down again and badly mangled in the process.[37] Most of the Continentals cut their horses free and fled to the surrounding swamps, including commanders Huger and Horry.

Vernier was destined to suffer a far crueler fate, and was carried inside a nearby tavern where he was jostled and screamed at by several troopers of the British Legion as he lay dying. Tory Charles Stedman said Verenier was "mangled in the most shocking manner" and a second witness, Anthony Allaire, was shocked at the actions of Tarleton's troopers in Vernier's dying moments.[38] The French patriot suffered a pitiful death as he lay thrashing in pain, heckled by his captors, and cursing friend and foe alike in his final moments. In all, fifteen Americans were killed and sixty-three captured in the attack. Ninety light dragoon horses were also captured along with forty crucial wagons loaded with supplies destined for Lincoln's Continentals in Charleston.

After the reverse at Monck's Corner, the Continental Light Dragoons fell back to the east and regrouped. Beyond the loss of nearly one hundred horses, they were also now short on swords, saddles, accoutrements, and provisions. Worse still, they had been caught off guard and on foot–a cardinal sin for light horsemen. Carbines may have helped but carbines had always been hard to come by in the Continental ranks and equipment returns don't show any present while the 3d served in the southern theater.

The principle fault in the defeat at Monck's Corner was the failure by two commanders, General Huger and Colonel Horry, to post a sufficient guard on the road, and not posting the infantry on the same side of the river as the cavalry, where they could have delayed the attack long enough for the cavalry to mount. Ironically, General Huger had just sent a letter to Thomas Rutledge two days before the attack wherein he decried the fact that the British cavalry were always covered with infantry support and unassailable![39] In fact, the American cavalry could have easily been wiped out if some of the light dragoons had not been up and in the act of breaking camp when Tarleton arrived.[40] After the battle a surviving member of Vernier's command, Captain Lebrun de Bellacore, apparently still had complete faith in both William Washington and his regiment and wrote a letter to General Lincoln, requesting that he be posted with Washington and his light dragoons, "where the military discipline is so well kept."[41]

Back in Charleston the news was even worse for Lincoln and his besieged Continentals. By now the British had fully invested the peninsula north of Charleston and commanded the majority of the harbor. Food was running low within the city and, barring a miracle, most everyone knew it was simply a matter of time until Charleston fell to the British. The only course of action open to Washington and the cavalry was to try and keep an overland escape route open east of Charleston via Georgetown and the Santee River.

Into this cauldron of gloom, uncertainty, and low morale stepped Lieutenant Colonel Anthony White, formerly of the 4th Light Dragoons. White had since taken command of the 1st Light Dragoons, and since his commission as a Lieutenant Colonel pre-dated William Washington's, he now assumed overall command of the remaining 1st and 3d Light Dragoons. White and Washington knew one another well from their days in the 4th under Colonel Moylan; however, there is no record of a friendship having existed between the pair during their service in the north, nor is there any recorded animosity. It's doubtful the amiable and outgoing Washington ever enjoyed the calculating company of Anthony White.

Since Washington's appointment to the 3d, White had enjoyed some success in the north when he led a raid against Westchester, New York, in early August 1779. White commanded some one hundred dragoons and fifty infantrymen in the operation and quickly captured a large number of Tories. He then turned the column back for their lines, but one of his prisoners escaped and made his way to where Tarleton's British Legion and the Queen's Rangers were camped. The Rangers and the Legion quickly mounted and took out after White's column with the hope of intercepting the Continentals.[42] White had just managed to cross his exhausted troopers over a bridge at New Rochelle, New York, and wisely posted his infantry behind a stone wall flanking the bridge when the British troopers approached. The British saw White's troopers on the far side and tried to charge across the bridge only to be mowed down in a volley of musketry fired by the hidden American infantry.[43]

The action closed and White's command made it back to the American lines, though they lost a good portion of the prisoners along the way. Despite the loss of so many prisoners the affair was viewed as a success due to the repulse of the British horse. Even General Washington gave his former wayward aide some guarded praise, "White and the infantry appear to have acquitted themselves with much reputation" and the victory helped White obtain command of the 1st Light Dragoons by the close of 1779.[44]

Now in the Carolinas, White was of course eager to impress, and when Governor Rutledge ordered all available troops to assemble at Lenud's (pronounced *Le-news*) Ferry on the north bank of the Santee River he was quick to respond. White soon formed a plan in which he would take the remaining Continental cavalry south of the Santee on an expedition to sweep the reported British foraging parties clear of the area.[45] A promise of support for that operation came from Colonel Abraham Buford, whose Continental Infantry had just arrived from Virginia but were too late to gain Charleston's lines and help in the city's defense.

The cavalry crossed to the south bank of the Santee and met at Lenud's Ferry on the evening of May 5. The following morning there was no sign of Buford, but White opted to go ahead regardless.[46] According to John Gore of the 1st Light Dragoons, Lieutenant Colonel White and Major Jameson "with servants in disguise went among the Tories, where they soon received information on the British."[47] Armed with this intelligence, the Light Dragoons then headed for the Elias Ball plantation, where they easily captured a British foraging party of over a dozen men from Tarleton's British Legion. Prisoners in tow, the Continentals promptly turned about and headed back for Lenud's Ferry. Unfortunately for the Continentals, Mr. Ball, the owner of the plantation, escaped.

Shortly after the Continental departure, Lieutenant Colonel Banastre Tarleton was out on patrol with one hundred and fifty dragoons when he was met by Mr. Ball. Ball quickly explained the morning's events and gladly volunteered to lead Tarleton by the shortest route to Lenud's Ferry.[48]

Meanwhile, on the Continentals' return to Lenud's Ferry, Buford was seen on the far north bank of the river, but that was over two hundred yards away and too great a distance to be of any support. The Continentals' horses had now traveled twenty-five miles and could use a rest and some forage. Lieutenant Colonel White ordered the dragoons to dismount, unbridle, and feed their horses on the river bank. However, Washington was of a different mind altogether, and Sergeant Lawrence Everhart of the 3d Light Dragoons recalled that Washington "strenuously objected" to White's decision to halt on the riverbank.[49] The earlier defeat at Monck's Corner still loomed large with Washington and his men, and the idea of halting with a river to their backs and no infantry support while Tarleton was known to be in the area was seen as not only dangerous but monumentally ignorant.

Nevertheless, White's commission as Lieutenant Colonel was nearly two years senior to Washington's, and the mission across the Santee was White's to command. If White's complacency was due to his previous victory in New York, it seems as if he had forgotten that his success at New Rochelle was predicated by his attending infantry and the fact that he had both a wall and a funneling bridge between his dragoons and the pursuing British cavalry, an entirely different situation than he currently faced with the Santee at his back, a pine forest to his front, and no foot support at hand. Given White's personality traits, he may have been feeling his oats after capturing the foraging party on his first outing in the Carolinas and more inclined to dismiss Washington's recommendations to swim the horses across the Santee.

Regardless of the reason, White exerted his authority and rejected Washington's argument to swim the horses over immediately. Instead, White ordered the horses unbridled, fed, and rested; his orders were executed and thirty minutes later pistol shots split the air.

Once again Tarleton's men came thundering down on the dismounted Continental Light Dragoons. British swords thudded and slashed as the Continentals desperately tried to bridle their horses in the ensuing panic. This time the attack came in broad daylight, on the open bank of a deep river and there was nowhere to hide. Captain Baylor Hill of the 1st Light Dragoons recalled the confusion:

> In an instant we [saw] the approach of the British horse in full speed; every man took his own way they coming on us so suddenly . . . I endeavored to bridle a horse standing just by, but the noise of horses straining, hollowing of men and firing, it was impossible to bridle him.[50]

Hill then took off on foot and was ridden down and captured. White, Washington, and Jameson swam to the far side of the Santee where Buford's infantry stood by helplessly. Others drowned in the attempt to cross the river and still others fled for the safety of nearby swamps alongside the river bank. Thirty men were killed, wounded, or captured. Estimates vary on the number of horses taken, from fifty to the entire corps.[51] Figures aside, Washington wrote that he had but twelve men mounted and fit for duty after the rout.[52] In a single charge Banastre Tarleton had wrecked the Continental cavalry and curbed any threat of mounted Continental operations occurring in the Carolinas for months to come.

Charleston surrendered a week later, and with it over five thousand men and arms fell to the British victors. It was the worst defeat of American forces in the entire war. Yet even that wasn't the final play in the campaign.

On May 29, Tarleton and his dragoons caught up with Colonel Buford's retreating Virginia infantry at Waxhaws, South Carolina. Tarleton called for Buford to surrender, but Buford declined and instead opted to form his four hundred Continentals in a line on open ground and receive the enemy cavalry charge.[53] Tarleton attacked in classic hussar fashion with flanking parties to each side, while his best horsemen, the 17th Light Dragoons, charged straight up the middle.[54] If Buford had followed the tactical standard of the day and given the command to fire against Tarleton's charging cavalry at fifty yards, he would have more than likely broken Tarleton's central charge and perhaps won the day. Instead he held his men's fire until the 17th was at a full gallop and only ten to fifteen yards away.[55] A galloping horse covers 33 feet per second, and even a direct shot to the brain wouldn't drop a surging, adrenaline-charged horse on a dime. The result was a wave of wounded and dying horses that came thrashing and kicking into Buford's line to break it wide open.

In the ensuing mayhem of screaming horses, cursing troopers, and crunching sword blows, Tarleton rode forward and had his own horse shot from under him–just as one of the Continental officers was carrying forth a white flag to ask for quarter. Tarleton's men thought their leader had been killed with a trick and went into a "vindictive asperity not easily restrained," as they hacked and chopped down every Continental soldier in sight even as they pleaded for quarter.[56] Unhurt, Tarleton got back up on his feet and stood by watching as his men continued to kill Buford's surrendering Continentals.

Of Buford's four hundred men, one hundred and thirteen were slain outright, one hundred and fifty were so badly wounded they couldn't be moved, and another fifty were carried off as prisoners. Tarleton's command suffered five men killed, fourteen wounded, and cited the loss of some twenty horses.[57] It may be that Tarleton felt a fearsome reputation would help him in subjugating the rebel Whigs, and if that was the case he was wildly successful in his bid for gaining a reputation. Americans soon branded him a monster and the terms "Tarleton's Quarter" and "Buford's Play" became bywords for a fight to the death. Tarleton's dogged pursuits and headlong tactics had indeed earned him a great deal of success, yet despite his new reputation it had been simple luck more than any inherent evil that governed Tarleton's latest three victories; both Monck's Corner and Lenud's Ferry were profoundly influenced by stumbled-upon intelligence and dismounted adversaries, and the third success at the Waxhaws was largely derived from Abraham Buford's misguided tactics.

Nevertheless, Buford's defeat seemed to signal the end of resistance in South Carolina, and Sir Henry Clinton sailed back for New York in June. His campaign had been immensely successful, and his new southern strategy of crippling the American economy and ending the war seemed well in hand. Sir Henry waved goodbye as he exited Charleston's harbor and left behind his second in command, Lieutenant General Charles, Earl Cornwallis, to mop things up in the Carolinas.

Seven

COURTS, CAMPAIGNS, AND BACKCOUNTRY

"The attempt to rally routed cavalry, whilst pursued close by the enemy, is generally found to be fruitless; everyone cries halt, but no one ceases to fly."–Emanuel von Warnery, Remarks on Cavalry

As Sir Henry Clinton was sailing for New York, William Washington was already in North Carolina starting the lengthy process of rebuilding the 3d Light Dragoons. No doubt Washington was still seething at White's decision to dismount on the wrong bank of the Santee, and praying for another chance to get at Tarleton, but he'd first need to rebuild his regiment and, as with his prior rebuilding of the 3d, the funds were again hard to find. Congress approved some funding but also recommended that the states of Virginia and North Carolina contribute as well, and the state funds were not nearly as forthcoming, as the process proved to be painfully slow.[1] While the weeks ticked by and the days grew warm, there was often little to do other than relive the former campaign, and Washington slowly became embroiled in a controversy with Lieutenant Colonel White.

Courts of inquiry had long been a part of Anthony White's military career and he promptly called for one following the defeat at Lenud's Ferry to clear his reputation. Eighteenth-century courts of inquiry were unique affairs whereby an officer could call a court together to essentially try himself and clear his name if he felt it necessary, and the records show Lieutenant Colonel White was a seasoned defendant.[2] In fact, White thrived on courts of inquiry and when he wasn't a defendant himself, he would often volunteer to sit as one of the jury panel or serve as the presiding officer. White was predictably cleared by this latest court and while no official blame was ever assigned for the defeat at Lenud's Ferry, that didn't change the attitudes of the light dragoons who had stood on the bank of the Santee when Tarleton's men arrived at the gallop. Opinions flew openly through the ranks and White soon had one of Washington's officers from the 3d, Lieutenant Presley Thornton, arrested for making disparaging comments about his character. Thornton was tried and duly convicted, White approved the sentence, and Thornton was removed from service. This seems to have been the final straw for Washington, who until now had taken no action against White for the folly displayed on the Santee. However, cashiering one of his junior officers was simply too much for Washington to stomach and he now made a move to sidetrack White once and for all.

Military protocol wouldn't allow Washington to press his own charges against White, so instead Washington waited until the majority of all general officers were away on military business and sought out Colonel Gideon Lamb of the North Carolina state militia, who, though he wasn't a Continental officer, technically outranked both Lieutenant Colonels White and Washington.[3] After speaking with Washington, Colonel Lamb ordered Lieutenant Thornton arrested a second time and a general court martial formed to retry the Lieutenant. Lamb also ordered White arrested on charges brought forth by Washington.[4]

This must surely have enraged White, who hated any accusations made against his character, but he was forced to suffer arrest until a court was convened. No doubt White was eagerly looking forward to his trial and the chance to clear his name. He promptly called forth Colonel Abraham Buford to contest

Washington's rumored charges. A court was assembled, but the presiding judge found the trial had to be postponed due to missing witnesses, ostensibly Washington and his officers, who were somehow unavailable just two days later when the court was convened. White's trial was then suspended until the lengthy process could be repeated and a court-martial again formed whereupon Washington could be found and called on by the court to exhibit his charges against Lieutenant Colonel White. This, too, surely enraged White, because he couldn't reconvene his trial and clear the charges against him without Washington first exhibiting the exact charges for which Colonel Lamb had ordered White's arrest.[5]

No doubt angering White still further was the fact that Washington next left Halifax to go on campaign in early October, without first exhibiting White's charges before a court. This left White in a state of arrest and, in a final slap to White, Washington and his 3d Light Dragoons left for the front with White's sole mounted and fit-for-duty troop of 1st Light Dragoons assigned to Washington.

Three months later, White was still in the rear with the cavalry reserve, waiting for his trial to reconvene, while Washington remained at the front on campaign–this had likely been Washington's goal all along, as it kept White in the rear where Washington probably thought he was best served. White had finally met his match in the courts and the added bonus, at least from Washington's perspective, was that Washington still retained White's one troop of 1st Light Dragoons.

On December 28 an angry and exasperated White bypassed the adjutant general and sent a letter directly to the new department commander decrying that Colonel Lamb, at Washington's behest, illegally ordered his own arrest and that Lamb had further interfered in Lieutenant Thornton's arrest. To halt the "malicious intentions and base designs of his enemies," White demanded that his court-martial be reconvened, Colonel Lamb's conduct be investigated, and Lieutenant Thornton be rearrested.[6] However, by this time Washington was actively engaged with the enemy over a hundred miles to the west and had proved to be an invaluable part of the campaign; the adjutant general sent a new letter that directed Washington to write back from the front with the charges and any evidence he had pertaining to the trial. It wasn't until late January that White was finally tried by a court behind the lines while Washington remained at the front and continued to prove his worth before the enemy.

White was acquitted by the court, but the judgment was disapproved because the court included matters in their determination that were not included in the original charges.[7] The verdict was thus clouded with doubt and reservation. However, rather than restart the whole process again, White was officially released from his arrest and ordered to travel to the Moravian settlements near Salem, North Carolina, where a detachment of 1st Light Dragoons were convalescing. Once there, White was directed to forward fifty horses to headquarters while any of his dragoons still fit for duty were to be sent on to Lieutenant Colonel Washington as soon as possible. The troop of 1st Light Dragoons that had departed in October would remain under Washington's command, and White was ordered on to Virginia to continue rebuilding his regiment in the rear.[8] And finally, Lieutenant Thornton's commission was reinstated.[9] This was surely the best Washington could have hoped for when he first approached Colonel Lamb back in September. Not surprisingly, White and Washington never served together again.

Through these initial trials and charges in August and September, Washington had continued recruiting, equipping, and training his regiment. Fortunately for Washington, Thomas Jefferson and the state of Virginia came through with the lion's share of the funding, and by early October the 3d Light Dragoons were marching south. In addition to Washington's core force of 3d Light Dragoons, he also had one undersized troop from Nelson's Virginia State Cavalry plus the aforementioned troop from White's 1st Light Dragoons. In all, Washington counted 82 troopers, 6 sergeants, and 2 trumpeters "fit for service" and was marching south by October 3, 1780.[10]

It was a cobbled force, to be sure, and far from regimental strength. In official numbers it was closer to a single squadron of two troops, and returns show they were well equipped with clothing, boots, and swords but light on pistols and cartridge boxes.[11] There were no carbines listed, but the diary of Captain Baylor Hill made repeated references to officers hunting deer before the fight at Lenud's Ferry and some scattering of civilian fowlers may have been available on this campaign as well. The low numbers of firearms and high number of swords are clear proof that horses and broadswords were the primary weapons of light dragoons or Washington wouldn't have even attempted to take the field.

In the short time Washington had been away, the war in the south had undergone a series of changes at rapid pace. After Sir Henry Clinton departed, Lord Cornwallis had taken command of all British troops and started to branch out from the South Carolina low country and into the state's interior, or backcountry, as it was known. The British soon established a series of forts and outposts that stretched in a broad arc from Augusta, Georgia, on the western border to Georgetown in the east on the South Carolina coast. Former members of the rebel militia were ordered to come in, swear allegiance to the crown, and be issued paroles which allowed them to return to their homes as prisoners of war. The British continued to hold to the belief that only a small percentage of South Carolinians were true rebel Whigs, and that there was a great "silent majority" of loyal Tories that inhabited the state's interior which had long been oppressed by Continental troops and powerful low country rice barons.[12]

This was partially true, but in reality a quarter of the population was Whig, a quarter was Tory, and the remainder could go either way.[13] What the British further failed to realize was that South Carolinians had been governing themselves for the past four years without Mother England and doing quite well for themselves. Much of South Carolina's backcountry was still a true frontier, and during the Crown's absence several successful expeditions had been carried out by the rebel Whigs against the Cherokee, who had made a series of raids against Whig settlements. It was a stunningly foolish misjudgment for the British to think that a well-armed and self-reliant frontier people, who had been free from foreign authority for the past four years, were going to readily accept a summons bidding them to come forward and, in effect, kiss the rings of British officers and gloating Tory neighbors. Once again England had horribly misjudged the American character.

Instead of signing paroles and surrendering, bands of Whig partisans soon began staging a series of mounted attacks on British supply lines and outposts. Tories were quick to respond with their own punitive raids against the Whigs, and the backcountry was quickly engulfed in a civil war that often had more to do with personal vendettas than the Revolution itself. British outposts were undermanned to deal with these turns of events, and backcountry oaks were soon dressed like vicious Christmas trees as bodies swung adrift from stout oak limbs, often adorned with the crude signs and scrawled placards of swift backcountry judgments.

As this violence was steadily building across the southern frontier, the Congress back in Philadelphia was forming a new army of Continentals to drive southward and recapture the vital port of Charleston. Funds were approved, troops were assigned, and Major General Horatio Gates of Saratoga fame was given command.[14] Gates moved south with a mixed force of militia and Continentals and met Lord Cornwallis outside of Camden, South Carolina, in August 1780. The fight rapidly degenerated into an American disaster as the American militia on the left flank proved unable to stand against the British regulars in an open field of scattered pines.[15] The remaining Continentals were driven by British bayonets and finally broken with a brilliant flanking charge made by none other than Banastre Tarleton and his vaunted green dragoons.[16] Gates's entire force was driven from the field in a rout, yet despite this severe blow to the American cause, the backcountry Whigs continued their resistance against what they now saw as a foreign occupation by the King's troops and their Tory quislings.[17]

Backcountry skirmishing continued to escalate in the southern interior as bands of roving horsemen swept across the frontier to attack distant targets and then vanish as quickly as they struck. Militias practiced lessons learned fighting the Cherokee and Shawnee and acted more as mounted infantry than true cavalry, as they would ride unseen to battle, dismount, and fight on foot from superior positions gained through the speed of their horses.[18]

In early October several groups of Whigs rode overland from the mountain Watauga settlements and joined with other partisan bands from the Piedmont. The combined force of nine hundred men dismounted at the base of King's Mountain and attacked a similar sized force of British provincial infantry under the command of Major Patrick Ferguson. Casualties quickly mounted among the British provincials who fought on open ground along the top of the ridge while Whig riflemen fired from cover on the tree shrouded hillsides in shifting, multipronged attacks. The ridge line was soon awash with rolling volleys of rifle and musket fire and Ferguson fell to a hail of rifle balls that killed him instantly and ended the battle. Sadly, the sharp crack of rifle fire continued for some while before the Whig commanders managed to wrestle control of their men.

When the shooting finally ended there were some one hundred and fifty dead Tories and an equal number too badly wounded to be moved, while the Whigs suffered over twenty men killed and another sixty wounded. The surviving Tories were rounded up and a drum head trial commenced. Thirty-six men were sentenced to hang but only nine suffered the verdict. Their victory complete, the Whigs then mounted up and vanished back into the frontier.[19] Word of Ferguson's defeat at King's Mountain spread through the backcountry with the speed of a sewing circle secret and suddenly the crushing British victory at Camden was reduced to little more than an unpleasant memory.

Shortly after this victory William Washington and his refitted light dragoons rode into the American lines and once there they were promptly assigned to a new corps of light troops under the command of a Continental Army legend: Brigadier General Daniel Morgan.

Daniel Morgan was a rare breed among General officers in the Continental Army. He was not a man of education, extreme wealth, nor born to a well-connected family. Instead he was a former wagoner who stood over six feet tall and had a two fisted reputation as a frontier brawler, gambler, and drinker.[20] He'd served as a civilian teamster for the British in the French and Indian War and had reportedly received a sentence of four hundred lashes for decking a British sentinel.[21] He liked to joke that the drummer had miscounted and the British still owed him a stroke! In later years Morgan was confident, but no longer foolhardy, and demonstrated a natural gift for tactics, having first learned to fight Indians on the frontier and later adopting those same lessons against the British. He had served in a number of northern campaigns in the first half of the war and the American victory at Saratoga in 1777 was in part due to his coordinated use of riflemen and musket-bearing infantry at the Battle of Freeman's Farm.[22] More than anything Morgan was a fighter who sought to surround himself with others of the same mindset whether they were rich or poor, from north or south, enlisted Continentals or volunteer militia.

Morgan was now serving under General Gates in the southern theatre where he had recently been given command of a "flying army," a period term describing a collection of fast moving light troops detailed as a mobile strike force.[23] Within this corps were three infantry companies from three different states; Virginia, Maryland, and Delaware under Captains Bruin, Brooks, and Kirkwood, while General Morgan commanded a collection of four rifle companies from Virginia under Captains Tate, Combs, Buchanan, and Rockbridge.[24] The addition of Washington's light dragoons gave the force a powerful mounted threat that would also provide infantry cover for Washington's troopers–a feature sorely lacking in the past. In fact, the defeats at Monck's Corner and Lenud's Ferry had helped prompt the Continental Board of War to reform the light dragoon regiments into "Legions" with attending light infantry companies for security.[25] Washington's attachment to the flying army served much the same purpose and more often than not Washington's troopers would come to be paired with Captain Robert Kirkwood's company of the Delaware Line.

Captain Kirkwood had served in nearly every major engagement of the war from Long Island to Monmouth Courthouse and on through to Camden while never rising above a company grade officer.[26] This wasn't due to Kirkwood's performance by any means but rather the Delaware Line had been so decimated that there simply weren't enough surviving members to warrant Kirkwood's promotion above captain. He was tough minded but beloved by his troops and was a soldier's kind of soldier; not the sort of veteran infantryman who would always get on well with others and certainly not the sort who would typically get along with an officer of light dragoons. However Washington was a former infantryman himself and not the preening, lofty type of elite horseman some light dragoons aspired to be and the record shows that Washington and Kirkwood would fight and march side by side through countless miles in the coming southern campaigns.

In early November Morgan's new flying army made a foraging and reconnaissance patrol down into the South Carolina backcountry, penetrating deep into the no man's land of feuding Whig and Tory militias between Charlotte and the key British forts of Camden and Ninety-Six.[27] The patrol went as far south as Hanging Rock, less than a day's ride from Camden, before turning about and returning to New Providence without any consequence. At the end of November, Morgan mounted a second expedition into the same region and, after having gained confidence in Washington's abilities, detached Washington and his light dragoons to try and take Rugeley's Mill, a fortified backcountry strongpoint held by a local Tory militia commander named Henry Rugeley.[28]

Washington arrived just after dark on December 1st and found that the position was far more fortified than expected. It was more stockade than mill with a large fortified barn enclosed within a surrounding wall of stout pine logs and peppered through with loop holes and sally ports from which to fire muskets. A towered platform was erected in the center of the walled barnyard to allow for a second tier of musketry to rain down on any attackers, and the whole enclosure was lined with abatis to prevent a cavalry charge.[29] Inside was an unknown number of men but the sally ports were bristling with musket barrels and Rugeley quickly refused Washington's call for surrender.

Washington knew he couldn't take the position with cavalry alone but he soon formed a plan and sent his men out of sight and sound. He had them cut down a pine tree, form the log to the shape of a six-pounder cannon and scald it black with torch and soot. A baggage wagon was dissembled and the "cannon" was mounted on the running gear's axle.[30] Washington next dismounted a small section of troopers to serve as "matrosses" and had them haul the pine cannon back up toward the walls of the fort in plain sight of the defenders inside.

Washington then picked out a veteran ranker and sent the man forward with a second summons for surrender. He added the stipulation that if Rugeley didn't surrender this time Washington "would blow them across the mill pond."[31] One can assume the veteran ranker added a few choice words of his own to the request and Colonel Rugeley instantly surrendered the fort without a shot being fired. One hundred men filed out with clubbed arms and Washington promptly burned the fort to the ground. Washington and his dragoons then reversed their march to North Carolina with prisoners in tow and on their arrival in camp a *feu to joie* was fired in their honor.[32] Sergeant-Major William Seymour of the Delaware Line declared Washington's pine cannon "was the best piece in Christendom." [33]

Morgan's flying army next went to witness General Gates surrender command of the Southern Department to Major General Nathanael Greene. The newly appointed General from Rhode Island took command on a cold autumn day in the frontier hamlet of Charlotte, North Carolina. Greene was asthmatic, walked with a pronounced limp, and was a former Rhode Island assemblyman.[34] His father was a devout Quaker and a very prosperous merchant who taught his son the family business from the ground up. However, the young Greene had a penchant for questioning authority and after his father's passing Greene was suspended from the Society of Friends for attending "a Place in Coneticut of Publick Resort." The rebellious Greene was unrepentant and wrote that the Quaker's constrained manner of education had created "a fine Nursery of Ignorance and Superstition."[35]

Greene may have appeared sickly, but he was aggressive, resolute, and straightforward; a true revolutionary with a disciplined mind and a keen eye for logistics. General Washington recognized the Rhode Islander's abilities early in the war and it was with the greatest confidence that Greene was appointed to command the Southern Department.[36] Three years before in New Jersey, then Captain William Washington had led the vanguard for Greene's division and captured the Hessian battery in the narrow streets of Trenton. One can only wonder if Washington and Greene didn't share a few words about prior campaigns when they met again in Charlotte.

The southern army Greene received from General Gates was ill equipped, undisciplined, and in a state of poor morale. On paper they numbered 2,300 but over five hundred were absent, absent sick, or on detached duty.[37] Worse still, even this undersized force was eating their way through what little provisions were available in the heavily foraged countryside.[38] Greene realized he needed to move his army to keep it fed but he also had to bear in mind that the British under Lord Cornwallis were within only a few days march to the south at Winnsboro, South Carolina. He also knew that Cornwallis had plans to invade North Carolina next and that additional British reinforcements were soon expected from Charleston.

Greene first prepared for the worst and sent survey officers to map an escape route north into Virginia in the event Cornwallis attacked sooner than expected. Once he had an escape mechanism in place, Greene sat down and devised a plan that would: one, regain the initiative; two, make Cornwallis hold where he was; and three, allow the Continentals to restock their provisions. In the end Greene could only devise one way to accomplish all three goals and decided to divide his weaker force in the face of a greater enemy.

Such a plan went against the most basic principles of warfare, but Greene had not come to the decision lightly.[39] He aimed to send Morgan and the flying army to the west, which would threaten Cornwallis's left flank and keep the British from moving north. At the same time Greene would take the remaining ill provisioned Continentals seventy miles east where provisions were more plentiful. This way if Cornwallis moved in force to the west after Morgan, he would leave the interior of South Carolina open to invasion by Greene's force. If Cornwallis came after Greene, then Morgan could sweep into Cornwallis's rear or assault the backcountry posts from the west. Greene wrote the following describing his decision:

> It makes the most of my inferior force, for it compels my adversary to divide his, and holds him in doubt as to his own line of conduct. He cannot leave Morgan behind him to come at me, or his posts at Nintey-six and [west] would be exposed. And he cannot chase Morgan far, while I am here with the whole country open before me.[40]

The key to Greene's strategy lay with Morgan's flying army; they had to threaten Cornwallis's western flank without getting too close, and still find enough forage and provisions to subsist in one of the most violent and remote sections of the Carolina frontier. More than anything they would need to gain the support of the clannish Whig militias who were used to writing their own brand of backcountry justice; men who were at constant odds with their equally nefarious Tory counterparts. General Greene wrote that: "The Whole country is in danger of being laid waste by the Whigs and Tories who pursue each other with as much relentless fury as beasts of prey."[41]

The flying army left Charlotte on December 21 with William Washington's eighty plus dragoons at the head of the column.[42] The size of Washington's force was constantly fluctuating around this time. In the past month alone Nelson's State Dragoons had returned to Virginia, Major Richard Call had brought down new recruits from the 3d's staging depot at Halifax, and a dozen deserters from the borrowed detachment of 1st Light Dragoons had been captured and returned to the ranks.[43]

Morgan's force headed west from Charlotte, but after nearly a week of solid rains the normally poor backcountry roads were reduced to little more than slick ribbons of miring red clay twisting through the steep hills and bare winter woods. Progress was painfully slow but Morgan's force made it across the Broad River with no enemy opposition and entered the heart of the Carolina backcountry. William Seymour of Kirkwood's Delaware Company described the trip as being very difficult and the backcountry as a harsh, difficult land of swamps and hills, inhabited by hardscrabble frontiersmen living in crude log cabins.[44] Provisions proved to be as rare as expected and though some Whig militia came in to join Morgan's flying army the numbers were far less than Morgan had hoped to see. As Morgan listened to the men coming in he soon learned that the low numbers were in part due to the absence of one Andrew Pickens.

Colonel Andrew Pickens was a renowned Whig militia commander, veteran Indian fighter, and wealthy land speculator. At the start of the war, Pickens played a key role in suppressing Tory activity along the Georgia and South Carolina border when he led the American militia to victory at the battle of Kettle Creek.[45] After the fall of Charleston, Pickens had sworn out a British parole rather than risk losing his considerable land holdings in the Cane Creek area of western South Carolina. He had since suffered an attack on his property by a British officer named James Dunlap and for this act felt his parole was no longer valid, but the former commander had still declined all requests to rejoin the war and many men in the area were swayed by the course Pickens decided to take.[46]

This situation was further complicated by the intimidating presence of a large force of some four hundred Georgia Horse Rangers who were lurking in the backcountry. These horsemen were commanded by a Tory Colonel named Thomas Waters and they had recently made a name for themselves by razing and burning a large swath of Whig farms in Wilkes County, Georgia.[47] This roaming force of Tory cavalry kept many Whig militiamen at home to protect their own farms and served as a severe deterrent to Morgan's recruiting efforts. Despite Water's presence, Pickens eventually decided to come in, most likely at the behest of Major James McCall, a friend and fellow veteran of the Cherokee Wars who now commanded a force of South Carolina state dragoons already in Morgan's camp. Yet even

Pickens's presence didn't instantly inspire the backcountry Whig militias to leave their homes and families undefended with Water's Horse Rangers at large, and so Morgan still lacked the numbers he needed to truly threaten Lord Cornwallis's western flank.

Disappointed but undaunted, Morgan made camp once he was west of the Broad River and Washington's troopers soon caught a band of Tories who were out on a raid of Whig homesteads. This was Washington's first true glimpse of the brutal state of affairs in the backcountry and it seemed to trouble him deeply: "The distress of the Women and Children stripp'd of everything by plundering Villains cries aloud for redress."[48]

Washington had certainly seen his share of civilian hardships over the past four years of war, and his anger hints at a greater injustice taking place here in the backcountry, something darker, harsher, and more depraved than the simple larceny and robbery he most certainly witnessed citizens suffering in New York, Pennsylvania, and the Jerseys. He was also shocked to find that one of the captured plunderers had come from a good home and had apparently turned his back on the admittedly wide common boundaries of moral behavior allowed during a war. In response, Washington had the captured Tories sent back under armed guard for General Greene to pass formal sentence upon.

Then on the 27th of December word arrived that Waters's infamous Georgia Horse Rangers were out on a raid of the nearby Fair Forest Creek settlements. These Horse Rangers were the same party that had earlier burned a swath of Whig farms in neighboring Wilkes County, and Morgan wrote Greene that he had identified a large body of Tories to the south that were "insulting and plundering the good people in that Neighborhood."[49]

Washington and his dragoons took out two days later with Morgan's full blessing. Riding with Washington's Continentals were a mixed group of two hundred state dragoons and mounted militia under commanders James McCall, Thomas Brandon, and Joseph Hayes.[50] The force rode south with a vengeance, pounding down backcountry tracks and trails and fording a series of wild creeks and swollen rivers. They covered over fifty miles in a day and a half and caught up with the Georgians at a frontier trading post called Hammond's Store in present day Laurens County, South Carolina. Thomas Young of the South Carolina militia wrote the following account as Washington and his men arrived:

> When we came in sight, we perceived that the Tories had formed in line on the brow of the hill opposite to us. We had a long hill to descend and another to rise. Col. Washington and his dragoons gave a shout, drew swords, and charged down the hill like madmen.[51]

Young isn't clear if Waters's men were mounted or not, but Morgan later wrote the Tories "flew to their horses."[52] Whether the Georgians were forming a dismounted firing line or attempting a mounted front by squadrons, Washington didn't allow them time to get comfortable. He directed the militia to the flanks, called for his men to pull swords, and charged straight for the Georgians.[53] The Tories broke as Washington's dragoons piled into them at a gallop, broadswords struck in whipping blows, and the Tories were cut to the ground in heaps. The fact that the Georgians never fired a shot lends strong credence to the theory that they were forming a mounted defense rather than a dismounted firing line. The state dragoons came barreling in on the flanks, slashing and hacking at the Tories with swords and tomahawks, and likely shooting others with rifles and fowlers as they began fleeing the carnage.

All told one hundred and sixty Tories were killed or wounded, and forty taken prisoner. Colonel Waters and the remainder escaped into the woods. Neither Washington's Continentals nor the state militia suffered any notable casualties. Such a discrepancy nearly always indicates a massacre and Hammond's Store is no exception. Whether Morgan and Washington viewed Waters's men as outlaws or combatants is hard to ascertain. Morgan described them as "insulting" and "plundering" innocent civilians and Washington's recent capture of a party of backcountry "villains" had clearly aroused his sense of justice. In contrast to Hammond's Store, Washington took the entire Tory garrison at Rugeley's Fort earlier that same month without injuring any prisoners.

Certainly the reputation of the Georgians as barn burners did them no favors at Hammond's Store, particularly with the local state dragoons accompanying Washington's men, but it doesn't excuse the event and Washington is ultimately responsible as the commander of the mission. Thomas Young, a mere seventeen years old himself, offered a chilling description of young men hardened by war:

> T]here was a boy of fourteen or fifteen, a mere lad, who in crossing the Tiger River was ducked by a blunder of his horse. The men laughed and jeered at him very much, at which he got very mad, and swore that boy or no boy, he would kill a man that day or die. He accomplished the former. I remember very well being highly amused at the little fellow charging round a crib after a Tory, cutting and slashing away with his puny arm, till he brought him down.[54]

The war in the backcountry was as harsh as its surroundings. Right or wrong, William Washington had cleared the countryside of Colonel Waters's Georgia Horse Rangers and the badly needed Whig militias came pouring into Daniel Morgan's camp.

Eight

BATTLE AT THE COWPENS

"The manner of charging the enemy is to be the same as directed in the evolutions; namely to advance at a brisk trot, and then to fall into a full gallop, taking care at the same time to keep their ranks and files well closed."–Regulations for the Prussian Cavalry

CHARLES CORNWALLIS PASSED NEW YEAR'S DAY AT Winnsboro, South Carolina. He'd been educated at Eaton and Cambridge, owned an estate in Kent, and was a member of the House of Lords.[1] He had turned forty-two the day before, and was likely wondering just how his twenty-year military career had taken him to this far-flung corner of the globe where he was miles apart from any sort of the refinements he'd grown accustomed to. Each day he was flooded with reports, dispatches, and intelligences of the ever shifting backcountry situation and lately the news had been far from good.

Back in August, Cornwallis's victory at Camden over General Gates had been hailed from Low Country to London as a most brilliant affair of arms, and seemingly cleared the way for an invasion of North Carolina and ultimately Virginia. However since August things had changed. Cornwallis had beaten Gates handily, no one denied that, but the rebel Whig militias were another story. The Camden victory over the Continentals was followed by the Whig victory at King's Mountain and General Greene's recent division of forces had stalled any plans Cornwallis had for invading North Carolina, particularly with Morgan's flying army now perched on Cornwallis's western flank.[2] Colonel Waters's defeat at Hammond's Store was the worst blow yet, and the news of the Georgia Horse Rangers' brutal routing by Washington's cavalry was still reverberating throughout the backcountry.[3]

This must have been incredibly frustrating for Cornwallis, because in total forces he greatly outnumbered Greene's Continentals.[4] However, the British troops were scattered across two states and garrisoned a great circular line of forts and outposts that stretched northwest from Savannah to Augusta, Georgia, and back east across the frontier to the South Carolina coast at Georgetown; these were primarily fed, clothed, and equipped from Charleston via a scattered web of supply lines and depots that required an ever increasing number of guards and escorts to maintain. This significantly curtailed His Lordship's ability to launch an offensive blow at his spreading enemy. Still, Cornwallis had options available and tools to fit the bill. The first issue to be dealt with was Morgan's growing army in the west, and His Lordship sent his best troops to that sector under what he believed was his best officer for the task at hand, Lieutenant Colonel Banastre Tarleton.

Since his victories at Lenud's Ferry and the Waxhaws, Tarleton had continued to make a name for himself by running roughshod over Continentals and Whig militia alike at Camden and Fishing Creek. Tarleton was an outstanding horse soldier but he was more than that; he was bold, cunning, and cocksure. He was everything a light horseman was supposed to be, and more than willing to strut about as the *beau sabre* of all British cavalry. Recently, though, he had suffered a costly reversal from General Thomas Sumter's Whig militia at Blackstock's Farm. For the first time Tarleton's tactics of headlong charges had failed entirely.[5] Instead he'd been met by disciplined volleys of rifles and smoothbore fowlers that stopped him cold and compelled him to retire from the field. The following day he'd returned to renew the fight only to find that Sumter's troops had already withdrawn. The undaunted Tarleton conveniently claimed a victory and hid the true outcome of the battle from Lord Cornwallis.[6] When His Lordship picked Tarleton to chase down Morgan's flying army, there's little doubt the vaunted Green Dragoon jumped at the opportunity.

To go after Morgan, Cornwallis gave Tarleton his own flying corps of horse, foot, and artillery. For cavalry he had two hundred and fifty of his own green-coated British Legion dragoons and another fifty troopers of the indomitable 17th Light Dragoons with their tailed red coats and death's-head helmets. For infantry Tarleton had three hundred Highlanders from the 71st Regiment, one hundred seventy men from the 7th Royal Fusiliers, two hundred men from his own British Legion Infantry and a Light Infantry battalion composed of the 16th Regiment of Foot, remnants of the Prince of Wales regiment, and two additional light companies of the 71st Highlanders. In addition, he had a pair of mobile three-pounder cannons called "grasshoppers," with two crews of artillerymen and mounted drivers.[7] All together the force consisted of over twelve hundred men of proven ability, the cream of Cornwallis's army, and Tarleton fully expected to annihilate Morgan's flying army in short order.

For his part, Morgan was now assembling one of the largest collections of American militia ever seen in the backcountry as every day brought more men into camp. Rifle-bearing Whigs rode in from North and South Carolina, Virginia, and Georgia to fight with Pickens and Morgan. Including his Continentals from the flying army, Morgan had a total force hovering around 2,000 men.[8]

As the militia came in, Morgan continued talking with them. Many were veterans of prior fights with Tarleton, and Morgan understood the value of the knowledge these men held of his enemy. Most Continental officers spurned the frontier militia and viewed them as little more than unwanted stepchildren, but Morgan was a frontiersman himself, and he especially wanted to talk with the men who had helped defeat Tarleton at Blackstock's Farm; men like James McCall, Thomas Brandon, and Benjamin Roebuck. As Morgan listened and learned from these backcountry veterans, he steadily developed a tactical plan for dealing with the hard-charging "Bloody Ban" Tarleton.[9]

By mid-January, Morgan reached a popular staging point for cattle drovers that straddled the Green River Road. Known as the Cowpens, the open fields were composed of a series of small, undulating ridges and were bordered by a ravine on one side and weed-choked springs on the other. These opposing features served as natural barriers to keep cattle collected before driving them to market. As Morgan rode the fields he realized these same natural barriers would protect any force deployed within from mounted flank attacks. Morgan also knew Tarleton was closing fast and he decided to fight here on ground that suited his battle plan.

Morgan intended to array his forces in three lines. The first would be made up of backcountry riflemen known for their marksmanship. The second, situated one hundred and fifty yards behind the first, would contain the majority of the militia under Andrew Pickens. A third line farther back would be composed of Morgan's Continentals under Lieutenant Colonel John Eager Howard and supported on the flanks by veteran riflemen. From his talks with the backcountry veterans, Morgan expected Tarleton to attack his position head-on, and his plan called for the first line skirmishers to harass the British approach and fall back to Pickens's second line. This second line of militia would aim for the epaulettes of British officers and deliver two volleys into the teeth of the British advance before withdrawing to the rear where they would regroup and reload. Morgan was trusting Howard's third line of Continentals would hold Tarleton's men in check, wearing them down with concentrated blasts of trained musketry while Pickens rallied his militia and reentered the fight.[10] Lieutenant Colonel Washington would command the cavalry reserve composed of the Continental Light Dragoons and state militia horsemen under Majors James McCall and Benjamin Jolly, all of which would be posted in the rear, ready to exploit or plug any breaks in the lines.[11]

That evening Morgan ordered cattle slaughtered to feed his troops and prepare for the coming fight; he walked among the campfires and joked with the militia and kept laying out his plan until all understood their part. The militia wouldn't have to stand before the British bayonets. Instead they only needed to give two fires, and then withdraw to the rear, reform, and come back again on the flanks. Morgan knew the militia's horses would be held nearby, and if the battle went badly, they would run for their mounts and ride away. He also knew that was one reason why they were willing to fight in the first place, as the horses gave them an escape route, and he continued to joke with them and cheer them up well into the night.[12] They needed to give two fires, he told them again and again, and then come back in on the flanks for the crucial final blow–two fires and then reform for victory.

Lieutenant Colonel Washington was busy as well. At this point he had some eighty light dragoons and their horses to get squared away for the expected fight and he also needed to attend to the militia troops of James McCall and Benjamin Jolly. McCall was a tough-minded frontier dragoon who'd fought at Blackstock's Farm and had already impressed Morgan by helping sway Andrew Pickens's decision to come into camp. His troop of backcountry dragoons was also one of the few militia units armed with broadswords and able to fight from the saddle as true cavalry.[13] Like Morgan, Washington realized the value of good local men and recognized McCall's abilities in the raid on Hammond's Store. Major Jolly was another flinty backcountry veteran who'd made a positive impression and Washington picked Jolly to call for a second company of volunteers out of the men who rode at Hammond's Store under Colonels Hayes and Brandon.[14] Washington then equipped these new volunteers with forty swords stored in the 3d Light Dragoon's baggage.[15] Between McCall and Jolly there were roughly ninety state dragoons, enough to form a separate squadron of militia horse.[16]

The next morning Morgan's men were up well before dawn. Scouts kept a constant report on Tarleton's approach throughout

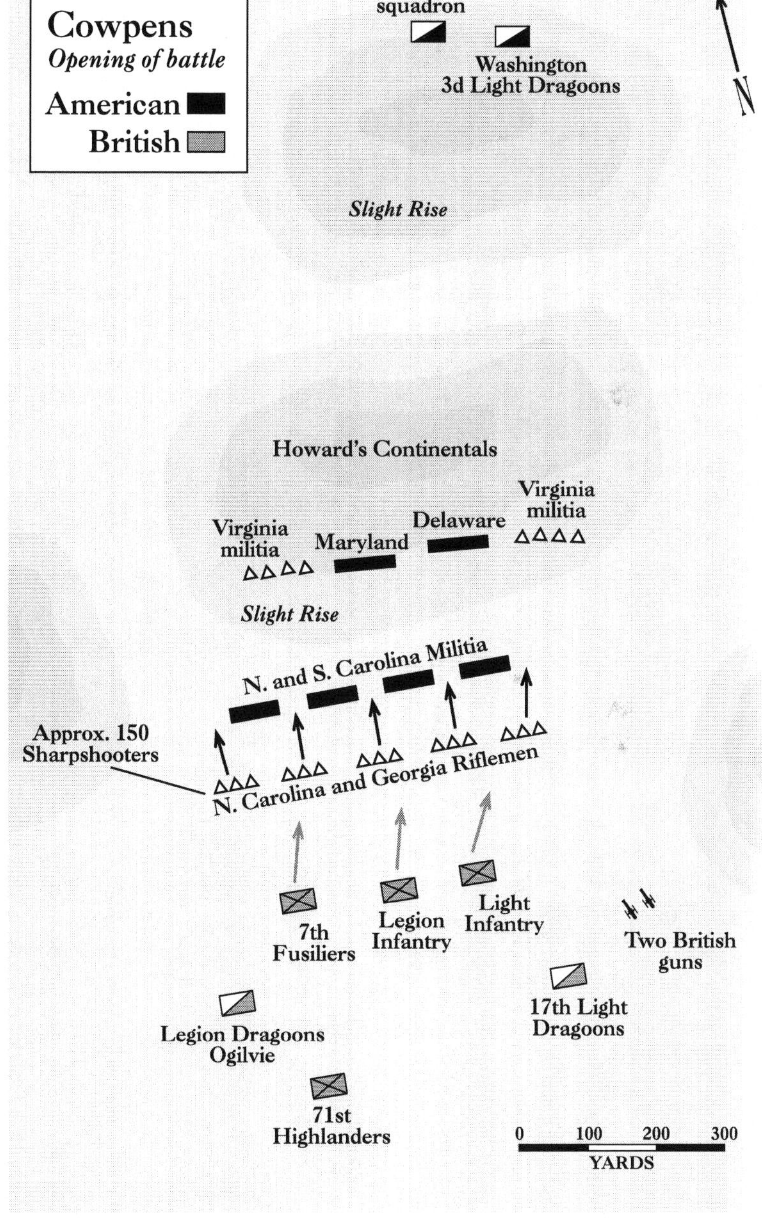

Cowpens
Opening of battle
American
British
Militia squadron
Washington 3d Light Dragoons
N
Slight Rise
Howard's Continentals
Virginia militia
Maryland
Delaware
Virginia militia
Slight Rise
N. and S. Carolina Militia
Approx. 150 Sharpshooters
N. Carolina and Georgia Riflemen
7th Fusiliers
Legion Infantry
Light Infantry
Two British guns
17th Light Dragoons
Legion Dragoons Ogilvie
71st Highlanders
0 100 200 300
YARDS

the night, and Morgan had his men in their positions before the sun even lit the horizon.[17] First contact was made with the British by a ten-man vedette sent from Washington's own 3d Light Dragoons.[18] The leader of the vedette, Sergeant Lawrence Everhart, was a personal friend of Washington's, and as Everhart closed in on Tarleton's van in the thick, predawn woods his horse was shot out from under him. Dragged before Tarleton, Everhart was asked if Morgan would stand and fight. Everhart hedged the numbers and sagely replied that they would if able to keep but a few men together. Tarleton then boasted that if they did it would be another Gates's defeat as in the Continental disaster at Camden the year before. Everhart brashly answered back that he hoped to God it would be another Tarleton's defeat, referring to the recent action at Blackstock's Farm. Just what the ever game Tarleton said in reply is lost to history, but he did order Everhart's wounds be dressed by a British surgeon.[19]

The rest of Everhart's vedette rode back to the American lines and warned of the coming British assault. Just as dawn broke the horizon, the sound of rifle fire split the morning air as a forward party of British Legion Dragoons came in range of Morgan's first line and quickly retired under the riflemen's fire.[20] Tarleton then edged forward in the early light, briefly studied Morgan's lines, and–as expected–decided to attack immediately. He directed the Light Infantry battalion to the right, his Legion Infantry to the center, and the 7th Fusiliers to the left. Lieutenant Henry Nettles' troop of 17th Light Dragoons was formed in rear of the right flank behind the light infantry, and on the left Tarleton placed a troop of British Legion cavalry under Captain David Ogilvie. The two artillery pieces came forward to support the infantry's advance and the 71st Highlanders were posted as a reserve in the rear along with the remaining two hundred Legion Dragoons.[21]

The British infantry moved out at a trot and swept forward until they came within range of Pickens's militia, who promptly opened a rolling fire by battalions.[22] The lethal American volleys stunned the British but they dressed their ranks with cool professionalism and continued to press ahead. Only one militia battalion managed a second volley before Pickens ordered the militia to withdraw and clear a field of fire for Howard's line of

Continentals. When Tarleton saw the rebel militia withdrawing to his right he promptly directed Nettles's troop of 17th Light Dragoons to exploit the moment and charge the retreating Americans.[23]

Nettles's men rolled forward eagerly; it was a light horseman's dream of firm ground with broken infantry before them and they went to work at a gallop. They cut through the militia and instantly created a panic in the American rear as they charged forward, hacking and slashing at the fleeing riflemen. There were only fifty troopers under Nettles, yet Robert Long of the rebel militia mistakenly thought he was being attacked by "200 or 300 cavalry" and James Collins remembered thinking "my hide is in the loft" as the expert 17th threatened to turn what had begun as a planned, orderly withdrawal into a panicked flight for the militia's horses.[24] A rout was about to ensue that would quickly ruin Morgan's battle plan.

Watching this transpire from behind Howard's third line was William Washington, no doubt standing in his stirrups, leaning forward in the saddle, and waiting as he marked Nettles's troopers passing his front and spreading out in pursuit of the fleeing militia on his left. This opening flank on the 17th was the opportunity every veteran of Lenud's Ferry had been coveting for months, and revenge was now but a short charge away. Swords scraped free, spurs came back and the 3d Light Dragoons rolled forward en masse at the open left flank of the British 17th. By now some of the leading elements of the fleeing militia had reached their horses and they started to open a scattering fire on the British dragoons just as Washington's men slammed home and started cleaving the British from their saddles like a tumbling of dominoes.[25]

> Col. Washington's cavalry was among them, like a whirlwind, and the poor [British] fellows began to kneel from their horses . . . The shock was so sudden and violent, they could not stand it, and immediately betook themselves to flight; there was no time to rally, and they appeared to be as hard to stop as a drove of wild Choctaw steers going to a Pennsylvania market.[26]

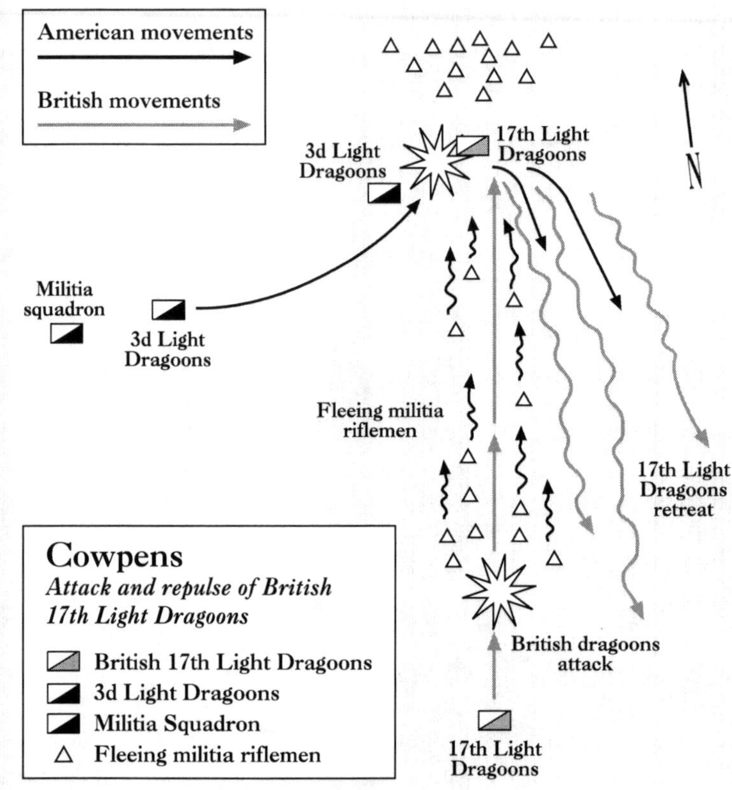

When Washington struck all three elements of the previously mentioned horse charge trinity were in play; speed, surprise, and momentum, and Cornet James Simmons of the 3d Light Dragoons recalled counting eighteen of the British Light Dragoons down on the ground at the point of attack.[27] Washington's troopers next rallied and rolled on, pursuing the 17th until they overtook the British artillery drivers posted on the British right flank. The British drivers refused to yield and the light dragoons shot down the artillery horses with their pistols.[28]

Washington then brought his men back to the rise behind Howard's line, re-joining McCall's and Jolly's waiting militia squadron that Washington had left in reserve to cover his attack on the 17th.[29] Washington simply hadn't needed to commit his entire command to attack Nettles's scattered troop of the 17th. Frederick the Great, the eighteenth-century master of smoothbore battle tactics, wrote that light horsemen should first attack opposing cavalry with a reserve in place, and only commit their entire force once they recognized disorder among the enemy.[30] This was prudent, battle-tested counsel and Washington employed this same principle when it fit the situation, as at Rantowle's Creek and again here at the Cowpens.[31]

The dismounted American militia was now free of threat and began to rally and reform in the rear as Washington let his own horses gain their breath while the infantry fight heated up before Howard's line of Continentals.[32] Advancing in the wake of Pickens's militia, the light infantry battalion, the Legion Infantry and the 7th Fusiliers pressed forward and began trading musket volleys with Howard's Continentals. As the two sides traded fire, Tarleton decided to bring up the 71st Highlanders on his left and flank the right of Howard's line.[33]

Leading the 71st's attack was Ogilvie's troop of British Legion Cavalry which promptly charged forward and cut through a company of North Carolina riflemen posted on Howard's flank.[34] Ogilvie's men charged after the North Carolinians and opened a gap on the American right that allowed the Highlanders to swing in on Howard's now open flank.

Seeing this new break in the line, Washington sent the militia squadron under McCall and Jolly to attack Ogilvie's troop while Washington and his light dragoons held fast in reserve to cover Howard's growing fight with Tarleton's infantry.[35] Riding with the militia squadron that January morning was Thomas Young:

> I soon found that the British cavalry had charged the American right. We made a most furious charge, and cutting through the British cavalry, wheeled and charged them in the rear.[36]

The two companies of mounted militia struck the single British troop with swords aloft and broke the green dragoons wide open, then wheeled about and struck again. This second wheel and closing attack is solid proof that McCall and Jolly were leading seasoned horse soldiers, and not a fresh collection of eager militiamen out on their first lark against the enemy. British Lieutenant Roderick McKenzie recalled how Ogilvie's British Dragoons charged "the right flank of the enemy" but were charged in turn and "compelled to retreat in confusion."[37]

But even as the militia squadron swept forward a fresh disaster was in the making on Howard's line. A mix-up of orders occurred as Howard's officers tried to re-fuse their flank and face the Highlanders now sweeping down on their right and Howard had no choice but to march his men back toward the rear so he could halt and reform. Smelling blood, the Highlanders broke forward in pursuit. Morgan was furious and came galloping over to Howard where he loudly demanded to know what exactly was going on.[38] Howard assured Morgan that his men were not beaten and just needed to be redressed. Morgan then turned about and directed Howard to reform in front of Washington, who was still holding his Continentals in reserve atop a small rise in the rear.[39]

The crux of the battle was now fast approaching. Washington watched the ragged pursuit of the Highlanders running forward in clumps of threes and fours, which were in turn creating disorder across the entire British line, and realized an opportunity was in the making. "They're coming on like a mob," he quickly told a courier he sent galloping for Howard, "Give them one fire and I'll charge them."[40]

The Highlanders continued to clamor after Howard's men, closing to within thirty yards before Howard ordered his line to suddenly turn about and fire. A solid sheet of smoke and fire blasted out point blank at the Highlanders and when the smoke cleared fully half the Scots were down on the ground.

Howard called for a bayonet charge and Washington's trumpets split the air. Spurs came back yet again and Washington led his dragoons around Howard's left to pitch into the right flank of the British infantry.[41]

Thomas Young and the mounted militia were just rallying from their charge on Ogilvie's dragoons when Washington was rolling forward: "At this moment the bugle sounded. We, about

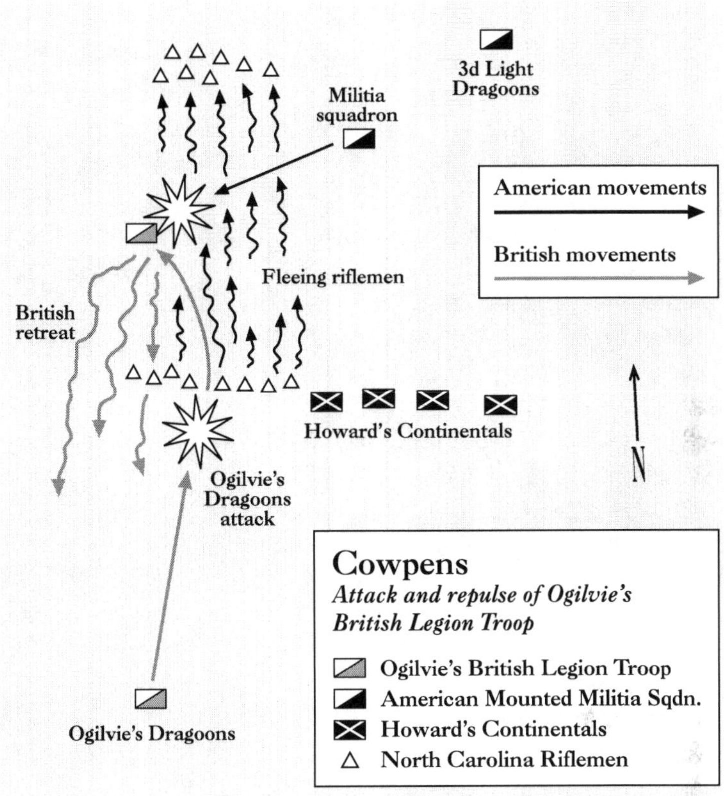

half formed and making a sort of circuit at full speed, came up in rear of the British line, shouting and charging like madmen."[42]

Amid cries of "Tarleton's Quarter!" and "Buford's Play!" Washington's light dragoons galloped into the British ranks and brought their broadswords crashing down. The attack instantly broke both the Light Infantry and the Legion Infantry, and drove them back on the 7th Fusiliers, a rippling effect as the fleeing British troops piled roughly into their comrades and masked their fellow soldiers from firing at the Continental troopers. As Washington's dragoons were chopping and hewing their way through the British right, Howard's men were driving into the Highlander's in a growing brawl of dirks, bayonets, and musket butts.

Banastre Tarleton sat watching from across the field and couldn't believe his eyes. In the span of mere minutes the fight had gone from certain victory to near certain defeat. First the 17th Light Dragoons had been routed on the right, then Ogilvie's troop came streaming back on the left, and now his infantry was being ridden over by the swirling horses of Washington's Light Dragoons. Tarleton turned to his reserve of two hundred British Legion Dragoons. They had seen no fighting so far and with a spirited charge could possibly turn the tide and save the day. Tarleton called for a charge but his men didn't budge. The victors of Camden, Monck's Corner, Lenud's Ferry, and the Waxhaws saw Washington's men riding down their fellow soldiers and balked. They sat watching as Howard's men drove the Highlanders before them and Pickens's militia came streaming back onto the field per Morgan's initial battle plan and began firing at targets of opportunity. It was simply too much for the Legion Dragoons and they turned about and galloped away to leave Tarleton standing in their wake. Tarleton later wrote, "[A]ll attempts to restore order, recollection, or courage, proved fruitless. Above two hundred dragoons forsook their leader, and left the field of battle."[43]

Desperate, Tarleton continued to seek a mounted force to stem the American tide and managed to rally a collection of mounted couriers, staff officers, and some forty survivors from the two prior charges of Ogilvie and Nettles and led them forward in a last-ditch effort. "Fourteen officers and forty horsemen were, however, not unmindful of their own reputation, or the situation of their commanding officer. Colonel Washington's cavalry were charged, and driven back into the continental infantry by this handful of brave men."[44]

This ad hoc force of British horsemen made a spirited charge that briefly checked Washington's ranks of light dragoons driving the British infantry and managed to reach some of Howard's Continental infantry.[45] Tarleton's claim that his charge drove Washington's light dragoons anywhere was later denied by both Lieutenant Colonel Howard of the Continental line and Captain Roderick McKenzie, a British infantry officer captured at Cowpens.[46] In reality Washington's men were focused on the

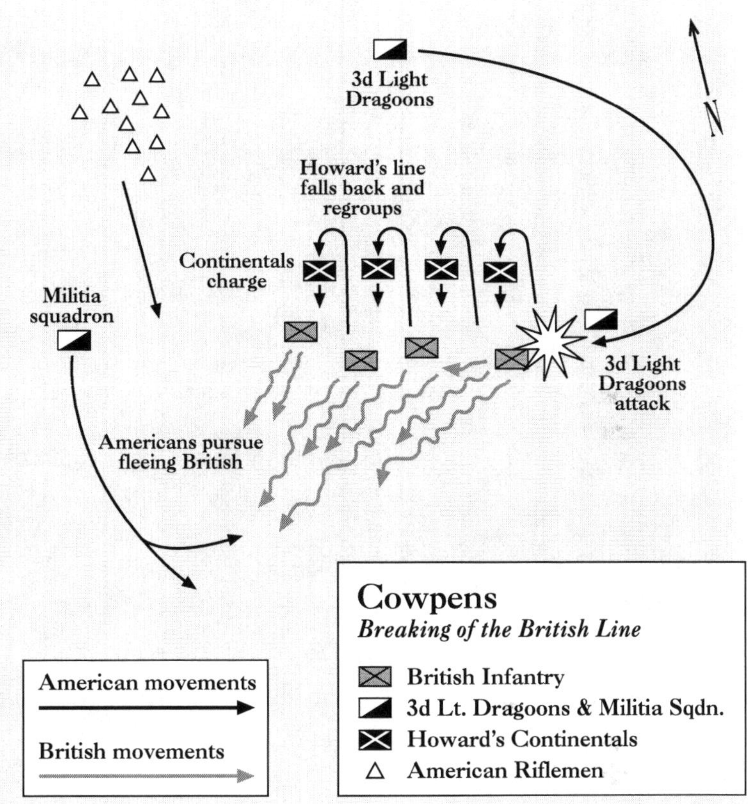

British infantry when Tarleton attacked but they swiftly rallied, counterattacked, and repulsed Tarleton's charge as quickly as it struck. Tarleton now knew the jig was up and drifted back away from the field, still not believing his eyes and likely spellbound by the disaster taking form about him as he trailed behind his dragoons.

At this point most Continental officers were busy taking prisoners, but William Washington was instead watching three trailing British officers on the far side of the field. Two of them were clearly officers of the British 17th in death-headed helmets, but the third officer must have struck a chord with Washington as he clapped spurs to his mount and took out after this trio of British officers at a gallop. He outdistanced his fellow horsemen and, according to the regimental history of the British 17th Light Dragoons, came on with the shout, "Where is now the boasting Tarleton?"[47]

The eighteenth century was still a chivalrous age; dueling was an accepted tradition and officers, particularly cavalry officers, were known to meet in private combat between the lines. The tradition would continue well into the Napoleonic era but on this day British chivalry was decidedly lacking as not one but all three British officers turned about and made for the lone Washington. Rashly or not, Washington had made the challenge and it was now too late to turn back as he spurred straight on and closed with the three enemy officers in a swirling exchange of sword blows.

Luckily for Washington, help was on the way. Sergeant Major Mathew Perry of the 3d Light Dragoons galloped into the ongoing melee and slashed Lieutenant Nettles of the British 17th across the arm to knock him out of the fight.[48] Moments later a pistol cracked and the second officer of the 17th, Cornet Thomas Patterson, reeled in the saddle and peeled off, mortally wounded from a snap shot fired from Washington's waiter–a young steward too small to wield a sword.[49] Meanwhile, Washington had closed with the third officer and traded blows; the officer lunged, Washington parried the thrust and broke the enemy officer's sword in the process. Washington may have also landed a glancing cut on this officer as the adversaries whirled about.[50] The enemy officer then wheeled out of range, drew a pistol and shot Washington's horse before galloping off the field.[51]

The best description of this affair comes from Lieutenant Colonel John Eager Howard, who wrote the following corrective account to author William Johnson in 1822:

> Now take Washington's own account of this. As he advanced Tarleton's cavalry showed no disposition to face him, and Tarleton with his officers threw themselves into the rear, and perceiving that Washington was very near and ahead of his troops, he with two of his officers wheeled about and charged upon Washington. The three advanced abreast and one of them

aimed a blow the effect of which was prevented by Sergeant Perry who coming up at the instant disabled this officer. On the other side an other had his sword raised when the boy came up and with a discharge of his pistol disabled him. The one in the center who it is believed was Tarleton himself made a lunge which Washington parried & perhaps broke his sword. Two of the three being thus disabled the third then wheeled off and retreated ten or twelve paces when he again wheeled about & fired his pistol which wounded Washington's horse–Thus the affair ended.[52]

Until now it had always been thought that it was Washington's sword broken in this duel of officers, but the subject of the key sentence in this account is clearly Washington's adversary, and as it follows, the possessor of the broken sword: "The one in the center who it is believed was Tarleton himself made a lunge which Washington parried & perhaps broke his sword."[53]

A thrust blade always suffered the hazard of being parried and binding in an opponent's webbing or saddlery and if the thrust was made at speed as when the third officer "charged upon Washington" the blade could easily twist, bind, and break as the two parties passed on speeding horses. Once the enemy officer's sword was broken he wheeled out of range, drew a pistol and took a shot at Washington. If it were Washington's sword that was broken in the exchange, the officer would have closed in and dealt a blow–not wheel out of range and fire a pistol. A second source lends further evidence for this scenario and comes from 3d Light Dragoon James Kelly, who wrote that "Washington made a hack at Tarlton & disabled Tarltons fingers & glanced his head with his sword."[54] Kelly was a long-serving veteran of the 3d, and if Washington had somehow clipped the enemy officer with his sword in this quick brawl of darting horses and ringing blades, it also follows that the officer might wheel out to a safer distance and draw a pistol.

Another account from the footnotes of William Johnson's *Sketches of the Life and Correspondence of Nathanael Greene*, Vol. I, states that it was Washington's sword which was broken in this swirling melee but Howard's corrective letter to Johnson is more descriptive and was written in reply to Johnson's book.[55] Though less plausible, it is possible that Washington landed a blow with a broken blade and compelled this third British officer to withdraw to a safer distance and draw a pistol. Either way, Howard's letter states that Washington believed he was trading blows with Tarleton, as does Johnson's account, and James Kelly's statement reveals he did as well.

Washington left no written record of the action but clearly spoke to Lieutenant Colonel Howard about the affair. Tarleton however, remained silent on the subject and to date no one can positively confirm or deny his participation in this battlefield duel. Tarleton was one of the first to publish his memoirs after the war but they were seen as self-serving by many of his fellow British officers.[56] In his memoirs, Tarleton went into much detail of the battle at Cowpens but of this particular phase he only made the false claim that he and his ad hoc force of horsemen drove off Washington's dragoons, which, as mentioned previously, was disputed by veterans on both sides.[57]

It would hardly bode well for Tarleton to admit that he refused a challenge of single combat from an enemy officer and instead charged forward with a three to one advantage in an attempt to kill his challenger; only to fail even in that. Instead three British officers were defeated by Washington, a sergeant, and a young boy too small to swing a sword–hardly the sort of thing one mentions when building their reputation!

As Tarleton, or whoever this third lookalike officer was, galloped off, Washington, still caught up in the heat of the moment, climbed down from his wounded horse and spun about on his waiter in a rage. Washington's standing orders were to engage the enemy with swords alone and he now demanded to know why his waiter had fired a pistol. When put to the matter the young waiter stammered that "he was obliged to do it to save the life of his Colonel."[58] After several seconds of reflection, and possibly a quiet word or two from Sergeant Major Perry, Washington cooled down and forgave the young man.[59]

Meanwhile the rest of Washington's men had been riding the field and securing prisoners. A native of South Carolina, Cornet

James Simmons of the 3d Light Dragoons came across Sergeant Everhart, the morning vedette commander captured before the battle, who was still being held captive by some of Tarleton's men. As Simmons and his troop approached, a British soldier raised a pistol to shoot Everhart in the head, but Everhart raised his hands as the pistol fired and the ball ripped through his arm and glanced off his skull. Simmons had the pistol-wielding British soldier shot and killed on the spot. Everhart survived the wound and the war.[60]

Elsewhere the British infantry was surrendering in droves. Lieutenant Colonel Howard dismounted to receive the swords of the Highland officers and when he went to remount a Captain Duncanson of the 71st Grenadiers began to pull and claw desperately at Howard in a begging panic and nearly unhorsed him. Howard angrily asked the panicked Highlander what he was about and Duncanson replied "that they had orders to give no quarter, and they did not expect any; and as my men were coming up, he was afraid they would use him ill."[61]

Howard took pity on the pleading Highlander and had Duncanson placed under the care of a sergeant. Other Scots were far angrier at the defeat. Major MacArthur of the 71st told Howard that he had been: ". . . an officer before Tarleton was born; that the best troops in the service were put under 'that boy' to be sacrificed."[62]

All told, over one hundred British soldiers were killed, two hundred wounded, and another five hundred captured, along with two pieces of artillery, thirty-five wagons, a traveling forge, and all their music. In short it was Lord Cornwallis's entire flying army of fast movers and light infantry, the very cream of his forces in the backcountry, less the Legion Dragoons who fled the field. American casualties were numbered at one hundred and forty men.[63] For their roles in the battle Congress awarded a gold medal to General Morgan and silver medals to Lieutenant Colonels Washington and Howard. It was the greatest tactical victory of the war for American arms.

Washington however, was far from done and he and his light dragoons soon took out after the fleeing Tarleton in a bid to chase down Tarleton and his Legion Dragoons. They pursued him over twenty miles but were purposely misdirected by a woman whose husband had been impressed by Tarleton as a guide, and therefore Washington failed to come up with Tarleton.[64] Legend holds that when Lord Cornwallis learned Tarleton had lost his flying army, his best trained and fastest moving troops, he grew so angry that he broke his own sword in two.[65] Whether the tale of Cornwallis's sword is accurate or not is debatable; either way, Cornwallis certainly realized the war in the Carolinas was quickly growing out of hand.

Nine

FLIGHT AND FIGHT

"During the retreat, a few small parties, composed of the best and bravest men, are to be advanced toward the enemy, in order to skirmish with them, and thereby to facilitate the movements of the main body."–Regulations for the Prussian Cavalry

THE BATTLE OF COWPENS WAS THE FINISHING TOUCH TO A string of victories for Washington and his 3d Light Dragoons. Washington had rescued a regiment that had suffered repeated misfortune both before and after he took the reins. The losses at Monck's Corner and Lenud's Ferry had been two crippling blows and, while not Washington's fault, he certainly shared the blame as the 3d's commander. Following the loss at Lenud's Ferry, Washington cobbled together a force of eighty riders and took the 3d back into the fight, joining forces with Morgan and changing his luck. The pine cannon deployed at Rugeley's Mill was a brilliant ploy and was followed by the routing of the Georgia Horse Rangers at Hammond's Store. Washington's performance at the Cowpens rightfully earned him a congressional medal, and if anyone had ever doubted his abilities they were now silenced by the ringing of church bells and the calls of town criers as news of the victory at the Cowpens spread across all states north and south.

Yet the war on the southern front was about to escalate radically. Lord Cornwallis now left South Carolina's affairs in the hands of Lieutenant Colonel Nisbet Lord Balfour and Lieutenant Colonel Francis Lord Rawdon, and took to the field with fresh reinforcements from Charleston in a bid to chase down Morgan and recapture his force of fast-movers lost at the Cowpens.[1] Fortunately for the Americans, Morgan had already anticipated such a move and he had the prisoners on the march soon after the battle, managing to cross the rain-swollen Catawba River well ahead of the British who arrived on the 30th of January.[2]

Heavy rains had fallen for two days and the British could only stare at the flooded watercourse of floating trees and debris that offered no passage in its current state. Safe on the north bank, Washington and Morgan rode down to Beattie's Ford where they met with General Greene. Greetings were exchanged as the officers dismounted and sat on a log to hold an impromptu field meeting with General William Davidson of the North Carolina Militia.[3] As the officers sat talking, British cavalry arrived on the south side of the Catawba and soon began galloping up and down the banks in frustration. They could see the American officers sitting in plain sight but well out of musket range, and there was no crossing the river in its flooded state. The British were simply two days late and they could only curse and stare at the distant collection of American officers through their spyglasses.

The meeting concluded quickly, Morgan and Washington rode back to their column, and Greene did the same–yet in that brief span of time, General Greene had scratched out a plan in the wet dirt of the river bank that would plot the course of the war for the next month and a half. General Davidson and his militia would contest the British crossing on the Catawba as best they could while Morgan marched his Continentals to the town of Salisbury. From there they would link up with Greene's northbound force of Continentals moving up from Cheraw. Once united, they would turn north for Virginia and reinforcements.[4] Greene knew he wasn't yet strong enough to stand against Cornwallis and his new reinforcements from Charleston, and it was imperative to keep Cornwallis from recapturing his light infantry lost at Cowpens. Therefore, a retreat north toward provision rich Virginia was his best option. This was the same route he had ordered mapped upon arriving in the Carolinas, and along the way Greene would scour all food and forage available to deny it from the British while collecting every boat, ferry, and bridge plank at the countless river crossings between the Catawba and Virginia.[5]

Green's retreat became known as the Race for the Dan, after the Dan River, which crosses the Virginia-North Carolina border. Washington and his light dragoons formed part of Greene's rear guard along with the newly arrived cavalry and light infantry of Lieutenant Colonel Henry Lee's Partisan Legion. The twenty-five-year-old Lee was from one of the wealthiest of Virginia families and a graduate of the College of New Jersey, one day to be known as Princeton University. He was a smart and calculating officer and well known for the American victory at Paulus Hook.[6] In addition to Lee and Washington, the Continental rear guard included the Virginia, Maryland, and Delaware infantry companies from the fight at the Cowpens, and all were placed under Colonel Otho Holland Williams of the Maryland line.[7]

In a strange twist of fate, Morgan wouldn't be a part of Greene's soon-to-be-famous retreat. The legendary rifleman had survived years of frontier hardships and countless battles but time and cold weather eventually caught up with Morgan and he was forced to retire from action due to a severe bout of rheumatism that crippled him shortly after his meeting with Greene on the banks of the Catawba.[8]

While Greene laid his plans, Lord Cornwallis went about trying to increase his speed of march and ordered the great majority of his wagons burned, leaving only the most essential for food, ammunition, and military stores.[9] The usually heavy traveling British infantry burned scores of tents, spare blankets, and equipment, barrels of rum, extra rations, and even officers' comforts in a drastic effort to lighten their load.[10] However, the mere shedding of equipment couldn't turn regular troops into light infantry.

In the British Army grenadiers and light infantrymen were select troops, hand-picked from the regular "hat companies" of each line regiment and formed into separate flank companies of elite soldiers.[11] Grenadiers were selected for size and strength and specialized in shock tactics and bayonet work. Light infantrymen were picked for fleetness of foot and shooting ability, and trained in specialized skirmishing and quick march tactics. The light infantry companies were then often banded together in fast moving "light" battalions. Cornwallis's actions on the banks of the Catawba did make for a faster moving column, but no amount of wagon burning would replace the loss of trained light infantrymen. While the new replacement regiments did contain some light infantry companies, their numbers came nowhere near to matching earlier levels and the British were never quite able to catch up with Greene's Continentals during the march to Virginia. Washington's Light Dragoons and Lee's Legion Cavalry skirmished constantly with Tarleton's Dragoons and the British van, and, along with Williams's light infantry of the rear guard, fought scores of mounted and dismounted feints, delaying actions, and ambuscades at every creek crossing and turn in the road–repeatedly forcing the pursuing British to halt, form up and take the time to go forth and clear an enemy that had often already taken flight.

At times Cornwallis's men were just hours behind Greene's column but, lacking a sizeable body of light troops, the British repeatedly came up short and were never able to recapture the prisoners lost at Cowpens, nor bring the Continentals to heel.[12] The last of Greene's men crossed the Dan River under torchlight in the early morning hours of February 14. Soon after the final boat landed on the northern bank, the bedraggled British advance arrived to find yet another deep river before them without a single bridge, boat, or ferry to be had for miles around. Foot sore, half-starved, and bone weary, Cornwallis's makeshift flying army was forced to turn south and beg provisions from the local populace.[13] The Race for the Dan was over, and the British had clearly lost the contest.

Now safe in Virginia, Washington and the rest of Greene's Continentals could enjoy a few days' rest as scores of Virginia militia began heading for Greene's army in droves. Washington and his veterans knew this would be only a brief respite, and there was much to be done in preparing for a new campaign. As always, the brutal wear and tear on the horses had thinned Washington's ranks, and his light dragoons were soon scrounging the countryside for replacements. Luckily, Washington and Greene found an ally in Virginia governor Thomas Jefferson, who allowed Greene to grant powers "to such persons as you shall think proper for impressing horses for your dragoons."[14] In less than a weeks' time, Washington's men were ready to take the field along with the rest of Greene's Continentals. Re-kitted and reinforced, Greene re-crossed the Dan on February 22 and began advancing into North Carolina with his cavalry in the lead.

Waiting in and around Hillsborough was Lord Cornwallis and his British troops who'd been welcomed by the local citizenry with a tepid enthusiasm at best. Much of the countryside had already been picked over by Greene during his retreat to the Dan. What supplies remained were few and far between, and not readily surrendered by farmers and families still in the grip of winter. Regardless of sentiments, Cornwallis took what he needed, which only amplified the local feelings against him. The situation was not at all helped when a force of some four hundred Tories were cut down by the combined forces of Lieutenant Colonel Henry Lee and Captain Joseph Graham's state dragoons. These Tories were some of the few Crown-friendly forces left in the area and, while on the march to join Cornwallis's ranks, they apparently mistook Henry Lee's green-coated Continentals for Tarleton's green-coated British dragoons. Lee played the deception to the hilt and nodded his thanks as the Tories stepped to the side of the road to let their "loyal friends" over take them and pass by.[15] As Lee reached the head of the Tory column the slaughter commenced and the surprised Tories were cut to ribbons in a matter of seconds.

Soon afterward a second, separate twist of fate caused still more damage when a group of Tories from Rowan County, North Carolina, approached Lord Cornwallis's camp and were mistakenly charged and cut down by Tarleton's men.[16] These twin cases of mistaken identity, the first cleverly intentional and the second wholly accidental, doused what little active support remained for the Crown in central North Carolina.

Once again the British were losing the battle of local perceptions. In a war where many campaigns would only total a few thousand combatants on each side, the inhabitants' views and opinions were far more critical than in the densely populated battlefields of Western Europe where supplies were readily available and populations were ten or twenty fold those of the American South. The campaigns of the Carolinas raged across vast frontiers with limited resources and crop yields that could only support small-sized armies, yet the outcomes of these campaigns would determine the course of vast areas of land far larger than many European kingdoms.[17] Whether the British high command realized such an aspect of the war existed is unclear, but they seem to have repeatedly fallen on the foul side of public opinion throughout the conflict.

In the meantime Greene and Cornwallis continued to stalk one another across the North Carolina Piedmont in a deadly game of capture the flag, and each side's advance guards fought daily skirmishes among the tall forests and winding roads tracing back and forth between the Haw, Deep, and Dan rivers. By March 6 the American flying army was posted on the south side of the Haw River while the main force of Greene's army held to the north. Cornwallis smelled opportunity and sent a large force of cavalry under Lieutenant Colonel Tarleton and an accompanying infantry force under Lieutenant Colonel James Webster to cut off and destroy Greene's advance corps of fast movers. Fortunately one of William Washington's patrols spotted the movement and Washington informed Colonel Williams of the British intent.[18] Colonel Williams quickly turned his command back about on the road for Weitzel's Mill, which led to an important ford over Reedy Fork Creek on the way to the Haw River.

With the British hot on Williams's trail, Washington, Lee, and Captain Graham's North Carolina dragoons drifted back to form a rear guard and protect their slower moving infantry.[19] Williams galloped ahead to form a line ten miles farther on at the Reedy Fork while the cavalry and two companies of militia riflemen attempted to hold the British van at bay. A running, ten mile fight ensued on the twisting forest roads as the British drove ahead in an effort to bowl past Washington's dragoons and the American rear guard and bring Colonel Williams's prized light infantry to heel.[20] Despite the best efforts of Tarleton and Webster's British van, the mixed rear guard of the Americans held the British at bay while constantly giving ground and drifting back in a deadly sequence of skirmishes, bluffs, flank fires, and quick charges amid the clay roads and stark winter woods.

The rolling fight eventually came within range of Williams's now-ready position at the ford of the creek where Williams had posted additional militia forces before the ford, while on the far bank he'd ranged his Continentals and Preston's Virginia Militia on the bluffs overlooking the watercourse. Washington and the American cavalry splashed over the ford and the militia opened a heavy fire in the face of the closing British infantry. Realizing Williams's Continentals were just across the ford, and the rifle-bearing militia was now without dragoon support, Webster's men charged headlong into a volley of rifle fire, absorbed the casualties, and continued on at the quick step before the riflemen could reload.[21] Lacking bayonets, the slow-loading riflemen could only turn and flee. Many were hard-pressed to make it back across the creek as Webster's men drove ahead until they were in turn checked by the fire of Preston's Virginia Militia, who today were attended personally by Henry Lee, and Williams's waiting Continental infantry posted on the elevated bluffs on the far side of the creek.[22] The firing grew hot and smoke soon engulfed the creek from bank to bank as the American militia scrambled up the steep banks to try and reach the safety of Williams's main line before being overtaken by the hard charging British. Not all the militia made it, and some were said to drown in the creek just feet from Williams's position.[23]

Once the scattered remains of his militia were finally across, Williams put his infantry in motion and the American cavalry again formed a rear guard as Williams's infantry retreated from the ford with the whole of his force marginally intact.

Meanwhile, British artillery had deployed on a hill overlooking the ford, British infantry were across the creek, and Tarleton was now forming his dragoons for a charge on the retreating

Americans. Captain Graham of the state dragoons later recalled the action and it remains one of the best first-hand descriptions of cavalry and light infantry acting in concert during the war:

> A column of the enemy's infantry, came on to the ford, and Tarleton with his cavalry came through. . . . [And on] the rise of the hill sounded his bugle.
>
> As soon as it was heard, Col. Washington, yet in his position on the right, about forty poles[24] from Tarleton, sounded his bugle also, and Major Rudolf, at the head of Lee's corps on the left sounded his. Upon this Washington's and Lee's cavalry went off at a canter, meeting each other in the road, about twenty poles in Tarleton's front. As they met, they wheeled up the road in a gallop (though in good order) after Col. Williams. Tarleton was halted on the hillside, and suffered them to pass without moving. The infantry on the opposite hill kept firing until they were out of view. When Washington and Rudolph came to Williams's rear, they turned out of the road, about sixty steps on each side, along his flanks. His men were marching briskly, and the cavalry officers gave orders that if the infantry was charged by the enemy in the rear they should wheel and take him in each flank. Washington himself and eight of his troopers took the rear.[25]

The British were now across the creek in force but still held at bay by the solid screen of revolving light horsemen directed by William Washington.

Despite their best zeal and determination the British were forced to surrender the chase in the face of the American rear guard and Williams's flying corps made the Haw River without further incident. Greene's prized regulars had been saved, but the militia had suffered a higher rate of casualties than Williams's Continentals, and many in the militia felt they had been sacrificed. There was a good deal of truth in the claim as Williams had indeed pulled his prized light infantry back across the ford to protect them before the militia. This was a cold fact and Williams's move would have been fully supported by General Greene as it was imperative that he keep his Continentals safe at hand to go against the trained British regulars of Lord Cornwallis. However the men actually serving in the militia didn't agree with Greene's standing sentiments, and, as quickly as Greene's ranks had swelled with militia they now drifted away and Greene's dreams of a battle with Cornwallis seemed to vanish with each new gap in the ranks at morning parade. "I am vexed with the militia," wrote Greene, "they desert us by the hundreds."[26] The rapidly shrinking American force now drifted along the banks of the Haw as their commander tried to determine his next move.

Meanwhile, yet another issue came into play. The day after the fight at Weitzel's Mill, Washington and his fatigued horsemen were still on the front lines with Colonel Williams's flying corps of Continentals when Washington received orders from General Greene's quartermaster, Lieutenant Colonel Edward Carrington. Carrington ordered Washington to immediately send a mounted escort back to Carrington to aid him in a prisoner exchange scheduled for five days hence.[27] The orders came from Carrington, a commissary officer, and not General Greene. After the long-running fight at Weitzel's Washington felt his mounts needed rest and re-shoeing and so Washington in effect declined Carrington's request and sent to General Greene for confirmation of Carrington's orders.[28]

Also running through the ranks at this time was a rumor that the next set of rations and provisions designated for Colonel Williams's Light Corps was to be diverted by the quartermasters and instead sent to Lieutenant Colonel Lee's Legion. This rumor created such a stir on the front that Colonel Williams wrote a formal request that these provisions be run through the normal commissary channels rather than Lee's Legion, "to prevent uneasiness and trouble" among the Light Corps troops.[29] This same rumor may or may not have influenced Washington's reply to Carrington and his quartermasters, and unfortunately, Washington's written reply to Carrington's request has been lost to history and we are forced to inject our imaginations here. Rumors aside, Carrington viewed Washington's refusal as bordering on outright insubordination and reported the offense to General Greene.

Throughout the history of military campaigns, a rivalry has existed between the quartermaster corps who equip and feed the troops, and soldiers serving at the front. Nonetheless, General Greene was a former quartermaster himself and his ire was certainly piqued by Washington's response to Carrington. Greene wrote Washington a stern reprimand and ordered Washington to attend to the shoeing of his mounts with all haste. Greene then tempered the letter with a request that Washington attend Greene's headquarters at his earliest convenience so the pair might discuss the central role Greene had devised for Washington's Light Dragoons in the coming weeks.[30]

General Greene was indeed making plans. Despite losing a number of South Carolina militia, deliverance had arrived in the form of a thousand man militia brigade from North Carolina. Two more brigades of militia arrived from Virginia and they were in turn followed by a detachment of four hundred Continentals.[31] In addition, two units of state commissioned dragoons arrived to supplement Greene's cavalry. One was a thirty-man element from Prince William County, Virginia, commanded by Captain Thomas Watkins and the second was a forty-man company of North Carolina light horsemen under the command of a former French cavalry officer, the Marquis de Bretigny.[32]

Apparently Captain Watkins had first offered his services to Lieutenant Colonel Lee, but Lee reportedly turned Watkins down because his men were not "fine enough dressed."[33] Unlike Lee, Washington was cut from the same cloth as Daniel Morgan and far more concerned with the way Watkins's men were kitted and drilled than how they dressed. After a quick perusal he gladly accepted both Watkins's and de Bretigny's horsemen into his command.

With these new recruits Greene's army numbered over four thousand men and the general from Rhode Island decided to halt and offer battle at a tiny crossroads of bucolic fields and woodlots overlooked by the log-framed courthouse of Guilford County, North Carolina.

William Washington, c. 1783, by Charles Willson Peale. (*National Park Service*)

George Washington from a 1780 portrait by John Trumbull. (*Library of Congress*)

Nathanael Greene, c. 1783, by Charles Willson Peale. (*National Park Service*)

Casimir Pulaski in a late nineteenth-century historical portrait. (*Independence National Historical Park*)

Stephen Moylan [undated]. (*U.S. Army Quartermaster Museum*)

Anthony Walton White in a late nineteenth-century historical portrait. (*Appleton's Cyclopaedia*)

Banastre Tarleton from *The Westminster* magazine, 1782. (*Library of Congress*)

Lord Cornwallis from *History of the war with America, France, Spain, and Holland* [1786]. (*Library of Congress*)

Daniel Morgan, an engraving after John Trumbull's 1822 painting, *Surrender of General Burgoyne.* (*Library of Congress*)

Otho Williams, painted by Charles Willson Peale in 1782. (*National Park Service*)

Henry "Light-Horse Harry" Lee painted by Charles Willson Peale in 1782. (*National Park Service*)

John Eager Howard painted by Charles Willson Peale in 1782. (*Independence National Historical Park*)

Sir Henry Clinton, a French engraving, c. 1778. (*Library of Congress*)

Lord Rawdon from *History of the war with America, France, Spain, and Holland* [1786]. (*Library of Congress*)

"Colonel [William] Washington at the Battle of Cowpens," an illustration commissioned for *Graham's Magazine* in the 1840s. It is worth noting that it was William Washington's "waiter," not a fellow soldier, who fired his pistol in defense of Washington. (*Library of Congress*)

Ten

GUILFORD COURTHOUSE

"Cavalry, especially when two deep, is not very terrible in their attacks in front, and least so when against infantry. . . . The deeper they are, the surer to break through."
–Baron von Steuben to General Washington, October 23, 1780

General Greene knew Lord Cornwallis would be coming for him, and devised a battle plan at the courthouse crossroads based on Morgan's defensive tactics as used at the Cowpens. Like Morgan, Greene deployed his men in three lines, and each line stretched across the Great Salisbury Road to aid in the movement and support of each.[1] The first line was set behind a strong fence of stacked rails that bordered a large cornfield. The North Carolina Militia manned the length of the rails and was protected on either side by a strong Corps of Observation to keep the first line's flank from being turned. William Washington commanded the corps on the right, and Henry Lee a corps on the left, both men were ordered by General Greene to "give the enemy all the annoyance in your power."[2] Washington's Corps consisted not only of his horsemen but also Colonel Charles Lynch's Virginia riflemen, Captain Robert Kirkwood's Delaware Light Infantry, and Captain Phillip Huffman's Virginia Continentals.[3]

As at the Cowpens, this first line of militia was tasked with giving two fires to bleed the British ranks before withdrawing, targeting the epaulettes of officers and non-commissioned officers and sapping the strength from the predictably hard-charging British. Greene's second line, also of militia, was placed some three hundred yards farther back along the Salisbury Road. Like the first line it was bisected by the Salisbury Road but the second line was purposely posted in dense woods and heavy undergrowth to force the British regulars into a close range brush fight. Greene's third line was set yet another six hundred yards to the rear in the open fields west of the courthouse and centered atop a thickly wooded ridgeline overlooking the open fields. This third and final line was the strongest yet and composed of Continental regulars and artillery.

The fight began on the morning of March 15th as Lieutenant Colonel Henry Lee's Corps of Observation was sent forward to find the British advance along the New Garden Road. Tarleton and Lee's cavalry met in a running fight that soon escalated into a series of sharp infantry skirmishes.[4] After giving the British three strong checks, Lee fell back to his post on the left of Greene's first line and awaited the approach of the main British force. As the sun lifted toward noon the British advance was spotted coming down the Salisbury Road.

American artillery quickly opened fire and British troops began to deploy on the far side of the cornfield. British gunners responded in kind, and a long range artillery duel took place until the British infantry stepped forward and the American guns withdrew. American riflemen began firing at the approaching ranks of scarlet and white while the remaining North Carolinians held their fire, waiting until the British came within musket range.[5] British drums drove the scarlet ranks forward, and as the British closed the distance they hesitated just outside musket range and came to a sudden halt.

Months of cold marches and hard campaigning had led to this inevitable point of confrontation and the tension was palpable as both sides stared at the other in anticipation of the coming storm. Finally, a British officer rode forward and urged his men ahead with a shout.[6] The British charged forward and a vol-

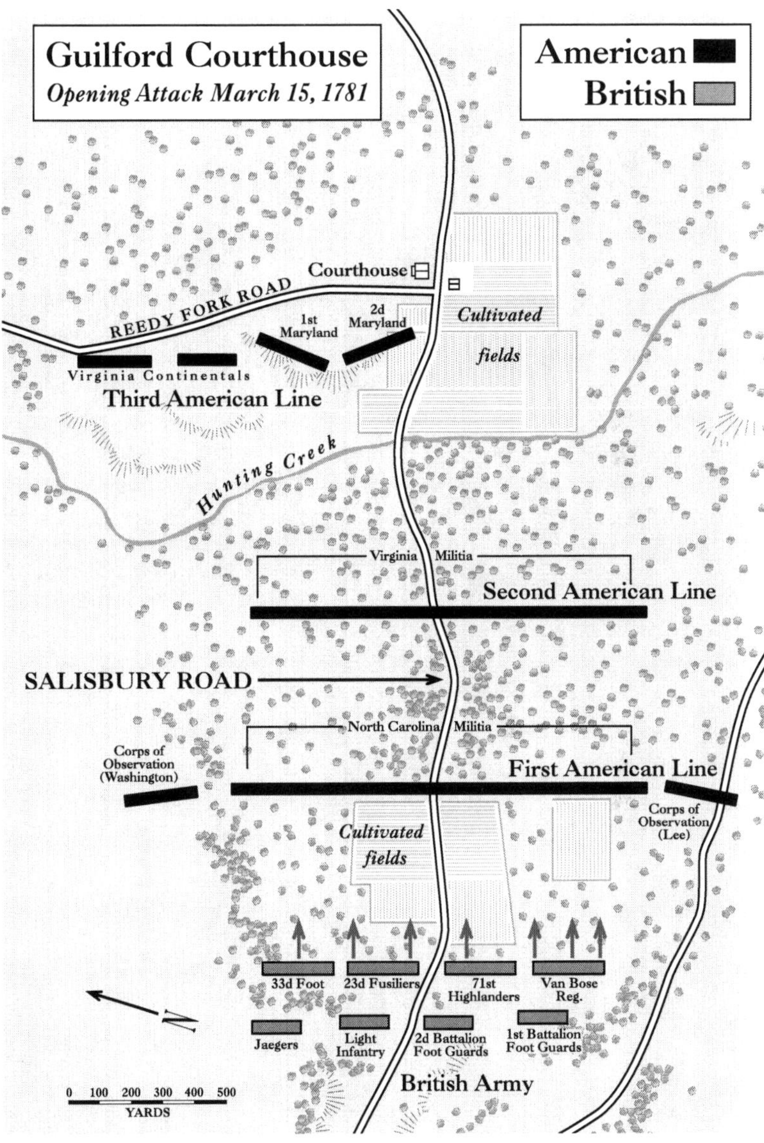

ley erupted from the American militia that ripped through the British lines like a reaping blade. However, British discipline held firm, as the scarlet-clad veterans turned a blind eye to their wounded, returned a volley, and charged forward before the militia could manage to reload. After giving but one fire, the vast majority of the North Carolinian militia turned and fled in the face of the coming bayonets.

As the first line broke for the rear, Washington's Corps of Observation began their fight on the right of the American line and opened a devastating enfilading fire across the leading British ranks. These deadly volleys quickly drew British attention and the 33d Regiment of Foot wheeled left to meet Washington's corps. Lord Cornwallis then sent his best skirmishers at Washington, the Hessian Jaegers, and a company of Guard's Light Infantry: "On finding that the left of the 33rd was exposed to a heavy fire from the right wing of the enemy, [Lieutenant Colonel Webster] changed his front to the left and being supported by the Yaghers and light infantry of the Guards, attacked."[7]

Now facing three British units, Washington pulled his corps back in a fighting withdrawal to keep from being cut off. Washington didn't fight his command in a true linear style but instead ordered his men to use natural cover and fire from behind trees, downed logs, and hillocks as the woods were so thick in these quarters that nearly all shots were fired inside fifty yards and well within the better range of a smoothbore musket. Any hopes Cornwallis may have held for quickly turning the American right now vanished in the face of blistering close range musketry and rifle fire, and the British advance ground to a crawl in the dense woods on the American right flank.[8] Washington would have been in the rear of this fight, directing traffic and dashing from flank to flank in the saddle, filing gaps in the makeshift line and watching to his flanks while exhorting the men to fire for effect and hold their ground.

The slower loading rifles were at a sharp disadvantage at this close range and casualties quickly mounted among Lynch's Virginians.[9] The lines seesawed back and forth in the heavy brush, and both sides dodged from tree to tree to fire on their enemies in short, sudden charges and hidden ambuscades.[10]

As Washington's corps struggled to hold Greene's right, Lieutenant Colonel Lee's Corps of Observation was soon engulfed in their own desperate contest against Lord Cornwallis's Hessian battalions on the American left. In the meantime, Cornwallis's now depleted center plowed ahead and engaged Greene's second line of militia waiting in the deep woods back behind the cornfield. Here the woods were as heavy and thick as the terrain in which Washington was fighting in on the right, and the battle quickly degenerated into a brutal series of close range volleys fired through dense underbrush. With the best of the British skirmishers engaged against Washington, this style of "Indian fighting" favored Greene's men considerably. This soon caused the regular "hat companies" of the British infantry to separate from one another and lose their momentum. Cornwallis wrote that the "excessive thickness of the woods rendered our bayonets little use and enabled the broken enemy to make frequent stands with an irregular fire which occasioned some loss."[11]

Scattered British officers, sergeants, and corporals rallied their men one by one and slowly pressed ahead in small sections to slug it out toe to toe and yard by yard with drifting groups of American militia and eventually cleared the woods before them, albeit in a definitively costly and piecemeal fashion.

As Greene's second line began to fall back, Washington and his Corps of Observation followed suit and began to withdraw. With their bayonets and quicker loading muskets, Huffman's and Kirkwood's Continentals pressed hard into the British infantry and temporarily gained ground to allow Lynch's riflemen to fall back under cover.[12] Sergeant Major Seymour of Kirkwood's Delawares wrote:

> Colonel Washington's Light Infantry was attacked by three British regiments, in which they behaved with almost incredible bravery, obliging the enemy to retreat in three different attacks . . . killing and wounding great numbers of the enemy.[13]

There is no accurate way of determining the number of casualties the British took on this flank, although four Jaegers were killed and another three wounded during the day's fighting. Lynch's Virginia riflemen suffered four out of eight officers hit along with eleven enlisted men killed and several more wounded throughout the course of the day.[14] While the riflemen were at a disadvantage due to the close nature of the fighting, it's highly unlikely the casualties were entirely one-sided.

As Washington's Corps of Observation withdrew to the third line, they naturally drifted north and right to clear Greene's line and continued to exchange fire with the pursuing Hessian Jaegers and British light infantry. Meanwhile, the first British troops began emerging from the fight with Greene's second line. These scattered British soldiers now halted as they exited the heavy woods and entered a large, open hollow that dropped away before them. Bisected north to south by Hunting Creek, this wide hollow stretched left and right, beginning to the south, or American left, with a series of cleared fields that slowly dropped to a ravine and more broken ground on the northern edge of the hollow on the American right. The far, eastern lip of the hollow was topped by a ridge of rough ground covered in trees where British soldiers could see portions of Greene's final line posted on the high ground of the ridge. What they couldn't determine was how strong this next American position would be.

Though largely hidden from view, Greene's third line of Continentals was very well posted. It began to the north on the American right, with two regiments of Continentals, the 1st and 2nd Virginia, followed by two regiments of Maryland Continentals with the veteran 1st Maryland toward the center, and the untested but larger 2nd Maryland anchoring the left flank and overlooking a series of open fields on either side of the Salisbury Road.

Augmenting the infantry were four, six-pounder cannons deployed in pairs. One battery was positioned with Lynch's Virginians on the northern flank under the command of Captain Ebenezer Finley; a second under Captain Anthony Singleton was posted to the south, in the midst of the 2nd Maryland, below the high ground where the courthouse was perched. The Reedy Fork Road ran along the ridge and paralleled the rear of Greene's line, allowing for the fast movement of troops from one flank to another. All in all, it was a strong position with overlapping fields of fire and Greene was confident he could deal the British a heavy blow here in the low ground below the ridge.

The first elements of British infantry to appear in force at the hollow's lip were from the 33d Regiment of Foot, many of whom had just endured the vicious firefight with Washington's Corps of Observation. These veterans quickly spied Finley's northern battery and, rather than waiting on fellow troops to come up in support, their commander, Lieutenant Colonel James Webster, led them straight for the battery. Exactly why Webster chose to attack without waiting for additional support is not clear and in reality there may have been multiple reasons. Authors Lawrence Babits and Joshua Howard believe line of sight may have been foremost.[15] From Webster's position the wooded terrain was concealing the majority of the main American third line and Washington's Corps of Observation had shifted out of sight to the north. Fatigue was another reason. Webster's men had been fighting and suffering casualties for a while now and when they saw what appeared to be a lightly defended battery across the open hollow, they might have hoped the end was at hand with one final, all-out push. Simple arrogance may have been a third reason, as every British soldier born believed British bayonets would always triumph over American musketry.[16] Whatever the cause for Webster's sudden attack, it would soon prove to be a remarkably poor decision.

Quickly formed, the 33d pushed down the western lip of the ridge and crossed the ravine where they were suddenly checked by a withering blast of musketry and artillery erupting from the American right and center. Webster's attack quickly broke apart under this sudden onslaught and his men spilled back across the ravine in the face of this heavy fire. Lieutenant Colonel Howard of the 1st Maryland stated that Washington brought his horsemen up at this opportune moment and the combined fire of Kirkwood and Lynch, along with the charging light dragoons, forced the jaegers and the British light infantry covering Webster's left to be "driven from their ground" and routed back, compelling Webster to re-fuse his flank by 90 degrees and take cover on the back side of a hill. This high ground proved to be a good defensive position and Webster stopped Washington's flanking infantry here, but Webster was now turned and "held completely in check" as he hunkered down behind the hill.[17]

Meanwhile, still more British troops continued to arrive at the hollow's western edge, and Howard said the 23d Fusilliers appeared across the hollow, but with Webster's flank turned they did not attempt much.[18] The next unit to form was the 2d Battalion of British Foot Guards, who streamed out of the southwestern corner of the hollow along the Salisbury Road on the American left.[19] As the Guards formed they heard Webster's ongoing fight to the north and instantly swept forward in support.

The British Foot Guards were composed of veterans from three of the finest regiments in the history of British Arms: the 1st Regiment of Guards, the Coldstream Guards, and the Scots Guards. Moreover, the Guards were long serving veterans of the American Revolution, having first arrived in America in 1776.[20] They were commanded by Brigadier General Charles O'Hara, a legend in the British army; however O'Hara had been shot through the leg in the close range fire fights along the second line, and command of the Guards fell to Lieutenant Colonel James Stuart.[21] Stuart was the son of a Scottish earl, a career soldier, and a veteran of the Seven Years War.[22] Great things were expected from the Guards and Lieutenant Colonel Stuart was determined not to disappoint. "Glowing with impatience to signalize themselves, [the Guards] instantly attacked." [23]

The Guards swept forward against the southern, left, flank of the American line, moving at the quick step with bayonets fixed and arms at the trail as they headed for the 2d Maryland.[24] These Marylanders, many of them about to see combat for the first time, were thrown into confusion by the rapid advance of the expert Guardsmen who suddenly halted within musket range and fired a quick volley with chilling precision.[25] Musket balls went sweeping through the Marylander's ranks, killing and wounding many and dropping two of the 2d's key officers. Already on the verge of panic, the raw Maryland troops managed to fire a volley but the result was a ragged, inaccurate fire that had little effect.[26] The Guards then gave a shout and charged forward with bayonets at the ready and the 2d Maryland broke for the rear; they abandoned friend and foe alike, and left Captain Singleton's battery to fend for themselves.

The Guards quickly rolled over Singleton's battery, and continued on in pursuit of the fleeing 2d Marylanders to angle in behind the 1st Maryland who were still keeping an eye on Webster's command to their front. Colonel John Gunby, the 1st Maryland's commander, now realized the British Guards had closed on his left rear and were poised to roll up Greene's final line altogether.[27] He quickly ordered the 1st Maryland to face about and engage the Guards in the open ground behind his left. Meanwhile, Colonel Stuart of the Guards started to call his scattered men back from their pursuit of the 2nd Maryland, and have them reform to fire a volley at Gunby's 1st Maryland.[28] The two sides fired at nearly the same instant, Gunby fell to the ground pinned beneath his dying horse, and Lieutenant Colonel John Howard took command of the 1st Maryland.[29] As the smoke lifted Howard ordered his men to fix bayonets and prepare for a charge. Colonel Stuart and his Guards were entirely focused on the 1st Maryland to their front when they were suddenly struck from behind by a thunderbolt.[30]

After helping pin Webster's men on the hill, there was little else for Washington's horsemen to do in that sector. As the firing increased to Washington's left, his attention was drawn to the Guards' attack and he moved down behind Greene's line toward the courthouse via the Reedy Fork Road.[31] When he saw the 2d Maryland break and the Guards pursue them onto open ground, he quickly recognized an opportunity; the Guards were acting alone, and would be temporarily disordered and focused elsewhere in their scattered pursuit of the 2d Maryland and growing skirmish with the 1st. He also knew Greene's final line was in imminent danger of being driven from the field. Charging the Foot Guards would be a risk–but any mounted charge was fraught with risk. Washington had also been given orders to "give the enemy all the annoyance in your power."[32] Rather than seek out additional orders, Washington chose to seize the initiative and wave his men forward.[33] He led them on at a canter in a column of fours and descended the ridge, in seconds Washington and the leading ranks gained the open ground north of the road and were in easy range of the Foot Guards' rear flank.

One has to remember the formation Washington led on the narrow roads along the ridge about the courthouse. He had roughly one hundred twenty troopers arranged in a column of fours, which makes for thirty ranks of four moving toward the enemy in close order. Each moving horse with trooper aboard was approximately three feet wide from knee to knee and therefore each rank of four was roughly twelve feet wide. At close order each rank of fours had to stay twelve feet back from the rank before them so that each rank, or set of fours, could wheel independently and the column could change front, direction, or even reverse itself, if needed. The average horse is around eight to nine feet in length, so the head to head spacing between each rank of four was roughly twenty feet. Multiply Washington's thirty ranks of four by twenty and you realize Washington's column was approximately six hundred feet, or two hundred yards long.

Lieutenant Philemon Holcombe recalled "leaping a ravine" in the assault and Washington likely dropped down off the wooded ridge within one hundred yards of the Foot Guards rear flank –point blank range for a cavalry charge.[34] As mentioned earlier, a line formation was preferred for a charge rather than a column. To change from column to line the front ranks of the column would break gait and allow the rear ranks to come up and form a line with a three deep front. However, at this range Washington couldn't slow down or he'd forfeit the element of surprise; if anything he needed to pick up the pace at this point. But to shift one hundred twenty cantering troopers from a column of fours already traveling at fifteen miles an hour into a three deep line of platoon frontage would require two hundred yards of ground Washington simply didn't have.[35] That would mean Washington's force would still be forming their three deep line formation when striking the Guards and his men would be focusing on dressing their ranks rather than engaging the enemy, a near certain recipe for disaster.

Washington had to attack–immediately. However, the risk of a charge in column was that a narrow front would be presented to the enemy and if any horses fell in the front rank, or stalled on impact, they would retard the progress of all behind like an accordion. To counter this, rearward troop commanders could

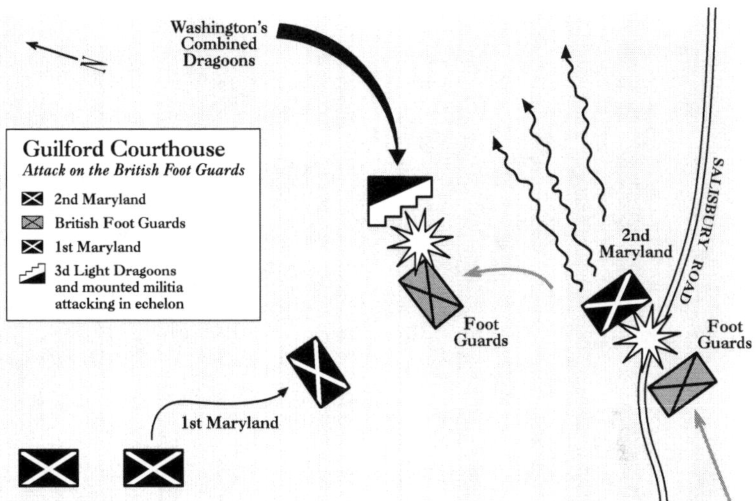

charge in echelon, with each troop column offsetting to the side, so they were not stacked directly behind the troop to its front.[36] This would also allow the attacking force to spread out the impact on the enemy as each column bore down separately, but still in league with the whole. Watching the attack from the northern end of the open hollow was Sergeant Major William Seymour of the Delaware Line:

> Colonel Washington, charged them so furiously that they either killed or wounded almost every man in the [Guards] regiment, charging through them and breaking their ranks three or four times.[37]

The offsetting columns of light horsemen closed to the croup and hit the Guards in succession to break and re-break the British ranks as each troop column plowed home at the gallop. Horses bowled men down like nine pins and troopers plunged through the guards atop wide-eyed horses turned wild with the moment. Broadswords followed with whipping blows that splayed skulls and shredded limbs in spreading waves of violence. Caught in flank and unawares, the British Foot Guards were broken, shattered, and scattered in less time than it takes to tell the tale.

The momentum of Washington's charge carried his men past the Guards and the 1st Maryland waited until the final horses had blown through the Guards' fleeing ranks before they pitched forward with bayonets at the ready. Many believe Lieutenant Colonel Stuart of the Guards was killed here by Captain John Smith of the Maryland line, due to the following account written by Samuel Mathis:

> Smith and his men were in the throng killing guards and grenadiers like so many furies Col. Stewart [sic] seeing the mischief Smith was doing made up to him through the crowd, dust an [sic] smoke unperceived and made a violent lunge at him with his small sword, the first that Smith saw was the shining metal like lightning at his bosom he only had time to lean a little to the right, and lift up his left arm so as to let the polished steel pass under it when the hilt struck his breast, it would have been through his body but for the haste of the colonel and happening to set his foot on the arm of a man Smith had just cut down, his unsteady step, his violent lunge and missing his aim brought him with one knee upon the dead man, the Guards came rushing up very strong, Smith had no alternative but to wheel round to the right and give Stewart a back handed blow over or across the head on which he fell; his orderly sergeant attacked Smith, but Smith's sergeant dispatched him; a 2nd attacked him Smith hewed him down, a 3rd behind him threw down a cartridge and shot him in the back of the head, Smith now fell among the slain but was taken up by his men and brought off, it was found to be only a buckshot lodged against the skull and had only stunned him."[38]

Though a bit overwrought, this is still an extremely compelling account until one discovers that Samuel Mathis wasn't at the battle of Guilford Courthouse. Instead, Mathis's eyewitness details came from his postwar business partner, the former Captain John Smith of the Maryland Continentals. Mathis didn't write this account until 1819, after his partner had died, and some thirty-eight years after the event.

There is no doubt Lieutenant Colonel Stuart was killed at the third line, but exactly how much swashbuckling took place in the wake of Washington's charge is a mystery. Sergeant Major Seymour's earlier account doesn't mention the 1st Marylanders; only the light dragoons. Nor does a second account–that of Banastre Tarleton, who was on the Salisbury Road waiting for his Legion Cavalry to come forward, and either saw the tail end of these actions or the entire attack.[39] "The ground being open, Colonel Washington's dragoons killed Colonel Stewart and several of his men, and pursued the remainder into the wood."[40]

Like Sergeant Major Seymour of the Delaware Line, Tarleton doesn't mention a sprawling, smoke-filled bayonet fight, which would certainly have captured his attention. Tarleton also had ample opportunity to talk with members of the Guards after the fight and didn't record Stuart's death as being any sort of extraordinary duel, only that Stuart was killed by Washington's men, and no doubt any mounted field officers of the Guards, such as a Lieutenant Colonel, would have been sought out and targeted by Washington's charging troopers, who may have cut Stuart off his horse but not killed him.

A third differing witness from Mathis's account was Lord Cornwallis who wrote the Guards were "charged and driven back into the field by Colonel Washington's dragoons . . ."[41] Cornwallis wrote his account just two days after the battle and doesn't mention a rollicking bayonet fight or "throngs" of "furies" either. Both Cornwallis and Tarleton's accounts were recorded in relatively immediate time frames compared to Mathis's thirty-eight year lapse.[42]

Captain Smith was later captured by the British and held under arrest for allegedly having killed a British officer at Guilford Courthouse and some works have claimed that this arrest was evidence of Smith having killed Lieutenant Colonel Stuart of the Guards. However, in a letter Captain Smith wrote to General Greene during his captivity Smith made no mention of Lieutenant Colonel Stuart and instead stated he'd been placed under arrest for allegedly murdering a British Captain and several soldiers "a considerable time after they were made prisoners" not during the heat of battle.[43] These same charges, that Smith "inhumanly put to death" a British officer and three privates after they had surrendered were also mentioned in another letter from

British Major John Doyle to General Greene and there was no mention of Lieutenant Colonel Stuart's death in this letter either. Captain Smith was later paroled by Lord Rawdon, which in effect cleared him of the charges.[44]

Still, it is possible that Captain Smith killed Lieutenant Colonel Stuart, and regardless who killed the Guard's colonel, the veteran 1st Maryland did most definitely attack with their bayonets and take advantage of the Guards' broken ranks created by the charge of Washington's Light Dragoons. Many of the Guards were bowled over and driven to the ground by the crush of horses and others willingly dove face down to avoid being poleaxed by the swinging dragoon swords only to be caught prone and pinned to the ground by the following Maryland bayonets. Lieutenant Colonel Howard of the 1st Maryland led the bayonet attack and stated dryly that numerous Guards "had been knocked down by the horse without being much hurt. We took some prisoners, and the whole were in our power."[45]

This was real war and the work was quick and brutal; it lacked the false glamour Mathis attached to it and that is why Howard, Seymour, Cornwallis, and Tarleton didn't mention a surging, sulfurous donnybrook between the Guards and Marylanders. Howard did claim later that "Captain Smith of the infantry killed a Captain Steuart with a horseman's sword… Steuart refused to surrender, I saw the transaction," in reference to Smith's encounter with Stuart, yet Howard's statement lacks Mathis's cliffhanging drama and instead reads as if Lieutenant Colonel Stuart was unhorsed and already compromised when the 1st Maryland closed.[46]

With the 1st Maryland now skewering the prostrate Guards to the ground, it made no sense for Washington to halt, reform, and come charging back through in a second pass as the chance for injuring the Marylanders was entirely too great. Instead, Washington kept his men headed across Hunting Creek where they spotted a group of British horsemen and turned for them next.[47] According to Lieutenant Colonel Howard, Washington pulled up and halted here while his men continued on because, "he lost his cap and there was something amiss with his saddle or bridle."[48] Knowing Washington's battle history it is unlikely that he would dismount simply to retrieve his helmet. It's far more plausible that his saddle had slipped when he was riding through the Guards, and for a horseman in combat a loose saddle or cut bridle rein from a British sword or bayonet, was an issue that required immediate attention.

As stated before, Cornwallis was now up and observing the fight from the hollow's edge and this may or may not have been the knot of officers Washington's men targeted. Either way his Lordship had seen enough of Washington's Light Dragoons for one day and ordered the newly arrived battery of Lieutenant John McLeod to open fire.[49] McLeod's guns opened with stiff volleys of grapeshot that killed Lieutenant Griffin Faunt le Roy of the 1st Light Dragoons and scattered the rest of Washington's command who turned and cantered back across the hollow.[50] Once remounted, Washington rode back to Greene's line and rejoined his command.

As Washington retired, still more British troops poured into the hollow. This act changed the game considerably and prompted the 1st Maryland to fall back toward the courthouse. Watching from atop the ridge, General Greene had a decision to make. His final line had held firm to the north but his southern flank was now wide open due to the 2d Maryland's panicked retreat. Historians will forever argue whether Greene should have advanced on the heels of the Guards' defeat and driven Cornwallis from the field but Greene really had few options. Though Greene's line had held to the north, Webster's mixed brigade still clung tenaciously to the hill at the northern end of the hollow and would have retarded any advance from that sector while on the southern end of the hollow, more enemy troops had appeared and were continuing to arrive by the second. Plus British artillery was now in place and Tarleton's dragoons were coming forward.[51] Greene had also not seen Lee's left flank Corps of Observation since the first line fighting, and with no ready reserves to deploy, an attack on Cornwallis would have been a gamble that bordered on folly.

Continental drums soon beat the retreat and Greene pulled his units out of line and fell back down the Ready Fork Road to the Speedwell Ironworks on Troublesome Creek.[52] Greene had lost all four of his guns to the British, and American casualties stood at ninety men killed and two hundred wounded. A vast number of North Carolina militia fled the lines after the fight and it's therefore hard to determine exact numbers in their ranks. However, Greene's Continentals were still largely intact and total battlefield casualties were around 7 percent of his force.[53] Among Washington's Light Dragoons the tally was low for what they had accomplished with three killed, eight wounded, and three missing.[54] The British on the other hand were in far worse shape and unable to pursue Greene's army after the fight. Lord Cornwallis's smaller force had won the ground but lost nearly a third of their numbers with ninety men killed and over four hundred wounded including five field officers. The heavy losses crippled Cornwallis's offensive capability and he'd also failed to destroy Greene's Army.

In much of the battle the Americans had relied on terrain, ambush, and Indian style fighting but at the third line, Greene's Continentals went toe to toe with some of the best infantry Britain had to offer and the tactics displayed in the turning of Webster's command and the repulse of the Foot Guards would have pleased the best of Europe's professional armies. No one would ever argue that Cornwallis lost the battle of Guilford Courthouse but Greene's Continentals walked away combat ready, knowing they had given as good as they got–if not better. On the other hand, the British were in deplorable shape. Short on food, tents and medical stores, they sat shivering in the open winter air, soaked by a steadily falling rain as they listened to the sounds of their own wounded dying around them. It's now over two hundred years after the battle but no one has ever put it better than British Parliamentarian Charles James Fox, who, after he read the field reports decried, "Another such victory would ruin the British Army."[55]

Eleven

HOBKIRK'S HILL

"The principle advantage of the cavalry exists in charging sword in hand."–Regulations for the Prussian Cavalry

AFTER "WINNING" THE BATTLE OF GUILFORD COURTHOUSE, Lord Cornwallis was forced to leave his wounded behind and begin a two hundred mile road march for Wilmington, North Carolina, where desperately needed supplies sat waiting courtesy of the British navy. General Greene followed after Cornwallis as far as the Deep River, watching his adversary and all the while reviewing his options.[1] Despite losing his artillery, Greene's core force of Continental infantry and cavalry had come through Guilford Courthouse largely intact and remained in good spirits. Unfortunately, the short-term militias that allowed Greene the numbers to give battle at the courthouse had concluded their terms of service and left for home, leaving Greene with roughly the same sized force of combat-ready troops as Cornwallis now had.[2] Greene was again dismayed by the fleeting nature of the militia, but his friend Joseph Reed cautioned him that a harsh attitude toward the militia would only alienate the countryside and cost Greene support in the future. Reed advocated looking upon the militia as an unloved wife, "be to their faults a little blind, and to their virtues very kind."[3]

William Washington had also lost his militia dragoons under Watkins and de Bretigny, but by now Washington was used to the constant turnover in the make do or do without world of a Continental soldier. As he crossed over the Guilford battlefield he came across an enemy cavalry sword lying on the ground, and Washington was so impressed with the piece that he had the blade sent to his executive officer, Major Richard Call in Virginia, who posted it on to Governor Thomas Jefferson. At Washington's request, Call put in an order for five hundred such blades to be manufactured, writing to Jefferson that "the sword is the most destructive and almost only necessary weapon a dragoon carries."[4]

Regrettably, the letter holds no details of the sword Washington admired, but went on to request additional help in procuring more horses, a constant problem given the hard service of light dragoon mounts. There were plenty of horses available in eighteenth-century North Carolina but the same standing orders that had stopped Washington from impressing civilian mounts on prior occasions were still in place, so the Continentals operated under a disadvantage compared to British cavalry such as Tarleton's who simply took what they wanted from Whig farmers.[5] Jefferson apparently made good on the request for the swords and Hunter's Manufactory on Rappahannock Forge produced one thousand horseman's swords "by order of Colonel Washington" by the fall of 1781. Unfortunately, Jefferson was less help regarding remounts. At a time when horse values were extraordinarily high and the Continental dollar had dropped drastically in value, it was commonly held that $100 of Continental script wouldn't even buy one's breakfast.[6]

Although General Greene secured permission from Jefferson for Washington to send horse agents into Virginia, the wealthy planters of Virginia's eastern tidewater community strenuously objected when their bountiful stables came to the horse agent's attention. The tidewater gentry quickly pressed the Virginia assembly to decree that only horses valued under $50–a ridiculously low sum for a horse given the war's spiraling inflation–were proper for the dragoons to take and that horses seized in violation of this restriction be valued at $5,000 in compensation to the owners.[7] Greene was livid at the imposed restrictions on Washington and his troopers who were fighting and dying to win the war and keep the British from subjugating not only the Carolinas but Virginia and the nation as a whole. Greene wrote in reply:

> the price fixed for the purchase of horses is very low–it would not purchase by voluntary sale a horse that I would trust a dragoon upon. . . . If horses are dearer to the Inhabitants than the lives of Subjects, or the liberties of the People, there will be no doubt of the assembly persevering in their late resolution.[8]

General Greene's remarks were largely ignored; then as now, good horses were harder to come by than swords.

As Washington and his troopers continued to scout the British withdrawal, Greene continued to study his options. With the cavalry of Washington and Lee at his side, Greene knew he could likely pin Cornwallis's retreating columns against one of the many river crossings en route to Wilmington on the coast; however, the loss of Greene's artillery at Guilford now created a need for caution. Greene also knew the British were sweeping up all available supplies on their march to Wilmington, and Greene didn't want to endure the same conditions he'd imposed on Cornwallis during the Race for the Dan. Greene could continue following after Cornwallis, harassing his march and dogging his flanks all the way to Wilmington, but in Greene's mind that served little purpose and he began to look southward instead.[9]

When Lord Cornwallis took out after Greene in the Race for the Dan, he left behind eight thousand men and a strong line of frontier forts and outposts that fanned out from Charleston across South Carolina's interior.[10] On paper those were imposing numbers but they failed to tell the whole story. Far from being secure, the string of interior British garrisons was constantly under attack from rebel partisans led by Francis Marion, Andrew Pickens, and Thomas Sumter. If these partisans continued to press the British garrisons, there was an excellent opportunity for Greene's Continentals to steal a march back into South Carolina and topple the British forts one at a time.[11]

It is not exactly clear who hatched the idea for reinvading South Carolina. On March 23rd Greene wrote Congress that "nothing will be left un attempted" in the Southern Department and went on to mention Sumter and Marion's recent successes in South Carolina.[12] Greene no doubt consulted his Continentals who'd fought prior campaigns in South Carolina: John Eager Howard, William Washington, and Otho Williams certainly all had a say as well as Henry Lee, who had most recently returned from operations in that quarter. Regardless of influence, it was Nathanael Greene that would bear the responsibility of any action and he would ultimately weigh the options and make the decision. One factor that weighed heavily on General Greene's mind was the amount of available forage and supplies in the sparsely inhabited backcountry of South Carolina, but assurances of support from General Sumter helped ease Greene's concerns in that regard.[13] In the end, Greene figured that if he turned for South Carolina and Cornwallis pursued him, then Greene would have relieved North Carolina of Cornwallis's presence without firing a shot, and Cornwallis would essentially be right back where he had started before the Race to the Dan. If Cornwallis didn't pursue and stayed at Wilmington, Greene felt the odds were ripe for taking the entire string of South Carolina forts, in effect liberating the vast majority of South Carolina and further isolating Cornwallis.[14] As Greene looked south he set his sights on the key British garrison at Camden and made his decision. On March 29 he wrote General Washington that he was "determined to carry the war immediately into South Carolina."[15]

The British commander at Camden was Lieutenant Colonel George Augustus Francis, Lord Rawdon. Just twenty-six years of age, Lord Rawdon had been born into an Irish peerage and grew up in the virtual lap of luxury. Tall, dark, and energetic, his portrait looks a bit homely by today's standards, but in his day he was reputed to be the ugliest officer in the British army.[16] Whatever his looks, he first saw combat as a lieutenant at Breed's/Bunker Hill in 1775, where he took command of his company after his own captain was shot. For the courage he displayed during his baptism of fire he was promoted to captain and given a company in the 63d Foot. Less than a year later he joined General Sir Henry Clinton's staff and saw further action at the battles of Brooklyn, White Plains, and Monmouth Courthouse. Lord Rawdon was then given his own regiment of Loyalist provincials, the Volunteers of Ireland, and promoted to Colonel.[17] He then accompanied his new command southward and arrived in South Carolina during the siege of Charleston where he quickly proved himself to his superiors and later turned in a solid performance under Lord Cornwallis at the battle of Camden.[18] Cornwallis had such faith in Rawdon's abilities that he gave Rawdon operational control over the line of backcountry posts when Cornwallis left to begin the Race for the Dan.

The post at Camden was the keystone in the line of backcountry British garrisons.[19] It commanded a crucial intersection of country roads and consisted of six redoubts, with a large stockade of high pine walls built in the center.[20] Aside from housing a large garrison force, Camden served as a stern reminder of the King's presence to all civilians in the area. Most of Camden's surrounding residents remained at least outwardly loyal to King George for the lucrative potential for trade with the garrison and many others provided Rawdon with a steady stream of news and information. By early April, farmers north of Camden began to report a large force of Continentals moving down from North Carolina.[21]

Greene arrived outside Camden on April 19 with a force of just over one thousand men and Washington's 3d Light Dragoons leading the van. After a brief skirmish north of town, Greene realized that Rawdon's fortified position was entirely too strong for him to take by assault or siege with the resources at hand and Greene decided to fall back and await the arrival of promised reinforcements from Thomas Sumter's South Carolina militia.[22]

Meanwhile, inside Camden's palisade walls, Lord Rawdon was hurriedly sending for reinforcements of his own from Lieutenant Colonel John Watson in nearby Georgetown.[23] After waiting several days without result, Rawdon decided to launch a surprise attack on Greene's men before the Continental position could be improved with artillery, more men, or proper breastworks.[24] Rawdon knew he was outnumbered and went about arming every man in his garrison: musicians, wagon masters, and surgeon's assistants–anyone who could load and carry a musket.[25] In addition to this amalgamated force of teamsters and musicians, Rawdon had four regiments of infantry; the 63d Regiment of Foot, the King's Americans, the New York Volunteers, and Rawdon's own Volunteers of Ireland. He also had a collection of Tory militia to draw from, plus a force of some sixty mounted infantrymen mostly pooled from the New York Volunteers. Kitted with broadswords, these horsemen were placed under the command of Major James Coffin, a native of Boston, Massachusetts, and a six year veteran of the war. All together, Rawdon's force totaled nine hundred fifty men and strict orders were given to march in absolute silence.

At 10:00 A.M. the twin columns left Camden and stole quietly through the thick, concealing woods along Pine Tree Creek. They didn't have far to go as Greene had just taken a new position a mile north of town on Hobkirk's Hill. More ridge than hill, the sandy eminence was covered in open timber and bisected by the Great Waxhaws Road. The hill was flanked to the east by a large spring that flowed down to form a swampy stretch of wooded ground that ran toward town. A second road ran southeast from the eastern side of the hill to Kershaw's Mill, and a third, more obscure road, ran directly into town from this eastern quarter and roughly paralleled the Waxhaws Road.[26]

Entirely unaware of these movements below were General Greene's men sitting atop their position on Hobkirk's Hill. They had just completed their morning drill and were enjoying their first full ration of food since having left North Carolina. The rations had been cause for a small celebration; arms were stacked and Washington's horses, now down to just some sixty odd animals fit for service, were tethered nearby on loose girths.[27] Recently both men and animals had seen hard service in marches through swamps and dense forests so choked with alder and pine as to barely admit the column to pass in single file.[28] A gill of rum was issued per man and the oily blue smoke of cook fires

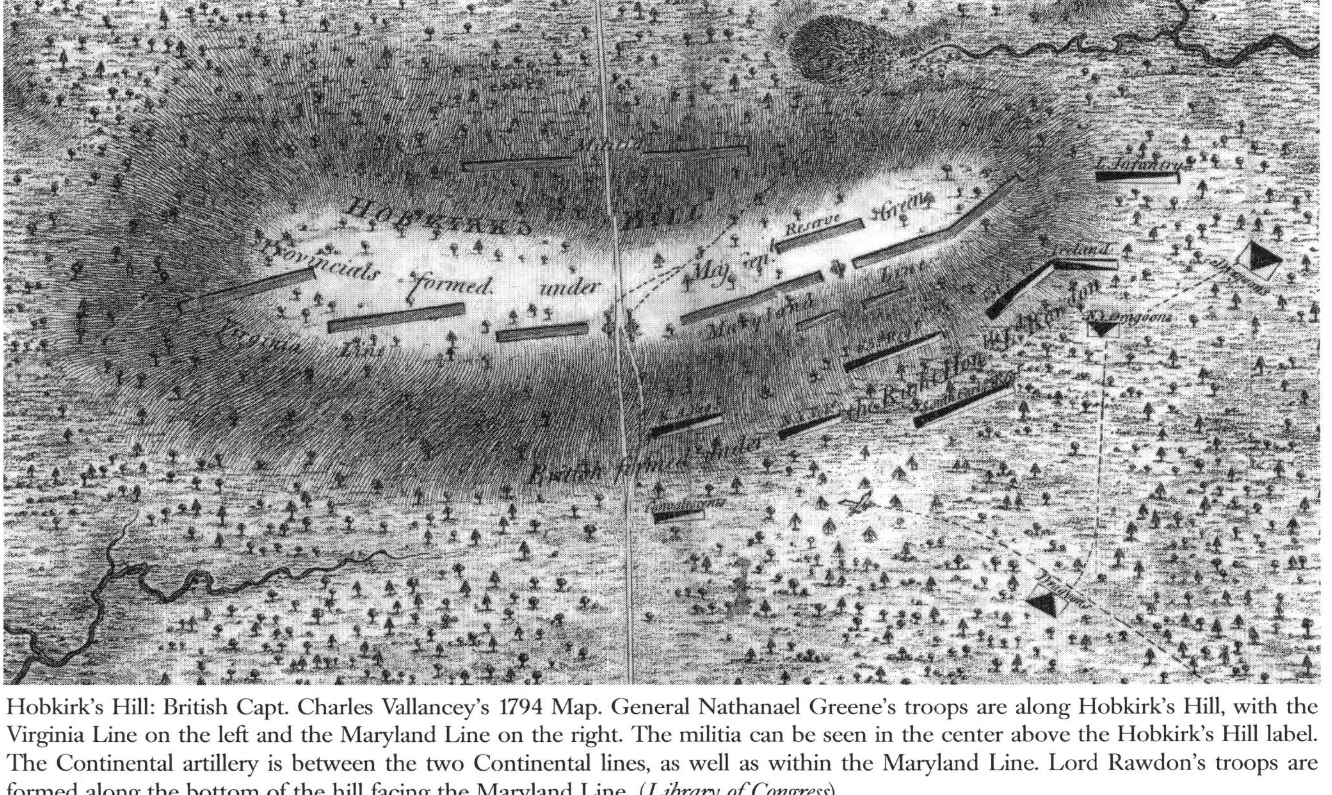

Hobkirk's Hill: British Capt. Charles Vallancey's 1794 Map. General Nathanael Greene's troops are along Hobkirk's Hill, with the Virginia Line on the left and the Maryland Line on the right. The militia can be seen in the center above the Hobkirk's Hill label. The Continental artillery is between the two Continental lines, as well as within the Maryland Line. Lord Rawdon's troops are formed along the bottom of the hill facing the Maryland Line. (*Library of Congress*)

soon wafted fragrantly through camp. After weeks of short rations and hard marches, all seemed briefly right with the world, and many were taking this rare opportunity to soak their tired feet and wash their clothes in the nearby spring when the sharp crash of musketry split the morning air.

Kirkwood's Delaware Company was the first to respond, quickly forming and rushing down the hill to assist the pickets stationed in the heavy woods below.[29] The firing increased as they went and what they found below was no simple skirmish between sentries but a stiff fight forming in the dense pines and brushwood. As Kirkwood's men returned fire, Greene began forming the rest of his troops for battle on the crest of the hill, many of them half-dressed and barefoot as they grabbed their muskets and rushed into action. The 1st Virginia formed the American right with the 2d Virginia tight to the road; extending east of the road was the 1st Maryland and forming the left was the 2d Maryland whose ranks ran down to the spring. Washington's Light Dragoons were quickly mounted and placed in reserve along with the North Carolina militia.[30] In a stroke of good fortune for Greene and his men, Colonel Charles Harrison's artillerymen had arrived earlier that very morning with three pieces of artillery and positioned two of the six-pounders along the Waxhaws Road and the third farther east between the two Maryland Regiments.[31]

Down at the base of the hill Kirkwood's men and the Continental pickets were caught in the midst of a "universal blaze of musketry" as concentrated British firepower eventually drove the stubborn Delaware troops out of the thick pines and into the more open woods at the slope of the hill near the Waxhaws Road.[32] Rawdon was urging his men forward just as they'd marched, bursting from the tree line in a narrow front with the 63d Foot on the right, and the King's American Regiment on the left.

The American gunners looked down at the concentrated mass of enemy troops advancing before them and opened fire. They shredded the tightly packed columns below with volleys of whistling grapeshot and blasted the British back into the pines. As the smoke cleared Greene saw the destruction wrought by his guns and felt the battle was practically won. Without full knowledge of Rawdon's forces below, he ordered his two center regiments, the 1st Maryland and 2d Virginia, to advance with the bayonet "and charge them in front" and then sent his flank regiments, the 2d Maryland on the left and 1st Virginia on the right, down the hill to take Rawdon's columns in either flank.[33] To complete his perceived rout of Rawdon, Greene sent Washington and his light dragoons forward with orders to "turn the enemy's right flank and charge them in the rear."[34]

Meanwhile, Rawdon was nearly beside himself with rage as the Continental artillery shredded his ranks before Greene's line. Rawdon had been informed that Greene had no guns, and now his men were paying the price for this false intelligence before his very eyes. Rawdon could see the Continentals charging forward and he quickly extended his front and ordered forward his reserves. The central, bayonet charging Continentals Greene sent forward soon masked the fire of his artillery and the British Provincials now rallied under the lack of grapeshot as Rawdon's own Volunteers of Ireland came up and added their fire against the Maryland ranks.[35] Aside from the 63d Foot, all of Rawdon's troops were American Tories fighting against fellow American Whigs in sharp exchanges of musketry that now harkened more of civil war than revolution. British troops were quick to take advantage of the thick woods covering sections of the hill and volley after volley crashed through the spring woods as men fired, bit open fresh cartridges, and hurriedly ran charges down barrels that soon grew too hot to hold with bare hands.[36]

As Greene's infantry rolled forward, so too did Washington and his light dragoons. They swept down around the hill in ranks and then spurred hard for Major Coffin's dragoons on the British right flank. Coffin's men were struck at the gallop by Washington's light horsemen and driven off in a sharp tussle of swinging blades and sprinting horses. Once Washington had scattered Coffin's men he collected his pursuing troopers and turned for the British rear but had a hard time gaining the enemy rear flank due to the "thick underwood in which it was enclosed."[37] Continuing on, Washington made a second charge farther down:

> After a spirited charge upon their Cavalry and dispersing them, [Washington] fell upon the rear of their Infantry, cut down a number of them on the field, and took upwards of two Hundred Prisoners.[38]

Unbeknownst to Washington, this "Infantry" deep in the British rear was in fact Rawdon's amalgamated corps of armed musicians, surgeons, and teamsters retreating toward Camden, and these men quickly surrendered to the hard charging light dragoons.[39] Also captured here were a number of British wounded from the initial fight between Rawdon's advance and Greene's forward pickets. Taking a large number of prisoners was no small feat in eighteenth-century arms, and given the timing and nature of Greene's orders, this is in all likelihood what Washington would have expected to see if Greene's ordered bayonet charge on Rawdon's front had been successful.

At this point Washington had three options: continue on, take prisoners, or cut down the surrounding enemy. But Washington could hardly pare his dragoons down into columns and files and hack his way through the tight pines and brushwood to attack an even greater hidden enemy force beyond, for which he no longer held any immediate knowledge.[40] Cavalry and thick woods never mix well, and such a move would be tactically dodgy at best and open his men to a rear fire from the throngs of armed enemy soldiers now wading about his dragoons with clubbed muskets. Nor could he ignore so many armed troops in supporting distance of the battle.

The final option of simply denying quarter and hacking down these surrendering enemy soldiers, some of whom were already wounded from earlier fighting, was apparently a line of honor Washington wouldn't cross.[41] Instead, some of his men began disarming the prisoners, officers started issuing paroles, and what were left attempted to keep watch and form a perimeter.

Meanwhile, the veteran 1st Maryland of Cowpens and Guilford fame were bravely advancing down the hill in the face of Rawdon's infantry. The Marylanders were striding forward with bayonets fixed and flags flying when Captain William Beatty, commander of the two right flank companies, was shot and killed. These two companies stalled as the rest of the regiment continued on, which in turn broke the regiment's front and created disorder. The 1st Maryland commander, Lieutenant Colonel John Gunby, ordered the center companies to halt and dress the ranks and realign the companies in proper range of their colors. The British charged forward at this very moment of redress and the disordered 1st Maryland broke for the rear in a panic.[42] On their left, the commander of the 2d Maryland, Lieutenant Colonel Benjamin Ford, was hit with a musket ball that shattered his elbow.[43] Seeing the veteran 1st Maryland fleeing in fright and their own commander painfully knocked out of action, the 2d Maryland took to their heels and the 1st Virginia on the far flank bolted in turn, streaming up the slope en masse, despite the shouts and pleas of their officers to stand and fire. Colonel Otho Williams, the Maryland brigade commander and a veteran of the battle of Camden stated:

> He who has never seen the effect of a panic upon a multitude can have but an imperfect idea of such a thing. The best disciplined troops have been enervated and made cowards by it. Like electricity it operates instantly.[44]

Now smelling blood, the British charged up the slope on the heels of the fleeing Continentals. Greene could hardly believe his eyes as he ordered the horse teams forward to limber their guns and carry the precious tubes to the rear. Lieutenant Colonel Gunby managed to rally his 1st Maryland and direct a few volleys but it was too little, too late. Lieutenant Colonel Samuel Hawes's 2d Virginia was the only unit to stand and they prevented the American withdrawal from becoming a complete rout until Greene himself ordered Hawes's men to withdraw least they be flanked and overrun.

Swept up in the tide of retreating troops, the American gunners mishandled their frightened teams and snagged the limbers in heavy brush. The horses began to panic and the teams had to be cut from the traces and the limbers were abandoned in the brushwood. Desperate not to repeat the Guilford loss of his cannon, Greene rushed forward to help save the guns and ordered

Captain John Smith's Company of Maryland Light Infantry to cover the guns' withdrawal.[45] Smith's men quickly grabbed the trail ropes by hand and took off at a trot down the Waxhaws Road. Witnessing this action was Coffin's dragoons, who were now rallied and reformed from their earlier bout with Washington's light dragoons. Spurs came back and Coffin's horsemen charged forward with swords aloft to make straight for the guns with a shout. Smith's men quickly dropped the ropes, turned about, and fired to check Coffin's troopers.[46]

However Coffin's men were pooled from veteran light infantrymen and not easily swayed. Coffin's game veterans reformed repeatedly, and with the aid of arriving British infantry, exchanged fire from front and flank to make a series of false charges that carried the action farther and farther down the road. The time bought in Smith's stand against Coffin allowed the guns to be dragged safely away but eventually Coffin's troopers baited the fire of Smith's dwindling rear guard and charged in to roll over and break Smith's ranks in a desperate fight of swords versus bayonets. The contest predictably ended with Smith's command cut to the ground and Smith taken prisoner.[47]

As these events transpired to the north, Washington was suddenly met by British troops turning back from Greene's shattered line. Washington now realized the tables had turned and his men quickly closed up and started to cut their way clear of the attacking British troops. With a cluster of prisoners in tow, Washington and his men looped past the British and rode after Greene's retreating army until they passed the American lines. Washington then delivered his prisoners into American hands and returned to the front where he and his men sallied forth and covered Greene's retreat by charging the British van and driving off any pursuing enemy.[48] Skirmishes continued in the wake of the American withdrawal until Greene finally halted on Saunder's Creek, some three miles north of his original position.[49]

American casualties for the battle of Hobkirk's Hill were twenty-five killed, one hundred and eight wounded, and one hundred and thirty-six missing for a total of two hundred and seventy. British casualties were thirty-nine killed and two hundred and ten wounded with estimates varying between eleven and seventy on the total number captured.[50] As the attacking force the British troops suffered a predictably higher rate of casualties. Unfortunately for Rawdon, trained troops were his most precious resource and the hardest to replace. He'd taken the field, but like Cornwallis at Guilford, failed to inflict a crippling blow against Greene's Continentals. Still, Rawdon was justifiably proud of his force and he wrote to his superiors that, "His majesty's troops behaved most gallantly."[51]

However the combat was far from over and that afternoon Washington and his light dragoons moved up with a party of infantry to make a scout against the British.[52] He found the British had posted a covering force near Greene's initial position on Hobkirk's Hill. Composed of both infantry and cavalry, this substantial British force occupied the ground Lord Rawdon had won that day in the time-honored custom of a victor holding the field after a battle. Washington studied the enemy troops on the field and quickly spied an opportunity in the making. He concealed the main body of his force in heavy woods beside the road and then sent a few files riding forward toward the British. Major Coffin and his dragoons gave chase *en masse* and Washington watched as the overeager British horsemen galloped straight into his trap. At Washington's command there was a blaze of musketry followed by a charge of light dragoons that swept half of Coffin's men from the saddle. Coffin's remaining ranks wheeled about and spurred back for Camden at a gallop. The covering British infantry guarding the battlefield followed suit and ran along with them.[53]

With the field now abandoned by the victors, Washington was able to steal forward to the brushwood and rescue the abandoned Continental artillery limbers, which had sat hidden and unnoticed by the British throughout the day.[54]

Twelve

REBELS RESURGENT

"All those who serve in the light horse, ought to be persons upon whom you can confide and depend; it is often on their vigilance and fidelity which depends the safety of a quarter, and even the whole army."–Emanuel von Warnery, Remarks on Cavalry

Some histories claim that William Washington's halt and brief capture of Rawdon's armed teamsters and musicians helped lead to the Continental defeat at the battle of Hobkirk's Hill. However, a quick view of the participant's correspondence clearly shows they thought differently.

Colonel Williams, the Maryland Brigade commander wrote:

"The cavalry led on by Washington behaved in a manner truly heroic . . . Washington is an elegant officer; his reputation is deservedly great."[1]

General Greene wrote to the Continental Congress:

"The Colonel's [Washington's] behavior and that of his Regiment upon this occasion did them the highest honor."[2]

To Henry Lee, Greene wrote that Washington:

". . . Never shone upon an occasion more than this, in the course of the day [Washington] made several charges, and cut to pieces their dragoons."[3]

And finally General Greene's aide, Major William Pierce said: "Colo. Washington was uncommonly active . . . and never upon any occasion exhibited a more brilliant instance of heroism and firmness."[4]

These simply aren't the sort of laurels thrown upon a commander whose actions help lose a battle!

Yet despite the performance of his cavalry, General Greene was still vexed over the loss of the battle and particularly the performance of his infantry that, despite holding high ground and enjoying artillery support, had been driven from the field. He wrote to Joseph Reed that he was "almost frantic with vexation at the disappointment," adding, "we should have had Lord Rawdon and his whole command prisoners in three minutes"[5]

The morning after the battle, Lieutenant Colonel John Gunby of the 1st Maryland took offense to the way Greene addressed his regiment at parade, and Gunby requested a court of inquiry be called to examine his own actions. Greene promptly agreed and a court was formed consisting of an officer from each arm: General Isaac Huger representing the infantry, Colonel Charles Harrison the artillery, and Lieutenant Colonel William Washington the cavalry. The panel found Lieutenant Colonel Gunby had been "active in rallying and forming his troops" but his decision to halt and reform his regiment was "unmilitary." The panel did definitively note that Gunby had rallied his men after their flight and directed several volleys before retiring.[6]

It might be that the panel took Lieutenant Colonel Howard's similar actions at the Cowpens into account. At the Cowpens, Howard had also ordered the Marylanders to retreat at a critical point in the battle. Like Gunby, Howard had made a retrograde movement to restore the order of his lines while in the face of the enemy, though in Howard's case the ordered retreat resulted in a sudden, near miraculous reversal of fortune that won the day. Any combat veteran will attest to the fact that luck can be a fickle mistress, and either way Gunby was a veteran officer of proven service and the panel merely censored him and never relieved him of command. Gunby's actions may or may not have been exceptional, but in reality there was plenty of blame to go around.

The battle for Hobkirk's Hill was a quick, violent, fast-paced affair and the close range and fluid nature of the combat greatly amplified any mistakes. Greene's letter to Congress after the battle shows that Greene thought to capture Rawdon's entire command outside Camden and the post as well: ". . . had we succeeded, from the disposition made, we must have had the whole prisoners as well as full possession of Camden."[7]

In Greene's rush to have it all, he pulled the trigger too soon and ordered his infantry to close with the bayonet while turning his cavalry loose in a bid to capture Rawdon's entire force. These actions masked his own guns from firing their crippling salvoes on Rawdon's charging infantry. This halt in artillery fire helped to allow Rawdon to rally and extend his lines in the face of the American bayonet charge, renew his advance, and break the 1st Maryland. Some historians feel that if Washington's force had still been held in reserve when the 1st Maryland panicked and broke, a direct charge by the dragoons might have covered the infantry's disorder and stemmed Rawdon's advance. Two of Washington's contemporaries, Colonel William Davie and Lieutenant Colonel Henry Lee also thought Greene mishandled the cavalry at Hobkirk's: "[H]ad the horse been still in reserve, not only would the forward movement of the enemy been delayed, [the American line] would have been restored to order, and the battle renewed."[8]

Neither Lee nor Davie were present at the battle, and these later judgments were all made from the safe ground of hindsight where what ifs are free to slowly take shape and gain crystal clarity: not during the heat of the battle when emotions were skyrocketing, couriers were flying about with varying reports, and powder smoke was obscuring the field. Yet despite a court of inquiry, the comments of contemporary officers and a string of glowing letters supporting Washington's actions, some historians continue to blame Washington for his part in the battle and claim that Washington's "disobedience" led to Greene's defeat, and Greene exaggerated Washington's actions in his report to the Continental Congress.[9]

Some of these criticisms stem from Colonel William Davie, who felt that Washington had wasted valuable time in his capturing and paroling of the British prisoners.[10] Davie, another of Greene's commissary officers, considered these men the "trumpery" of the British Army and Davie felt Washington should have cut them out of his path without delay and charged straight into the British rear. However, Davie was not at the battle, and in reality Washington was prevented from reaching the rear of the British lines by the dense underbrush that dominated that portion of the field. These same thick woods allowed Rawdon to sneak his approach march on Greene's position, and they also prohibited the cavalry's free operation and movement, either with or without prisoners. Another Hobkirk's veteran, Lieutenant Colonel John Howard of the 1st Maryland, disagreed with Davie's opinion of cutting down these prisoners and later wrote "I do not believe Davie would have done it." [11]

Washington executed Greene's orders to the best of his ability. He first engaged Coffin's dragoons and sent them flying. Given the fluid nature of mounted combat, Coffin was able to flee the point of attack, rally back to reform, and later attack Greene's artillery where he inflicted a number of casualties. Breaking and driving an enemy cavalry force is no small feat in itself, but if Washington failed at anything it was in not following up on his initial attack against Coffin and continuing his pursuit. Instead Washington moved on and attacked Rawdon's rear per Greene's orders but he quickly became bogged down by a surrendering drove of armed and wounded prisoners whose numbers far eclipsed his own light dragoons. In addition, he hit a wall of thick brush that effectively shielded his horses from gaining the British rear. Washington was then too far away to support the 1st Maryland when they broke under the stress of the firefight, and the resulting panic that swept through the Continental ranks turned the tables on the battle and nearly caused Washington to be captured in kind. Washington then cut his way out of the British rear, passed his own lines, delivered his prisoners into American hands, re-passed his lines, and again engaged the enemy to cover Greene's retreat. Later that evening he stole forward, laid an ambush that crippled Rawdon's cavalry, and recaptured the American artillery limbers left behind in the battle.

Washington may not have been perfect, but Greene was fortunate to have a light dragoon of his caliber at his side and knew it. The praise Greene and his officers "heaped" upon Washington was just and well-deserved but the greatest compliment of all may have come from the British Commander, Lord Rawdon, who mistakenly thought Washington's light horsemen far outnumbered Coffin's dragoons when in fact they started the battle with near equal numbers. Rawdon wrote: "We pursued them about three miles, but, the enemy's cavalry greatly surpassing ours as to number, horses and appointments, our dragoons could not risqué much, nor could I suffer the infantry to break their order in hopes of overtaking the fugitives."[12]

This indirect praise is telling. Rawdon apparently felt his dragoons were so out-matched and out-horsed that he checked not just his own dragoons back from an all-out pursuit of a defeated and fleeing enemy, but his own infantry as well, lest they suffer an attack from Washington's light horsemen. Lord Rawdon clearly recognized William Washington's actions and abilities for what they were, as did General Greene, Colonel Williams, and Lieutenant Colonel Howard.

Meanwhile, just as Greene had made up his mind to turn south and head for South Carolina, Lord Cornwallis had been wrestling with what action would be best to take after marching from Guilford Courthouse and reaching his cache of supplies in backwater Wilmington.[13] It was Cornwallis's opinion that North and South Carolina would never be fully conquered without first subjugating Virginia–the primary source of supplies for Greene's recent campaigns in the American south–and any efforts spent in the Carolinas would yield but marginal returns until Virginia was fully under British control.[14] To that end Cornwallis decided to leave both Greene and the Carolinas for someone else and instead marched north to join the ongoing British efforts to subjugate the Old Dominion.

Cornwallis's commander, Sir Henry Clinton, strongly disagreed with Cornwallis's decision to abandon the Carolinas but the electrifying reports of Rawdon's victory at Hobkirk's Hill now reassured Cornwallis of his own recent decisions.[15] Further news to support Cornwallis's move to Virginia came from Cork, Ireland, where three regiments of British regulars boarded ships for Charleston to support any future efforts by the British in South Carolina.[16]

Cornwallis made good time in his advance to Virginia and encountered little if any resistance between the Cape Fear and Roanoke rivers. Once in Virginia he joined forces with General Arnold in Petersburg and turned the cavalry of Lieutenant Colonels John Simcoe and Banastre Tarleton loose in raids across the Virginia tidewater. Ironically the very same horses the Virginia assembly had selfishly price controlled out of the hands of William Washington's horse agents were now captured from the shortsighted Virginia planters by British dragoons under Simcoe and Tarleton. These troopers were soon riding roughshod over the wealthy tidewater estates; burning, razing, and stealing everything that wasn't nailed down. These British horsemen became some of the best-mounted cavalry during the war and the resulting raids ravaged the countryside and threatened to bring Virginia to its knees. Any support Greene and his Continentals had been receiving from the state of Virginia now came to a sudden halt in the wake of Cornwallis's advance.

With the battle of Hobkirk's Hill behind him, Greene retreated farther up the Waxhaws Road while Washington and Kirkwood again paired up and moved toward the Wateree River opposite Camden, where they captured an enemy redoubt and set it ablaze.[17] In the meantime Lieutenant Colonel Watson and his British infantry drove out of Georgetown to hurry to Rawdon's assistance. After ducking both Lee and Marion in crossing the Congaree River he managed to reach Camden on May 7. Rawdon, now reinforced by Watson, quickly came out in pursuit and Greene fell back to high ground along Sawney's Creek.

At this point Greene was in great despair over the loss at Hobkirk's Hill, Rawdon's re-enforcement by Watson, and Sumter's continued absence. This combination of events was compelling Greene to begin planning a retreat to Virginia with

Washington's cavalry, while leaving most of his infantry behind in the Carolinas. Lieutenant Colonel Howard of the Maryland line would later write that Washington visited Howard in camp and expressed his deepest regrets at Greene's plans, claiming that the two friends might never meet again. The moment speaks of not only the strong bond forged under fire between brother officers, but also of Washington's deep and compassionate feelings for his friends. Howard recalled that these moments were so "impressed on my mind that I shall never forget them."[18]

However, war is anything but predictable, and before Greene could retire to Virginia he first had to try and check the hard marching advance of Rawdon and Watson. As Rawdon approached Greene's position on Sawney Creek, Greene had his infantry fire a number of volleys at the enemy and Greene then left Washington and Kirkwood poised as a rear guard to oppose the British advance while Greene retreated back to an even stronger position on Colonel's Creek.[19]

Now was the perfect time for Rawdon to send his cavalry in pursuit and Washington and his men eagerly stood in their stirrups in anticipation of the event; however Coffin's troopers were in no shape to make a charge after the heavy drubbing they'd received from Washington at Hobkirk's Hill. Rawdon could see his depleted corps of cavalry was no match for Washington's light horsemen waiting across the field and recognized that regardless of Watson's additional infantry, he wouldn't be able to bring Greene's quick marching army to heel until his own cavalry was rebuilt and again capable of offensive operations.[20] Though largely overlooked in historical accounts, this was no small matter in the ongoing campaign, and Washington and his men certainly recognized the import of their recent actions against the British horse at Hobkirk's Hill, as Rawdon now turned his back and marched away.

Dejected, Rawdon retreated back to Camden only to learn that his vital supply lines to Charleston were now under renewed attacks by the combined forces of Henry Lee and Francis Marion. Now that Cornwallis had left for Virginia there were far fewer options available; Camden was rapidly growing indefensible with the resources Rawdon held at hand and the young peer abandoned the crucial post just ten days after he won the battle of Hobkirk's Hill.[21]

Rawdon's unexpected retreat surely came as a godsend to General Greene, who now switched tacks back to an offenssive posture and stepped up the pressure on the remaining strong points in the British line of backcountry forts. First to fall was Fort Motte, a fortified plantation home that refused to surrender and was set ablaze with a rain of fire arrows at the orders of Henry Lee and Francis Marion.[22] Greene next divided his two lieutenants and sent Marion after Georgetown on the coast while directing Lee toward Fort Granby at present day Columbia. When both posts fell without a fight, Greene took aim at the final two major forts in the backcountry, Augusta and Ninety-Six. Augusta was already under building pressure from partisans under Andrew Pickens and Elijah Clarke and Greene sent Lee's legion of infantry and cavalry to help these ongoing operations on the western flank while Greene himself turned for the last remaining British stronghold; the fort at Ninety-Six.[23]

Greene sought to score a quick victory behind a rapid advance and he set out for Ninety-Six with Washington and Kirkwood leading the way. By now the men of Washington and Kirkwood were familiar partners and expert in their work. They skirmished with a number of less experienced Tory parties along the way, killing and capturing twelve Tories on May 21 and another eleven the following day when they closed on Ninety-Six's palisaded walls.[24]

Since the fall of Charleston the post at Ninety-Six had been garrisoned entirely by Loyalist provincials; one hundred fifty men from DeLancey's Volunteers, two hundred men from the New Jersey Volunteers, and two hundred Tory militiamen. The old fort had been named for its distance from the major Cherokee village of Keowee, and from its early days the post had been surrounded by heavy pine walls to guard against native attacks. The current Tory commander, Colonel John Cruger, had worked on improving its defenses by adding a deep ditch around the post's perimeter with wooden stakes and abatis ringing the ditch.[25] The eastern corner was connected to a large star shaped redoubt that allowed converging fields of fire down two sides of the stockade and another smaller redoubt served the same purpose on the western side and overlooked the post's water supply. Cruger also had three cannons inside the post and a large number of slaves on hand to serve as a ready labor force of sappers and miners within the walls.

Greene realized he couldn't storm such a strong position and turned over control of the siege to his chief engineer, Colonel Thaddeus Kosciuszko, who promptly set to the laborious process of digging parallel entrenchments in the rapidly climbing heat of the coming South Carolina summer. Kosciuszko's work parties would dig round the clock and Cruger's men would often sneak forth at night and try to ruin the investing trenches. The trenching process was pitifully slow and time dragged by as the daily temperature seemed to climb with each passing day. Greene appealed to Virginia for more troops, and perhaps a quick end to the situation, but with Cornwallis's well-mounted cavalry still roaming about on stolen tidewater horses, he could find no support from that sector. Instead the digging outside Ninety-Six scraped slowly but steadily on in the South Carolina heat.[26]

On June 8th Henry Lee arrived from Augusta with a string of prisoners in tow. Lee had done boon work in the past two months, reducing the British forts: Watson, Motte, Granby, and the twin posts at Augusta in turn. Ranging far and wide and working in concert with various militias, Lee had shown a brilliant aptitude for siege work and independent command. Glowing with victory, he reached the post at Ninety-Six on June 8 and lent his troops to Greene's ongoing efforts.[27]

With Lee's added presence, Greene redoubled his exertions; a mine tunnel was started to bury a charge beneath the fort's works and an additional trench was started against the opposite side of the stockade. All present were firmly convinced it would now be but a matter of short time before Cruger would have to surrender. However, on June 11 deplorable news reached Greene's camp. British reinforcements from Cork, Ireland, had landed in Charleston and Lord Rawdon was now headed north for Ninety-Six with a relief force of two thousand men.[28]

Such a force easily outnumbered Greene's Continentals and Washington and his light dragoons were sent south to link with

Thomas Sumter's militia in an attempt to slow Rawdon's advance and buy the necessary time for the siege to succeed.[29] Henry Lee and his Legion infantry were to remain at Ninety-Six but Lee's three companies of dragoons under Captain Michael Rudolph were directed to join with Washington's light dragoons.[30] Somehow through a "mistake" in orders Lee's cavalry under Rudolph remained at Ninety-Six with Lee, while Washington rode south with only his light dragoons and linked up with Thomas Sumter on the Congaree River.[31] Unfortunately, Sumter wasn't up to the task of directing the militia against Rawdon and sent a stream of conflicting and confusing orders to his various lieutenants.[32]

Washington now galloped west, but there was little he could do on his own before Rawdon's advance with no infantry. Sumter followed behind Washington at a slower pace, all the while waiting for his militia to come up and join him.[33] On June 17, Sumter sent two hundred men under Colonel Charles Myddelton to harass Rawdon's rear.[34] Guarding the rear of Rawdon's column was British Major John Coffin, Washington's quondam adversary from Hobkirk's Hill, who had since revamped his command with new levies and also had an additional force of "Hessian Horse" temporarily assigned to him.[35]

On the following day Coffin set an ambush for Myddelton's force at Juniper Springs, in the fork of the Augusta and Ninety-Six roads.[36] Myddelton, whose men carried few swords, first engaged a force of some two hundred Tories in their front and were gamely exchanging fire with this forward force when they were charged flank and rear by Coffin's dragoons. Myddelton's men were ill-fitted for close combat and Coffin's sword-bearing troopers charged in and cut the underequipped Whigs to pieces.[37] John Chaney, one of the handful of Whigs who even had a sword, was slashed three times with a broadsword in a fight with a "Hessian Dragoon," "whom he met in full charge." The Hessian was "well skilled in his sword exercise" and "greatly his superior." The Hessian's first blow cut Chaney's sword hand, a second harder cut landed across the wrist of the same hand; Chaney then wheeled his horse about to escape but was clipped with a third cut across his temple which dumped him to the ground. While the Hessian was focused on finishing Chaney off, a fellow Whig rode up unnoticed and "shot the Hessian dragoon dead in the saddle."[38] Elsewhere this unequal contest ended more poorly for Myddelton's men as the British and Hessians handily routed and scattered the Whig dragoons. Myddelton later returned to Sumter's camp with just forty-five horsemen.[39]

That same day Greene was forced to lift the siege at Ninety-Six and retreat toward Charlotte. Despite heroic attempts by his men to both storm the redoubt and mine the walls, Rawdon was now too close to chance any further investment without risking a battle between two enemies. Greene knew it was but a matter of days if not hours before Cruger would have to surrender, but the largely uncontested advance of Rawdon's greater force left Greene no choice in the matter and Greene had his men marching at 5 A.M. on June 19.[40]

After relieving Ninety-Six Rawdon decided to chase after Greene's numerically inferior force and quickly set out in pursuit. Washington and Lee now threw up a screen of dragoons between Rawdon and Greene, haunting the British advance and sending constant dispatches to Greene on the British movements. Greene gave ground easily behind his light horsemen as he set a rough course for Charlotte; crossing the Saluda, Little, Bush, Enoree, Tyger, and finally, the Broad River, where he left a rear guard of Lee's infantry, Kirkwood's Delaware Company, and a select force of hand-picked militia under Major Alexander Rose.[41]

Fortunately for Greene and the Americans, Rawdon's men were quickly exhausted in their efforts to keep pace with Greene in the stifling Carolina heat. Many fell out on the march from heat exhaustion and Rawdon soon turned back to Ninety-Six, empty-handed and drained from the attempt.[42]

Lee followed Rawdon back to Ninety-Six where he could keep an eye on him and inform Greene of any developments. At this point Greene could only hold in limbo as he didn't know whether Rawdon would try and maintain the post at Ninety-Six, abandon it, or attempt another pursuit; it wasn't until June 25 that Greene learned Rawdon was in fact retreating from Ninety-Six and heading south.[43] Rawdon had indeed wanted to keep the post but despite all the blood and treasure the British had put into Ninety-Six, American forces had swept the backcountry clear of any notable support and maintaining a single distant post without a fortified supply line would be next to impossible. Rawdon had no other choice than to abandon Ninety-Six and a lumbering wagon train of livestock, soldiers, slaves, and Tory refugees soon began making its way south for Charleston.

Greene was determined to strike Rawdon while he was on the march and sent word for Sumter to prepare for a move against Rawdon in the Congarees, the general area north of Orangeburg, south of Fort Granby (present day Columbia), and west of the confluence of the Wateree and Congaree rivers; Greene also instructed Lee to do likewise.[44]

Just as these plans were under way, Greene received word from Francis Marion that a second relief force of three hundred and fifty men under Lieutenant Colonel Alexander Stewart was marching north from Charleston to join Rawdon.[45] This column was composed of the famed 3d Regiment of Foot, or "the Buffs," as they were known among military circles.[46] Washington wrote to Greene about this new turn of events and his plans to head south and intercept Stewart's column of veteran British infantry. Greene quickly approved of Washington's plan and wrote to Colonel Lee to move southward and form a junction with Washington.[47]

Greene also ordered Lee to send Kirkwood and his Delaware Continentals to Washington that he might have a covering force of infantry in his operations against the British. Lee, however, didn't comply. He instead wrote Greene on June 26 and advised his commanding officer that Kirkwood should stay with Lee's Legion Infantry and Major Rose's foot soldiers–all of which were now with Lee–rather than join Washington, and that Lee would soon join Sumter in the Congarees. First, however, Lee promised he would make a "flourish" before Rawdon in the latter's retreat from Ninety-Six. Once he'd made his "flourish" Lee would then release the infantry to march down separately to the Congaree, where Lee suggested they could either join Greene, or link back up with Lee, again slighting Washington.[48]

Lee's refusal to release Kirkwood's company was not only a blatant rejection of his commanding officer's orders; it also severely hampered Washington's efforts before Stewart's column of infantry, and endangered the lives of Washington and his light dragoons who were only armed with pistols and broadswords as they moved south to intercept the much larger enemy column of British infantry coming up from Charleston.

However, Lee felt that he had some discretion in his advanced position before Rawdon; this was in part due to some flexibility in Greene's earlier orders and perhaps also due to Lee's recent stint as an independent partisan. Lee went on to report from his camp that part of his cavalry were currently out scouting the enemy while his other troops were "refreshing" themselves and "doing well for provision" but lacked both rum and salt. Lee also thought it worth mentioning that he hoped his presence in the area would help "hold up the idea of [American] superiority" among the locals and "intimidate the disaffected."[49]

Clearly the high-minded Lee didn't fancy the idea of relinquishing any troops to Washington, let alone following Washington's lead; Lee's commission pre-dated Washington's and therefore Lee outranked Washington through precedence. A new, more direct set of orders from Greene finally pushed Lee from his reportedly comfortable camp although Lee wrote Greene that, though he was moving toward Washington, he was still hanging before Rawdon, and in addition, he was overriding Washington's written orders to Kirkwood to fall in with the 3d Light Dragoons. Lee stated that he was keeping Kirkwood, along with his Legion Infantry and Major Roses's infantry, "lest an opportunity of striking might be lost" against Lord Rawdon for want of force.[50]

However Lee had infantry support outside of Kirkwood's company and this countermanding of Washington's orders, orders which had been approved by General Greene, was an affront to Washington. Lee tempered this move by pleading that Greene himself might do Lee a favor and intervene with Washington on Lee's behalf, "lest a stupid jealousy arise."[51] Certainly Washington would have viewed Lee's continued harboring of Kirkwood's company as far more than a "stupid jealousy" when riding into harm's way with no infantry support! If Lee was concerned enough to call for Greene's protection in the matter then he may have been dreading a future face to face encounter with the notoriously hard-charging Washington, "the Hercules of his day."[52]

Meanwhile Washington continued moving south to intercept Stewart's column. He wrote Greene informing the General that he was headed for the Congaree River and would attack Stewart if the opportunity arose. Washington wisely realized he'd get little support from Lee and asked Greene to order state cavalry under Lieutenant Colonel Hezekiah Maham, currently to the southward, to get before Stewart's relief column coming up from Charleston and then the two commands could form a junction and possibly curtail the enemy advance.[53] Greene supported Washington's plan entirely and urged caution on Washington's part. Greene then sent letters on June 29 ordering both Lee and Colonel Myddelton to join Washington at once in acting against Stewart's southern force.[54]

By this time Greene was also moving for the Congarees with his Continental infantry in tow while simultaneously directing the militias of Sumter, Pickens, and Marion to converge in the same area. It was paramount to Greene that Rawdon and Stewart be prevented from uniting so they could be defeated separately. Unfortunately for Greene his plans fell apart when Sumter, who always bristled at the thought of acting under anyone's direct command, used the excuse of having to repair to Camden for several days to "expedite the manufacture" of some swords being made by local blacksmiths![55] While to the south, the normally redoubtable Marion was having difficulties with his own command.[56] Marion's two Lieutenant Colonels, Hezekiah Maham and Peter Horry, had both been recently directed to raise regiments of state dragoons, and the pair were now bickering over the details of which troopers would be detailed to which command.[57]

In the midst of these martial shenanigans Greene's frustration was growing by the day. As Greene's own column of infantry closed in on the Congarees he learned that Rawdon and Stewart were planning a junction at Orangeburg, some thirty miles below the Congaree River. Word also arrived that Marion's Brigade was now finally taking the field to the south and so Greene decided to rearrange his plans and leave Stewart's smaller southern column for Marion's two regiments to deal with on their own while Greene threw all the rest of his forces at intercepting Rawdon's larger column coming down from Ninety-Six. Greene therefore ordered Washington, who was still acting alone despite all recent orders to the contrary, to ride northwest and secure the northern fords of the Congaree River above Orangeburg, ahead of Greene's march. Meanwhile Lee, with his larger force and requisitioned collection of infantry, would cover farther west, along the southern flank of the Congaree, in Rawdon's expected line of advance.[58]

On the same day Washington received his new orders portions of Lee's cavalry under Captain Joseph Eggleston surprised a detached British foraging party from Rawdon's column and took the whole party captive.[59] This was an outstanding feat of arms for Eggleston and his troopers, and Lee was quick to report that he had finally made good on his prior promise of a "flourish" against Rawdon. Unfortunately, Lee's flourish didn't interrupt Rawdon's actual march. Instead the Irish peer now pressed southward in earnest to link with Stewart. While Washington continued to screen the upper fords in anticipation of Greene's arrival, Lee cut Rawdon's trail at Congaree Creek, a southern tributary of the Congaree River.

Lee and his combined forces of infantry were now in position to deal Rawdon a severe blow but instead Lee withdrew them back out of the way after firing only a few "ineffectual shots" at Rawdon's advance.[60] Lee's timid action here is still a puzzle. Rawdon's column definitely outnumbered Lee's, but Lee knew Rawdon's men were distressed and near the point of exhaustion as they struggled across the ford which Lee's men had prepped with felled trees and other obstacles to create a daunting defensive position. It seems Lee's multiple forces could have certainly struck Rawdon's column to greater effect and at least retarded their advance, however Lee later claimed he was waiting on the militia to come to his aide, and had heard no news from Washington on the northern fords. Washington, who had an ego as well, was likely guilty of dragging his feet here–hardly a surprise given Lee's continued purloining of Kirkwood's infantry at Washington's expense.[61] However Lee's sudden caution to fight even a screening action here seems entirely incongruous with his earlier determination to hold onto Kirkwood and Rose's infantry "lest an opportunity of striking might be lost."[62] Lee continued to judge the risk of any attack on Rawdon to be too great a hazard to risk on his own, despite his knowledge of Greene's approach with the main force of Continentals, and Lee's combined forces again gave way at the next ford on Beaver Creek. Lee finally pulled his troops aside altogether and let Rawdon pass by unopposed.[63] Rawdon then marched unchecked into Orangeburg just as General Greene reached the Congarees with his Continental infantry in tow.

Meanwhile, Sumter was still not up and in the field, and Marion, now well on his march with Horry and Maham to the south, was quickly using up his horses in the brutal summer heat as he attempted to cover a sprawling spider-like network of roads and byways to block Stewart's relief column marching up from Charleston. In the end Stewart managed to slip past Marion's forces and link up with Rawdon before Orangeburg on July 7.[64]

Greene must have been outraged by these fumbling and disjointed events but he remained confident he could defeat both Rawdon and Stewart once he caught up with them, given his decisive advantage in cavalry.[65] He accordingly made camp at Beaver Creek and there marshaled together the forces of Washington, Lee, Myddelton, Sumter, Marion, Maham, Horry, Pickens, Kirkwood, and his Continental infantry under Otho Williams–altogether nearly two thousand men–and marched for Orangeburg. If there was any altercation between Washington and Lee it is lost to history, and given the larger looming issues it is far more likely that Greene honored Lee's request to speak with Washington, and any ill feelings were put aside in the midst of the ongoing campaign.

Greene now marched his collected army onto Orangeburg but to his chagrin and eternal vexation, he found Rawdon dug in along the bank of the North Edisto, with additional troops deployed in a strong brick building commanding the British lines.[66] The post offered no opening to an attack on any flank and Greene's powerful cavalry was entirely useless before such a prepared position. Wrapped in quiet fury, Greene ordered a retreat and turned his men about. He could comfort himself in the fact that though he'd lost the battle for Ninety-Six the post now lay abandoned and he had cleared the upper backcountry of British influence, but the latest maneuvers had all been for naught, and he still hadn't won a victory in the field.

It's doubtful his men cared one way or the other; they were hungry, footsore, saddle weary, and worn to a nub. Rations were so scarce that men were filling the void by spearing frogs and shooting alligators.[67] The core force of Greene's command was still Daniel Morgan's old flying army raised in the fall of 1780, the Delaware and Maryland infantry, and the 3d Light Dragoons. Since before Cowpens, these troops had seen near constant front line service and were now near the point of exhaustion. Uniforms were in tatters, equipment was failing, and horses were beginning to fade. All were in need of rest, resupply, and better rations. Now that the militia had finally turned out, Greene left them to harass the British on their own and turned his Continentals to rest and refit in the breezy high ground hills of the Santee's north bank.[68]

As Lord Rawdon watched Greene retreat he also turned his back on Orangeburg. He left a covering force at the new garrison and then retired to the streets of Charleston unmolested.[69]

Meanwhile, farther to the north, Rawdon's fellow peer, Lord Cornwallis, was giving ground as well. After a series of raids across Virginia, Cornwallis sparred with a weaker force of Continentals led by General Lafayette and fell back to the Chesapeake Bay. Under orders from Sir Henry Clinton in New York, Cornwallis searched the bay for a suitable port. After scouting several options, Cornwallis chose the handsome hamlet of Yorktown, Virginia, where he encamped to await resupply from the British navy.[70]

Back in South Carolina, William Washington and Henry Lee were both back in the field after a short rest, and, working independently of one another, combing the approaches to Orangeburg and Charleston. Now reunited with his familiar cohort Captain Kirkwood, Washington and his men shadowed the Edisto, Santee, and Cooper rivers and constantly harassed British lines of communication and supply. During these operations Washington and his men captured two detachments of enemy horse, and, in a later encounter, Captain Watt's single troop charged a troop of enemy cavalry and entirely routed them.[71] Understandably pleased, Greene commented on his cavalry in the following dispatch to Congress:

> The Corps of Horse under Lt. Colos Washington and Lee have at different times since I wrote you last taken 30 and 40 prisoners, and killed and wounded a number more, the greatest part of the whole were cavalry.[72]

Under increasing pressure from Greene's Continental horsemen, and state troops under Sumter and Marion, the British position at Orangeburg was considered to be in great danger and many of the British troops stationed there were pulled back closer to Charleston least Orangeburg be overrun.

Elsewhere, in Charleston proper, wartime politics were taking a decidedly ugly turn. The issue was over South Carolinian Isaac Hayne. Hayne had been a Whig militia officer serving in the Colleton Regiment. He was captured when Charleston fell and under threat of imprisonment had sworn an oath of loyalty to the Crown and returned home. Many American officers had sworn similar oaths and then returned to the fight against Great Britain when their homes had come under Continental control. When Hayne's property fell under the control of Greene's troops, Hayne considered himself free from his British parole and reentered the American militia. On July 5 Hayne led a raid outside Charleston and seized General Andrew Williamson, who was himself a former Whig militia commander that had since accepted protection from the British garrison at Charleston, and was now openly loyal in service to the crown. British dragoons gave chase, overtook the party, rescued Williamson, and arrested Hayne in turn.

Hayne was escorted under guard to Charleston and placed in the provost's prison. He was then questioned by a board of officers and sentenced to be hanged without trial.[73] Hayne protested, claiming the board's actions were illegal regardless of whether he was a British subject, or a prisoner of war who had violated his parole.[74] Lord Rawdon, and the British commandant of Charleston, Lieutenant Colonel Nesbit, Lord Balfour, both signed a proclamation condemning Hayne to death. Before Hayne's execution, many Loyalists appealed for leniency, including William Bull, the royal lieutenant-governor of South Carolina. Lords Balfour and Rawdon turned deaf ears to all pleas and Hayne was hanged without further trial despite the many protests.[75]

Hayne's execution deeply angered Whigs across the country, including William Washington, who demanded justice and wrote a spirited letter to Nathanael Greene calling for retaliation:

> Sir,
>
> The execution of Colonel Haines by orders of the Commanding Officers of the British Army . . . claims the Attention of his brother officers, & those I have the honor to command. . . . After deliberate reflection on the reasons offered for that sanguinary step they are of opinion that it was unjustifiable on every principle of justice & can find no security from being subject to a similar fate if the fortunes of war should throw them into the hands of an arbitrary foe, unless restrained by retaliation, the only argument that will avail with men whose minds are callous to every sentiment of humanity.[76]

Like revolutionaries before and since, justice was clearly an ideal Washington held dear. This is hardly a surprising sentiment for an individual who first picked the pulpit and later chose a revolution in its stead. Nor was Washington alone in his anger against the Crown courts of Charleston. American officers joined Washington in calling for swift retaliation for what they felt was the murder of a comrade who had surrendered expecting quarter, and many Continental officers serving under Greene signed a petition that called Hayne's execution a violation of civil and military law.[77]

However, Rawdon and Balfour felt that if the Crown was seen as too weak to protect their own, they might risk what little

Loyalist support they enjoyed. Legal and martial precedents were ignored and Hayne was marched to the gibbet as an example of the king's infallible rule. Once again British officials drastically misjudged the American temperament and created a martyr by killing Hayne.[78] General Greene responded with a public proclamation threatening to exact revenge on captured British officers in the future and penned a letter to Lord Cornwallis where he also threatened to suspend all protections covering prisoners by the currently agreed cartel.[79]

Fortunately this threat of future hangings reversed course and the final chapter in the Hayne affair played itself out as Lord Rawdon boarded a ship bound for England. The Irish peer could rightfully claim victories at Hobkirk's Hill and lifting the siege of Ninety-Six, and in his own mind the hanging of Colonel Hayne, but while in command Rawdon had lost all of South Carolina north of Orangeburg, a total of some twenty thousand square miles of territory. Everyone knew such a loss was a staggering setback for the Crown, and Rawdon took the gangplank home with his nerves shot through and his reputation in tatters.[80] With a final, shaky salute he passed his command to Lieutenant Colonel Stewart.

General Greene learned of Rawdon's departure while sitting at his camp in the High Hills of the Santee. He had now survived two British commanders in the Carolinas, Lord Cornwallis and Lord Rawdon, and freed the greater part of two states in doing so. He penned the following to his close friend General Henry Knox: "There are few Generals that have run oftener, or more lustily than I have done. But I have taken care not to run too far, and commonly have run as fast forward as backward."[81]

Thirteen

EUTAW SPRINGS

"All officers of the Cavalry must assure themselves that there are only two methods of defeating an enemy; the first of which, is by attacking them with the utmost impetuosity: and the second, by outflanking them."–Regulations for the Prussian Cavalry

By late August Greene's forces in and around the High Hills of the Santee River's eastern bank had increased to nearly two thousand men with troops arriving from both North Carolina and Virginia. In a switch from many former campaigns, the greater portion were Continentals, but even among the militia, the majority were combat veterans, having served at some point or another in the nearly constant eighteen month conflict ensuing since the British landed outside Charleston. Greene's new command was well balanced, composed of infantry, artillery, and cavalry. In addition to Washington and Lee's troopers there were state and militia dragoons under officers William Henderson, Wade Hampton, Charles Myddelton, Peter Horry, Hezekiah Maham, and Samuel Hammond. Given the overall experience of the force, and high proportion of cavalry, it was perhaps the strongest body of troops Greene had led since Guilford Courthouse and possibly since his arrival in the

Carolinas. Greene was now itching for a fight and William Pierce, an aide of Greene's wrote that, "Mischief is a-brewing by the General."[1]

On the British side, Lieutenant Colonel Alexander Stewart had taken field command of all British forces outside Charleston. Stewart was a career army officer who had just arrived in Charleston before leading the three hundred and fifty man relief column to Rawdon's assistance at Orangeburg. During that march he'd managed to slip Marion's forces and proven to be a capable officer. Stewart's force was nearly equal in size to Greene's, with a strong body of infantry composed of elements from nine regiments as well as five artillery pieces, and Major Coffin's small but spirited contingent of light infantry turned dragoons. Realizing he had to do something to maintain his steadily shrinking supply base, Stewart decided to mount a heavy expedition of roughly two thousand men up the western side of the Santee with the idea of creating a new forward post while collecting supplies.[2]

When Greene caught wind of Stewart's actions, he called in all his detachments and began moving to intercept Stewart's designs. Due to the flooded state of the Santee River, Greene first looped north toward Camden and crossed the Wateree River at Howell's Ferry while William Washington followed behind and crossed farther south to screen Greene's southern advance. Rejoined, they marched south down the west side of the Santee and along the way Francis Marion also linked with Greene, raising the American force to just over two thousand men. Greene's force continued south and made camp at Burdell's Tavern, just seven miles from Stewart's rumored position at Eutaw Springs.[3]

Eutaw Springs had earned its name for two freshwater springs that boiled up and ran into nearby Eutaw Creek. Near the head of the creek stood a fine brick mansion of two stories which served as a natural way point for travelers en route to Charleston.[4] The rumors regarding Stewart's position were indeed true and his massed camp of tight canvas tents spread out before the brick mansion like a vast quilt of white on green. The fact that Greene's army was able to steal so close to the British camp unnoticed was a true testament to the excellent work of

Greene's plentiful cavalry and their screening abilities. Stewart wrote to Lord Cornwallis that, due to rebel activity, it was impossible for his men to maintain their scouting patrols among the trails and bye-paths of the near woods and swamps.[5]

On the morning of September 8, Greene had his army on the move by 4 A.M. In the advance rode Lee's multiple troops of dragoons and his legion infantry along with Lieutenant Colonel William Henderson's South Carolina state troops. After daybreak a pair of Americans deserters reached the British camp and warned the British of Greene's approaching army.[6] Stewart responded by sending Major Coffin forward to investigate with his force of fifty mounted dragoons and an attending force of light infantry.

Lee's forward troop of cavalry under Captain James Armstrong had posted a vedette at the head of the American advance and they were driven in by Coffin's dragoons just a few minutes after sunrise. Armstrong sent word to Lee that he had made contact and then expertly gave ground before Coffin's combined force while Lee formed his infantry for a fight.[7] A sharp skirmish ensued as Coffin's light infantry came upon Lee's infantry posted in the road and then Lee's remaining horse troops looped around behind Coffin. Now charged front and rear, Coffin's infantry were quickly broken and a number killed and captured. Coffin's dragoons realized they were being flanked and turned about to gallop back and alert Stewart at the main British camp.[8]

Greene now drove his troops ahead and Stewart, forewarned of the American approach by Major Coffin, came out to meet him in the open timber stretching before the British post. Greene chose to attack in three lines, the first of militia, and the second two of Continentals with four guns moving in support. Henry Lee was posted on the right front with his combined Legion of horse and foot, along with Samuel Hammond's militia dragoons, and Lieutenant Colonel Henderson covered the left front along with Hampton's state cavalry. Washington would command the *Corps de Reserve* in the rear with two companies of Delaware Continentals under Captain Kirkwood attached as his infantry support.[9]

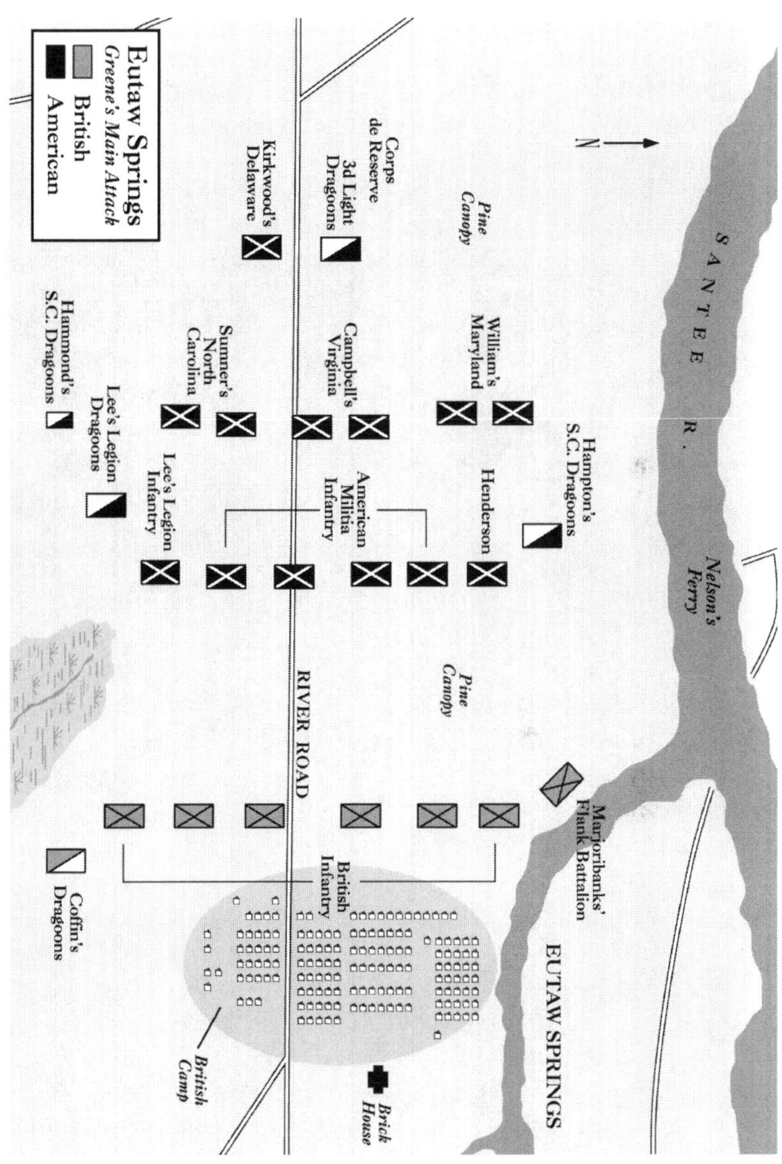

The *Corps de Reserve* was no insignificant posting and stood ready to be used at the commanding general's discretion. The reserve could be called to any point on the field to attack a resilient enemy position, countercharge an enemy breakthrough, or rout a broken enemy flank.[10] Greene trusted Washington, and his performance at Cowpens, Guilford Courthouse, and Hobkirk's Hill made him a natural choice for this crucial position.

The first American line drove the British before them and the fire soon ran from flank to flank in one of the bloodiest encounters of the entire war. The battle was fought over a series of gently undulating ridges that ran the breadth of the field, and tall long leaf pines stretched high over head to form a lofty canopy over the struggle below while most of the ground was open and free of underbrush. Limestone sumps dotted the field like pockmarks and were chocked tight with clumps of vegetation while thick stands of short black jack oaks were scattered about in clumps atop the ridges. The fighting seesawed back and forth beneath the canopy as casualties mounted and both sides threw in more troops. Greene ordered in General Jethro Sumner's North Carolina Continentals who pressed forward beneath a withering fire from the British. Many of Sumner's brigade were former militia who had run at the battle of Guilford and had since been formed into punitive battalions as a result and undergone extensive training.[11] Today they meant to clear their reputations and did so in earnest as they charged forward to trade close volleys with three British regiments: the 63d, the 64th, and Delancey's Loyalists. In just minutes, five company commanders and a field officer were hit as the British fire cut through the North Carolina ranks like a scythe and forced them to give ground.[12] The British smelled blood, and pressed ahead by companies and platoons and soon lost their own order in the pursuit which rapidly began to create gaps in their lines.[13]

Greene now committed his remaining Continentals. Lieutenant Colonel Richard Campbell's Virginians charged on the right and Colonel Otho Williams's Marylanders charged forward in the center. They rushed forward through enemy grapeshot and a shower of musketry with bayonets fixed and arms at the trail.[14] At forty yards Campbell's men fired a quick volley that fractured the British ranks before them and then swept ahead with the bayonet.[15] Drums rolled across the

American line, Sumner's men rallied yet again, and Lee's infantry pressed ahead on Campbell's far right flank.[16] A cheer swept through the American ranks and the British line now began to waver and then break entirely.

Colonel Campbell of the Virginians was shot and mortally wounded at this instant on the right but his troops continued forward despite the loss of their leader and the British were now bolting for the rear in what was looking to be one of the most complete victories ever won by Continental arms.

Now was the perfect time to send the light horse galloping after the fleeing British ranks and create a British rout that wouldn't slow down until it reached the gates of Charleston. However, Lieutenant Colonel Lee's dragoons, who were posted on that very flank with Lee in close support, somehow, didn't appear. At the very moment Lee's horsemen could have swept the field and rendered the British disorder irretrievable, they were unaccountably absent from their post. Colonel Otho Williams of the Maryland Line would later write that Lee's cavalry could have indeed done great execution had they been employed at this juncture.[17]

Nearly simultaneous with these actions was the ongoing fight on the British right flank which was composed of the handpicked grenadier and light infantry companies from three different infantry regiments. This, elite, three-hundred-man "flank battalion" was under the command of Major John Marjoribanks (pronounced marshbanks) of the famous 3d Regiment of Foot, the Buffs, and formed near a creek whose raised banks were overrun with a series of heavy thickets of scrub oak known as blackjack. The fire from Marjoribanks's flank battalion was creating disorder on the American left and Greene called for Washington and the *Corps de Reserve* to clear Marjoribanks's position.[18] At first glance it seems obvious that cavalry sent against infantry embedded in a tight thicket of shrubs would be a suicide mission, only attempted by a brash or foolishly aggressive commander, and many histories of the battle make no further conclusions. However some first-hand accounts contradict that conclusion and the cornerstone may lie with a few lines written by Lieutenant Colonel Henry Lee:[19]

> Marjoribanks now for the first time was put in motion, which being perceived, Lieutenant-Colonel Washington, with the reserve, was commanded to fall upon him . . . Washington promptly advanced to execute the orders he had received.[20]

One has to remember the goal of a cavalry charge was to ride through the enemy, shatter their discipline, and create a rout, therefore a body of light horse charging an enemy posted in a tightly wooded thicket was tactically ridiculous, akin to a battalion of infantry charging a twelve foot wall without ladders. Lee's statement implies that Marjoribanks's men may have swung away from the thicket of blackjack, or partially advanced out before it, to gain a better range or angle of fire upon the advancing American line. After witnessing the disorder visited upon the earlier advancing militia, Williams and his Continentals may well have given Marjoribanks a wider berth, causing Marjoribanks to extend in response. If that was the case, cavalry could make a charge against the extended portion of Marjoribanks's line and Greene's orders don't seem so far-fetched. Riding with Washington was 3d Light Dragoon George Hood who gave the following account of Washington's actions before the charge:

> The right wing of the enemy was the English Buffs, which fronted our left wing of militia–the fire was heavy, which caused our left wing to retreat–Morgan's [William's and Campbell's] Infantry with trail'd arm[s] too[k] their place, and commenc'd a heavy fire, and drove them back into line–By Col. Washington's orders we rallied the militia and brought them back into line–Col. Washington order'd them to keep their places; in a few minutes they would see him in front, among the Buffs, and then to cease firing.[21]

When Washington received orders to bring the reserve into play he knew better than to risk a charge on Marjoribanks's daunting position in the thicket. Veteran George Hood states that Washington decided to try and gain Marjoribanks's right rear flank and ordered Kirkwood's Light Infantry to move with him. Lieutenant Colonel Wade Hampton and his South Carolina state dragoons followed suit at Greene's behest:[22] "Washington

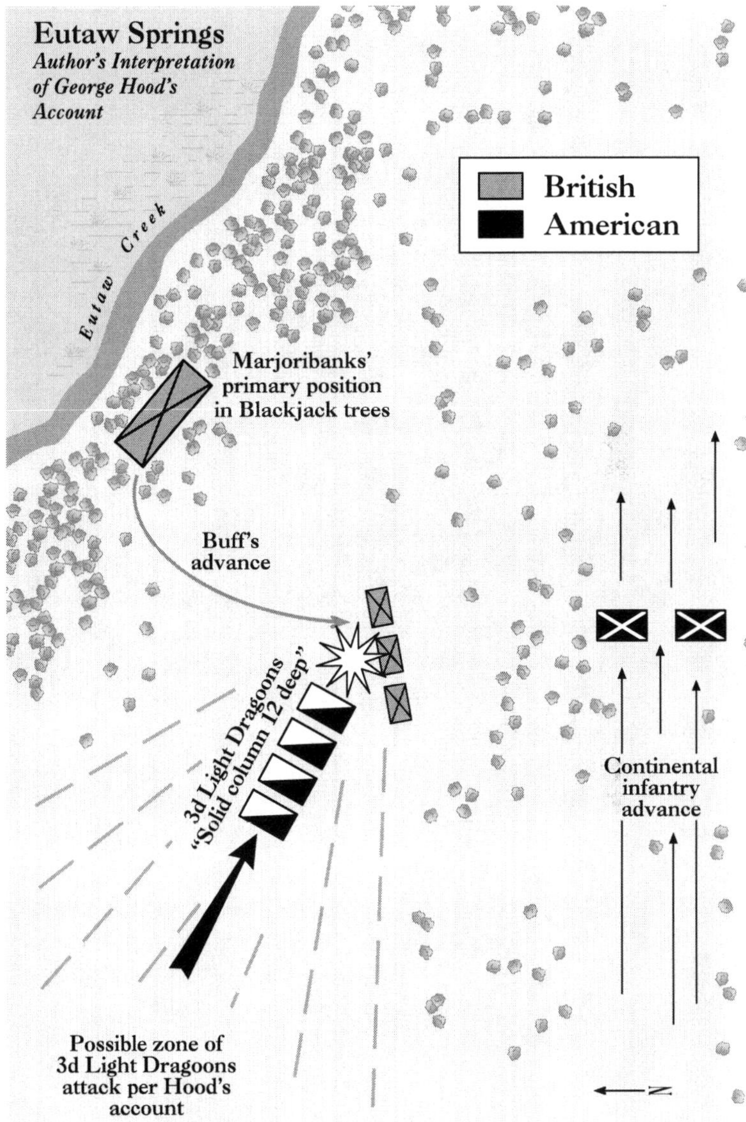

and Infantry went round and got in their rear–Washington and cavalry assisted by Wade Hampton and a company of mounted volunteers–also Geo. Griscom a Virginian with a company of mounted volunteers . . . was alongside."[23]

While the American infantry continued to press ahead, Washington came up in the rear of Marjoribanks's flank battalion and prepared to make a charge through the open timber. Hood's description "got in their rear" doesn't necessarily mean they were directly behind Marjoribanks's position, it could just as well mean they were past 90 degrees from the enemy's front. From this position Washington could probably see portions of the blackjack thicket, and elements of Marjoribanks's flank battalion extending out from the blackjack.[24]

Light dragoon George Hood said the 3d charged "in solid column 12 deep."[25] His description of a solid column twelve deep is hard to interpret with complete certainty. The squadron was the basic operating block of a light dragoon regiment. At Eutaw Springs, Washington had four companies, or two squadrons, and each company had approximately twenty to twenty-five troopers. A forty-eight man squadron in a column of fours would form a column twelve deep and such a slender, maneuverable column would certainly fit the bill for the open woods covering much of the battlefield. The second squadron could have been formed likewise, behind the first. As mentioned previously, such a formation would have been dangerously long and narrow for an assault. However, if the open tree cover allowed, Hood's description of a "solid column twelve deep" could have also meant all four troops were each formed three ranks deep, a standard for the day, and stacked in "solid column" one behind the other, yielding a column of troops in a broader eight file front and more resilient to musketry when closed up nose to croup for the final charge.[26] Nearly all of Washington's officers were struck down in the coming charge and this four troop, three rank formation would place the majority of the officers on the right flank of the column and put them at close intervals where a volley or rolling fire could sweep over them en masse: not from the thicket to their left, but from some extended portion of Marjoribanks's line.

Now formed and in range, Washington waved his men forward. Until now Washington and his men may have gone unnoticed by Marjoribanks but every light dragoon riding in the charge knew that was about to change as they brought spurs back and urged their mounts ahead.

The exact location of the thicket(s) in relation to Marjoribanks's men and Washington's charging column can never be known, and portions of the orginal field in this sector have since been flooded and now lie underwater. However, author John Marshall interviewed many veterans of the battle and later wrote that Washington broke the platoons on Marjoribanks's right but the remaining British retreated into the thicket.[27] Washington may have been hoping to mask the fire of the British by breaking the extended British ranks in the open and driving them back on top of their own lines within the black-jack, and this follows with what Marshall described. The tactic may have worked in some circumstances and probably did at the Cowpens. If that was the goal here it failed miserably as the British turned to see Washington's sudden approach at their rear and unleashed a storm of close range musketry that dropped officers, men, and horses alike. As at the Battle of the Waxhaws, such a late, close range volley would fail to halt the crush of galloping horses. Instead it would create a ghastly tumble of dying men and horses crashing and skidding into the British infantry and this is what 3d Light Dragoon George Hood describes: "We then charg'd the Buffs in the rear in solid column 12 deep–the slaughter was great on our side; but we cut through their line and wheel'd for the second charge."[28]

Hood's words clearly describe driving through the enemy ranks from the rear flank–after receiving a destructive volley–not halting before it as an earlier, prepared volley should have caused in a frontal attack, or halting and turning about before the thicket in the face of the British as other authors have surmised. A second participant, John Chaney, saw Washington "jump his horse into the midst of the enemy," not wheel away or fall short as if he'd charged into a mass of blackjack.[29] The 3d Light Dragoons then followed after Washington and "cut through" the British as best they could.

If Washington led the charge trooper Hood described, it would have made him a natural target. Washington's horse was struck by musket fire and collapsed even as others riding deeper in the column were shielded from the British fire. The momentum of the horses charging in unison would have carried them over and around wounded and dying comrades to plunge through the British Buffs in broken waves of swinging blades and thrashing horses that carried past with each succeeding rank of light dragoons hacking and spurring their way through.[30] The thicket now served as an anchor point for the British and preserved the remainder of Marjoribanks's battalion. After the horses rolled on, the British ran forward from the thicket and swarmed over the wounded light dragoons, including Washington who lay pinned beneath his horse.[31] Trooper George Hood wrote that he saw Washington as they wheeled to attempt a second charge: "defending himself among the Buffs, with sword in hand, but we had few men left and could not get to his Assistance."[32]

Washington was now in a fight for his life and managed to partly parry the thrust of a bayonet and only received a shallow wound to his chest rather than being run entirely through. He was then recognized by British officers and taken prisoner.

Two other probable casualties of the charge, Sergeant Major Mathew Perry and Trumpeter Lorentz Miller, were members of Washington's field staff and likely went down beside their commander as they were both later counted as prisoners.[33] John Chaney claimed a British soldier appeared to be in the process of stabbing Washington as he lay pinned beneath his horse but "one of his men rushed forward and cut him down with one blow."[34] This may have been a trooper in the later ranks, or it may have been either Sergeant Major Perry or Trumpeter Miller, and Sergeant Major Perry performed a similar feat at the Cowpens. Miller recalled being wounded five times. He was shot through the neck, bayonetted in the abdomen, and cut three times with a sword across his face and head. Any of Marjoribanks's officers would have enjoyed swatting their foot swords at a downed enemy light dragoon, especially if seconds before that same light dragoon had just come barreling down in an attack. If Trumpeter Miller had just cut down a British soldier as Chaney described, it may account for the multiple wounds he received.

The moments immediately following Washington's charge are best described by Colonel Otho Williams of the Maryland Line:

> The field of battle was, at this instant, rich in the dreadful scenery which disfigures such a picture. On the left, Washington's Cavalry, routed and flying, horses plunging as they died, or coursing the field without their riders, while the enemy with poised bayonet, issued from the thicket, upon the wounded or unhorsed rider: In the fore-ground, Hampton covering and collecting the scattered cavalry, while Kirkwood, with his bayonets, rushed furiously to revenge their fall. . . . Beyond these, a scene of indescribable confusion viewed over the whole American line advancing rapidly and in order: And, on the right, Campbell [now fatally shot] sustained in the saddle by his brave son.[35]

One of those downed in Washington's charge was Lieutenant James Simmons of the 3d Light Dragoons, who was shot twice in the hip and fell pinned beneath his horse where he called for quarter. "Oh yes, we'll quarter you" was the reply heard from the approaching British and Simmons was expecting the worst when his horse suddenly roused itself on instinct and galloped off to join the other retreating horses while Simmons clung fast to his neck and mane. In this fashion, Simmons made it back to some of his own men where his horse again fell down and died amongst his herd.[36] Simmons was fortunate and survived his wounds but others weren't as lucky; eleven light dragoons were killed and another fourteen were wounded.

Trailing behind Washington, Lieutenant Colonel Hampton made a charge that was also repulsed. On his heels came Kirkwood's two infantry companies with fixed bayonets, and Marjoribanks abandoned his position and retreated farther down along the creek to put an end to the enfilading fire pouring into the American ranks from that sector.

Elsewhere the battle continued on as the British line now fell back at all points and was driven through their camp of tents, lean-tos, and picket ropes set in the fields before the two story brick mansion.[37] By this point Washington was captured, his regiment's command structure was ruined, and his light dragoons were scattered and effectively out of the fight. Twenty-nine men out of eighty-three were either dead, wounded, or captured, and only one officer, Captain William Parsons, came through unscathed.[38] Some few of this total might have been injured in later fighting but after suffering such debilitating losses in men, mounts, and command structure it is unknown how many may have seen any additional action after the charge on Marjoribanks's battalion.[39] Yet there is one aspect of Washington's charge against Marjoribanks that has been overlooked, the *Corps de Reserve.*

Washington's orders were to clear Marjoribanks from the thicket with his *Corps de Reserve.* As George Hood stated Washington rode around Marjoribanks's flank with his Light Dragoons, Hampton's State Dragoons and Kirkwood's Delaware Infantry. If Hood's account is accurate, then it may be that the intent of Washington's charge was to drive Marjoribanks's extended line back into the blackjack and either cover or aid the movement of Kirkwood's slower approach–a classic screening action of light horsemen stretching back to Frederick the Great's legendary hussars.

Kirkwood's men did follow after Washington and Marjoribanks did withdraw from that section of the thicket and move down the creek. Kirkwood's men were also outnumbered three to one by Marjoribanks's battalion, hardly enough to carry the thicket on their own.[40] Nor could Washington charge alongside Kirkwood's slower moving infantry as that would have robbed his horses of any speed, surprise, or initiative.[41] Exactly what casualties Washington's horsemen inflicted upon Marjoribank's men is unknown, however this wasn't the first time Washington's men rode through enemy infantry and by day's end Marjoribanks's men suffered one hundred and six casualties.[42] At the very least Washington's charge disordered Marjoribanks's battalion before Kirkwood's men struck, as it would be physically impossible for two squadrons of dragoons to charge through even a portion of Marjoribanks's ranks without having a substantial effect on their order and discipline. Washington's charge on Marjoribanks ended in high casualties for the 3d Light Dragoons but the actions of Washington's overall command–the *Corps de Reserve*–were successful in carrying out Greene's orders of ending the enfilading fire sweeping across the American lines in that sector of the field.

It is true Washington's troopers paid a high price in delivering the charge but so did most of Greene's command in their efforts throughout the day. Estimates vary but Greene's overall casualties are figured as 692 of 2080 men engaged, for a percentage of 33 percent compared to Washington's own casualties of 34 percent.[43] Washington and his horsemen suffered the consequences of fulfilling the orders given but none more so than General Sumner's North Carolina Brigade which suffered roughly 44 percent in their brave assault against the British line which ended in Sumner's repulse.[44] General Greene later wrote of Sumner's brigade that he "could hardly tell which to admire most the gallantry of their Officers or the bravery of the Troops."[45] Greene also wrote in the same letter to Congress that "Col. Washington made the most astonishing efforts" in his charge against Marjoribanks.

In the end, Greene wasn't able to exploit the breakthrough gained by his men. While Washington was charging the British right, the British left flank was breaking to the rear. Greene sent for Lieutenant Colonel Lee's cavalry, posted on the American right, to attack the retreating British on their crumbling left flank.[46] Yet remarkably, Lee's normally redoubtable troopers were somehow "baffled" by the moment and unable to be marshaled into a coherent force to make a charge when the British left flank was hanging wide open.[47] Lee claimed that General Greene's aides, unbeknownst to Lee, had earlier ordered Major Eggleston, who was posted to command Lee's cavalry while Lee attended to his Legion infantry, to assist Washington's charge against Marjoribanks in the thicket on the American left.[48] And 3d Light Dragoon George Hood stated that "Major Henry Lee" briefly appeared on the American left but "the balls flew so fast" that the major commanding "the relief force" balked and "wheeled off, and did not come among us."[49] Hood presumably meant Major Eggleston or another officer commanding a section of Lee's dragoons and not Henry Lee himself. Lee claims this officer was Major Eggleston.[50] Hood and Lee therefore both place a portion of Lee's cavalry acting in support of Washington. Lee also stated that Captain Armstrong's troop of Legion dragoons was in place with Lee on the British left during

Eggleston's absence; Lee doesn't mention why Armstrong didn't make a charge.

Another theory for this criminal absence of cavalry survives from Lieutenant Colonel Samuel Hammond of South Carolina, who stated that he managed a successful charge with his small body of mounted militia that briefly cut through the retreating British infantry, but lacking any support from Lee's dragoons, had little lasting result. Upon his return to Continental lines, Hammond claimed Lee was trying to take command of Campbell's Virginia Brigade after Campbell was killed in the fight on the British left, and Lee was at that critical time embroiled in an unsuccessful argument with Campbell's subordinate officers.[51] According to Hammond, several of Lee's troop commanders were mortified by the affair, while Hammond felt that Lee was simply pursuing his own personal glory in too zealous a manner. Yet another witness, Lieutenant Colonel Howard with the Maryland Infantry, remembered seeing Lee about this same time on the American left, casting about the field for the artillery.[52] Other theories claim Lee's attention was simply focused too keenly on his Legion infantry, but none excuse this missed opportunity to rout the broken British ranks–be it Greene's, Greene's aides, Eggleston's, Armstrong's, or ultimately Lee's, responsibility.

General Greene's aide, Captain Pendleton said:

> The truth is, Col. Lee was very little if at all, with his own corps after the enemy fled. [i.e. when the British left crumbled] He took some dragoons with him, as I was informed, and rode about the field giving orders and directions, in a manner the General [Greene] did not approve of.[53]

Captain Pendleton eventually found Major Eggleston, presumably after his aborted attempt to support Washington, and Eggleston did make a charge on the British left but it came too late and well after the British had started to reform at the brick house and its surrounding ravines and gardens. Eggleston's charge was quickly broken here and driven back by Major Coffin's single squadron of resilient troopers.[54]

With commendable foresight, Lieutenant Colonel Stewart had wisely fortified the house when the battle began with a contingent of marksmen from the New York Volunteers and the sturdy brick house offered excellent cover and elevated firing positions from upstairs windows.[55] Flanking the house was a series of deep ravines and the sturdy brick mansion offered excellent cover and elevated firing positions from upstairs windows.[56] Marjoribanks's flank companies had simply retreated down the creek from their earlier position to the mansion and rallied with other units fleeing the fight on the British left, and all were now taking new positions in the gardens, thickets, and deep ravines about the brick mansion. Several valiant attempts were made by Greene's infantry to storm the house but all failed in the face of withering blasts of musketry that poured from the house and its surrounding cover.[57] Artillery was brought forward to batter the house into pieces and Lieutenant Colonel Howard recalled that he was wounded shortly after Lieutenant Colonel Lee was directing these guns up to the house.[58] Regrettably, the guns were laid in range of the British muskets, and Greene's gunners were cut down in a stream of fire. British infantry then rushed forward and captured the guns.[59]

Greene's forces were now starting to fall apart before his very eyes. They had suffered debilitating losses of both commissioned and non-commissioned officers and his command structure was in tatters. By this phase of the battle Greene was down to just one functioning cannon and his men were scattered across the field. Many of the Continental infantry pursuing the earlier British collapse had been forced to pass through the British camp which proved an unexpected and daunting terrain feature as the thick maze of tents, ropes, and stakes had broken all formation and order in the pursuing Continental troops. Upon clearing the camp these same troops came under fire from the British marksmen posted in the upper floors of the brick house which further eroded the Continentals' discipline.[60] Elsewhere Greene's men were running low on ammunition, others were dealing with herding about hundreds of British prisoners, and all were suffering greatly for lack of water. Under these scattered conditions and spiraling breakdown of command, Greene decided to call a retreat rather than feed more lives into the meat grinder before the plantation house.

Greene now turned to Hampton and his state dragoons to cover the retreat and sweep away Coffin's British dragoons. Hampton and his officers, now reformed from Washington's charge against Marjoribanks, collected all survivors on hand and charged forward in a blur of broadswords, a "sharp conflict, hand to hand was for a while maintained."[61] The two sides fought boot top to boot top in a whirling combat of crashing swords and wheeling horses before Hampton's dragoons finally scattered Coffin's troopers. However, the drifting fight carried Hampton's men in range of the plantation house and gardens where Marjoribanks's flank battalion and others had reformed, and the British now opened a severe fire upon Hampton's men in their pursuit of Coffin's retreating dragoons. The volleys were so intense that Hampton's second in command, William Polk, thought "every man killed but himself."[62] Several saddles were emptied as Hampton's men scattered before the house and gardens but they reformed out of range of the house and covered Greene's infantry as they began to fall back unit by unit.

The day's combat came to an end as Greene's army drifted back unchallenged through the ravaged British camp. Once through the maze of tents and bodies they posted a rear guard and began the long, seven mile march back to Burdell's Tavern.

Greene still hadn't won a battle but despite retiring many of his veterans felt they'd won a victory merely by breaking the British line and driving them with the bayonet. Victory had indeed been close at hand when the Virginia and Maryland infantry broke the British left and whatever the cause of Lee's Legion Dragoons' failings, many of Greene's officers believed this lack of action cost the Americans the battle.[63]

Eutaw Springs was the fourth time Nathanael Greene led American forces against the British. It was also his fourth defeat. Greene's own after action report is vague in a few areas and he still doesn't seem to have a firm grasp on Washington's actions three days after the battle. He claims Washington twice assaulted Marjoribanks, in two different actions, and at two different positions, the first of which Greene claims was a perfect success for Washington that sent Marjoribanks flying with no chance to rally. Greene then seems to have confused Hampton's later charge against Coffin and the resulting fire from the plantation house and gardens with Washington's earlier assault on the thicket.[64] It's possible some 3d Light Dragoons under Captain Parsons were engaged here as part of Hampton's force and their distinctive white uniforms led to Greene's confusion. Other first-hand accounts differ with Greene's considerably, including George Hood's, Otho Williams's, and Henry Lee's.

Still, it's hard to find fault with Greene. More than any one individual, Nathanael Greene was responsible for driving the British from the Carolinas and pressing Cornwallis to invade Virginia. This was a brilliant strategic success and clearly led to the end of the war. There is no doubt Greene reigns near the very top as a military strategist; his ability to see several moves ahead of his enemy within a campaign was extraordinary, yet his worth as a battle captain making quick decisions amid the swirling violence and ever-shifting chaos of eighteenth-century combat was lacking. Simply put he was a brilliant architect but a meager carpenter.

Nor had the battle been an easy day for Lieutenant Colonel Stewart and the British; combined British losses were 42 percent percent compared to Greene's 33 percent–a staggering percentage and a true testament to the discipline and expertise of Greene's men and officers. Stewart managed to wrestle a narrow victory but afterwards he so feared Greene would attack a second time that he burned his stores and abandoned the field with little more than his prisoners and ammunition in tow.

As he was withdrawing, Stewart ordered all muskets belonging to the dead and wounded be piled and burned lest they fall in the hands of the Continentals. Many were still loaded and they soon began to discharge from the heat of the flames. Stewart's men were still so spooked from the prior fight that this sudden "firing" caused a full blown panic in the retreating British columns as they thought Greene's men were attacking again! Gun-shy British teamsters were so alarmed that many cut the traces on their horses and fled the scene.[65]

Under guard in this very column, William Washington was briefly free from custody as his guards ran off in the ensuing panic. However, Washington had already formally pledged his parole; unless actually recaptured by his own forces he was honor bound to wait on his guards' return. He also had a bayonet wound to his chest and was badly bruised from his horse falling on him; sprinting back several miles toward the American lines might not have been an option. The British panic eventually died down, Washington's guards returned, and the British retreated to Monck's Corner where, ironically, Washington had been briefly captured by Tarleton's men over a year earlier and made good his escape.

This time his luck had run out and he penned the following note to General Greene:

> Eutaw. Sept. 8th, 1781
> Sir,
> I have the Misfortune to be a Prisoner of war, I am wounded with a Bayonet in my Breast, which together with the Contusion from the fall of my Horse which was killed makes me extremely sore: But I am in hope not dangerous. I shall be extremely obliged to forward the enclosed to Capt. Watts & permit my Cloathing to be sent in as soon as Possible Being informed by Col. Stuart that I am not to be indulg'd with Parole on any Latitude. I have been treated politely by many of the British officers.
> I have the Honor to be yrs.
> Very H. Servt.,
> W. Washington[66]

Fourteen

THE WAR WINDS DOWN

"I rejoiced unspeakably for my County."
–Henry Knox to Nathanael Greene

ONCE AGAIN GREENE HAD LOST A BATTLE BUT FORCED HIS enemy to give ground and Stewart's men were now formed in a lengthy column of jittery victors limping back to Charleston. The column made Charleston with little interruption and Washington and the other prisoners were turned over to the British garrison. Luckily for Washington, he was an officer of particular fame and the fetching Jane Elliot was soon allowed at his side to help nurse him back to health. In William's absence Jane had had no shortage of suitors, particularly from British officers and one admirer had even written a poem in Jane's honor:

Sweet harmonist! Whom nature triply arms
With virtue, beauty, music's powerful charms,–
Say, why combined, when each resistless power
Might mark its conquest to the fleeting hour?[1]

Bad poetry aside, it is extremely doubtful Jane would have welcomed any advances from an occupying enemy officer, especially given the intense hatred Whig families held for the Crown and its soldiers who constantly trespassed, impressed livestock, and took whatever provisions they required. Apparently, once Jane tilted her bonnet in William's direction she never switched tracks, and she now threw all her efforts at nursing William back to health even as he remained a prisoner under guard in Charleston.

After the fight at Eutaw Springs the British withdrew to the city and Greene sat above Charleston, ready to confront future British movements from within. Meanwhile in Virginia, the French fleet defeated the British navy off the Chesapeake Capes. Mere weeks after the battle of Eutaw Springs, Cornwallis was trapped and besieged at Yorktown. His Lordship surrendered his command to the combined French/American force on October 19, 1781. Among the British prisoners at Yorktown was William Washington's old enemy Banastre Tarleton; ironically, the two rival light horsemen were each destined to end the war as prisoners.

After the surrender at Yorktown, Cornwallis's army sailed for England and the war activity scaled down considerably while the two sides entered treaty negotiations. Charleston and New York both remained in British possession as the negotiations dragged on and skirmishes and foraging forays continued to take place outside Charleston for some time. The 3d Light Dragoons were forefront in many of these encounters though they never regained their strength prior to Eutaw.

Washington remained on parole during this period and the command of the British forces at Charleston switched from Lieutenant Colonel Stewart to Colonel Paston Gould, then General Alexander Leslie. Washington and Leslie had both fought at Guilford Courthouse and the two former antagonists slowly developed a mutual respect for one another. Leslie even trusted Washington's honor enough to allow him to leave the city and act as a liaison with General Greene, whose forces remained perched outside of Charleston.

Overtime Leslie grew to favor Washington so much that he allowed the marriage of Washington and Jane Elliot and the couple were wed on April 21, 1782, while Washington was still on parole. Washington's "lively" and "good humored" nature was clearly on display with Jane at this time and the couple was seen laughing and kissing in public as they doted on one another after their marriage. His competitive nature was also evident as Washington gambled at backgammon with fellow parolees and was seen racing horses outside the city gates.[2]

Washington served fourteen months on parole and was probably one of the first to shake hands with General Greene when his army marched into Charleston on December 14, 1782, after the British withdrawal. The war officially ended with the signing of the Treaty of Paris, September 3, 1783, and the last British troops sailed from New York on November 25, 1783.

By his marriage to Jane, Washington became a very wealthy man and instantly a member of South Carolina's elite planter circle. Jane's father had died in the spring of 1781, and Washington now had a lot to learn about tending rice fields and running a plantation. With the estate came the responsibility of managing several hundred slaves. William Washington was not alone in this postwar practice. Nathanael Greene, George Washington, Thomas Jefferson, and scores of other Continental officers and politicians owned slaves after the war. These others do not excuse the behavior but they do show evidence of a social and historical precedent that existed at the time of the revolution. The sad truth is that without slavery the American Colonies would not have won the war. The slave-tended crops of tobacco, indigo, and rice were a large part of what kept the early states afloat with foreign powers and secured the loans that allowed the United States to win its freedom from Great Britain.[3] All Americans, Northern and Southern, have that blood on their hands–and William Washington was certainly as guilty as any, if not more so, given his newfound rice wealth.

Washington proved to be an able administrator of his plantation and he and Jane were able to purchase a stylish townhouse in Charleston proper; the house still stands today at the corner of Church and South Battery. The couple had two children, Jane born in 1783, and William Jr. born in 1785. When not busy raising his children, Washington used his new wealth to breed racehorses. He was quite successful at this notoriously risky enterprise and helped form a number of race tracks and jockey clubs in and around Charleston. With such names as Trumpetts,

Ranger, Rosetta, Acteon, Flora, and Shark, his horses were known to all classes who followed the circuit and many were household names.[4] Washington was wildly popular with the people of Charleston and South Carolina alike and served in both the South Carolina House of Representatives and the Senate.[5]

He was a staunch Federalist and was selected to serve on Governor Thomas Pinckney's Privy Council, which acted as a legislative advisory board to the governor. Washington often voted outside the majority and differed from most by donating his legislator's salary to the charity fund for the poor of his parish.[6] In 1791 President George Washington visited Charleston and its surroundings, and William was there with other dignitaries to welcome the president to South Carolina. William now stood before the elder George as a man of means and a respected planter among his peers. Whatever gulf had existed between the two cousins before now seemed to evaporate as George toured William's plantation. The president even broke a standing rule to not stay at a private residence during his journey and spent the night at William's Sandy Hill plantation, where the pair reminisced about the war, horses, and, both the men now being planters, agriculture. Afterwards William and George enjoyed an ongoing correspondence of an entirely different tone than the terse, direct letters they exchanged during the war.

As William aged he spent more and more time away from Charleston and preferred to stay at his Sandy Hill plantation with Jane and his grandchildren. He died on March 6, 1810, at age 58 and was buried near Rantowle's Creek where he crossed swords with Tarleton's British Legion thirty years before. His wife, Jane, outlived him by twenty years.

Though many officers of the war wrote memoirs, William Washington apparently never did and not much more than brief campaign notes survive in his hand. Washington's fellow officer of the war, Henry "Light Horse Harry" Lee, did write a memoir after the war and Lee was not always kind to Washington in his work. Lee said of Washington that: "His occupations and his amusements applied to the body rather than to the mind; to the cultivation of which he did not bestow much time or application, nor was his education of the sort to excite such habits."

After insulting his fellow officer's intelligence, Lee switched tacks and praised Washington's achievements before again changing direction to claim Washington was better suited to hard combat than the "calculations . . . of means and measures" or the "sifting of intelligence" and followed with the statement that Washington's "system of discipline was rather lax and . . . subjected him to injurious consequences."[7] This was a mouthful even for the pretentious Lee and patently unfounded. Though full of much excellent information, anyone reading Lee's memoirs should be aware that Lee wrote them while sitting in a prison cell after being ousted from public office and publicly disgraced for a string of, at best, shady land dealings.[8] Lee was incarcerated for his larcenous behavior and excessive debts while Washington remained affluently comfortable in South Carolina and adroitly managed his plantation and racing stables.

Some historians have tried to compare Washington to Lee but it is a difficult exercise and largely similar to comparing apples and oranges. Despite the later nineteenth century moniker of "Light Horse Harry," Henry Lee's mark was made as a legion commander and partisan officer, not a light dragoon officer. Lee was a remarkable soldier and a superb partisan when out ranging on his own; his victories at Paulus Hook, Fort Watson, and the twin posts at Augusta clearly show his expertise in siege work and ground assaults. As a legion commander he led a mixed force of infantry and cavalry and Lee's focus was often directed to his infantry over his cavalry.

A closer comparison to Henry Lee would be Banastre Tarleton. Like Lee, Tarleton also led a mixed legion of horse and foot and both Lee and Tarleton were first-rate soldiers and highly successful. However, Tarleton seems to have held a preference for mounted combat that was lacking in Lee. As legion commanders Lee and Tarleton also had the opportunity to operate more independently and with larger numbers of troops than Washington ever had. Tarleton was twice the victor when he surprised Washington's men on foot but the fights at Rantowle's Bridge, the Cowpens, and Weitzel's Mill are proof positive that Washington was more than a match for Tarleton when both were in the saddle. Joseph Graham's insightful account of the fight at Weitzel's Mill shows us the simultaneous actions of Lee, Tarleton, and Washington and reveals Lee's tendency to want to fight with the infantry and allow his junior officers to command his horsemen. Meanwhile Washington is seen in the saddle just yards from the approaching enemy van, commanding the very rear element of the American rear guard with sword in hand–the epitome of a light dragoon officer.

A study of Washington's dealings with Anthony White in the courts, his ruse with the pine cannon at Rugeley's Mill, and his letter of protest over Isaac Hayne's execution, clearly show Washington was far from the impetuous, simple-minded horseman Lee implied. Harlem Heights, White Plains, Trenton, Brandywine, Germantown, Monmouth Courthouse, Rantowle's Creek, Monck's Corner, Lenud's Ferry, Rugeley's Mill, Hammond's Store, the Cowpens, Weitzel's Mill, Guilford Courthouse, Hobkirk's Hill, Eutaw Springs, and hundreds of daily scouts, skirmishes, vans, vedettes, reencounters, and rear guard postings attest to the fact that Washington was a keen judge of both character and circumstance or he never would have survived the war. Washington was a hard-charging, front-line soldier. His record was far from perfect, however, there are few soldiers of the revolution whose combat resume would eclipse Washington's, and far fewer who landed as many battle-turning blows on different fields.

It is true that Washington was aggressive and daring, that he led from the front, met the enemy sword in hand, and took great risks, but ultimately Washington was a light horseman, and light horsemen were expected to take risks and charge through the enemy. Timid horse soldiers are rarely mentioned in history, and when they are it is seldom a positive account. General Cornwallis, the British commander of the southern theatre for much of the war, understood this principle as much as anyone. Cornwallis was a career soldier who fought wars in Europe, Asia, and America. He squared off directly against Washington at Guilford Courthouse, and before that dealt with the repercussions of Washington's actions at Hammond's Store, the Cowpens, and the Race for the Dan. Long after the war his Lordship made a comment to a friend which summed up his former American enemy in the simplest of terms: "there could be no more formidable antagonist in a charge, at the head of his cavalry, than Colonel William Washington."[9]

This was no small praise when coming from a career officer who had seen action on three continents! Yet what truly separates William Washington from the Henry Lees or Banestre Tarletons of the world had little to do with the battlefield proper; William Washington was never running about tooting his own horn or desperately seeking the praise of his superiors, nor had he any driving desire to become a celebrity. Washington was a genuinely modest, plain-spoken, individual, who not only had the opportunity to do great things: he triumphed at them. If he didn't write a memoir at the end of the war, it was because he didn't see the need.

Washington was a hands-on commander, a soldier's soldier fully secure in his own image; when he posed for his portrait he did so without powdered wig or dressed hair, a novelty for most any field officer of his day, which shows what an honest, common sort of person he was at heart. The war was in the past in Washington's mind and he was content to let others write the history. In combat Washington always led from the front; after the war he retired to the ranks of private life. His marriage to Jane Elliot made him extremely wealthy and, coupled with his war record, he could have attempted almost anything in politics; instead he was happy just racing horses and serving his neighboring constituents.

At one point Washington was asked to run for governor of South Carolina and he turned the offer down flat, stating that he wasn't native to the state. This refusal dovetails entirely with Washington's personal experience. He fought a seven-year war for American independence: a war that in many ways was a basic quest for home rule. Washington simply couldn't see the justice in a Virginian leading the state of South Carolina. Every generation will have its simpering scions and sunshine patriots; what every generation needs are more bedrock Americans like William Washington.

NOTES

Prologue

1. "Cpt. William Pierce Jr. to General Nathanael Greene, 14 Sept. 14, 1782," *The Papers of Nathanael Greene,* Vol. XI, ed. Dennis Conrad (Chapel Hill, University of North Carolina Press, 2000), 660.
2. Ibid.
3. John Eager Howard ca. 1822, "Letter from John Eager Howard to William Johnson," Rocky Mount Collection, DuPont Library, MS on file at Stratford Hall Plantation, Stratford, Virginia. Courtesy of Dr. Lawrence Babits.
4. "William Washington to Nathanael Greene, Sept. 8, 1781," Conrad, *Papers of Greene,* Vol. IX, 306.

Chapter One: Fortune's Son

1. Stephen Haller, *William Washington: Cavalryman of the Revolution* (Bowie, Heritage Books, 2001), 1.
2. Ibid.
3. Willard Cochrane, *The Development of American Agriculture: A Historical Analysis* (Minneapolis, University of Minnesota Press, 1993), 28-32.
4. Louis Wright, *Everyday Life in Colonial America* (New York, Penguin, 1966), 195.
5. Elwyn Edwards, "Quarter Horse," *The New Encyclopedia of the Horse* (New York: Dorling Kindersley, 1994), 230-231.
6. Caroline Jones, "Fox Hunting in America," *American Heritage,* accessed June 28, 2013, http://www.americanheritage.com/content/fox-hunting-america/page=4.
7. John Durant, "Virginia"s Finest Horseman," *Sports Illustrated,* July, 2 1956, accessed June 29, 2013, http://sportsillustrated.cnn.com/ vault/article/magazine/MAG1132077/1/index.htm.
8. Haller, *William Washington,* 3.
9. John Galvin, *The Minute Men* (Washington, D.C., Brassey's AUSA, 1989), 38-40.
10. Haller, *William Washington,* 4-5.
11. A. J. Langguth, *Patriots: The Men Who Started the American Revolution* (New York, Simon and Schuster, 1988), 67-70.

12. Langguth, *Patriots,* 48-50, 50-65, 93-105.
13. Haller, *William Washington,* 3.
14. Langguth, *Patriots,* 188-193.
15. Merrill Jensen, *The Founding of a Nation* (New York, Oxford University Press, 1968), 457.
16. Lillian Miller, *The Die Is Now Cast* (Washington, D.C., Smithsonian Press, 1975), 205. Jensen, *The Founding of a Nation,* 644.
17. Langguth, *Patriots,* 222-223.
18. Pension application of Alvin Mountjoy, W8471.

Chapter Two: Harlem Heights

1. W. J. Wood, Introduction to *Battles of the Revolutionary War 1775-1781* (New York, Da Capo Press, 1995), xxi-xxvi.
2. "President of Congress to the Governor of Virginia July 22, 1776," Haller, *William Washington,* 11.
3. Langguth, *Patriots,* 380-383.
4. David Fisher, *Washington's Crossing* (New York, Oxford University Press, 2004), 106-107.
5. Thomas Emmet, *The Battle of Harlem Heights,* accessed June 28, 2013, Columbia University Digital Collections, http://www.columbia.edu/cu/lweb/digital/collections/cul/texts/ldpd_6219521_000/pages/ldpd_6219521_000_00000015.html?tog, 7. Henry Phelps Johnson, *The Battle of Harlem Heights, September 16, 1776,* accessed March 31, 2012, Google Books, http://books.google.com/books?id=MTdCAAAAIAAJ, 41-43.
6. "Adjutant General Joseph Reed to his wife," *Reed Papers,* Vol. IV, 59, N.Y. Hist. Soc.; Henry Commager and Richard Morris, eds., *The Spirit of 'Seventy-Six* (New York, Da Capo Press, 1995), 468.
7. Johnston, *The Battle of Harlem Heights,* 58.
8. Ibid., 82.
9. Quote from Captain Gustavus Wallace, in Johnson, *Battle of Harlem Heights,* 119.
10. Matthew Spring, *With Zeal and with Bayonets Only: The British Army on Campaign in North America, 1775-1783* (Norman, University of Oklahoma Press, 2008), 198-201.
11. "George Washington to Congress, September 18, 1776," *George Washington Papers at the Library of Congress,* Library of Congress, *Peter Force Collection,* ed. John C. Fitzgerald, accessed July 12, 2013, http://memory.loc.gov/mss/mgw/mgw3a/001/424423.jpg.
12. Johnson, *Battle of Harlem Heights,* 125.
13. Ibid., 138.
14. "George Washington to Congress, September 18, 1776," *Washington Papers LOC,* accessed July 12, 2013, http://memory.loc.gov/mss/mgw/mgw3a/001/424423.jpg.

Chapter Three: An American Crisis

1. W. J. Wood, *Battles of the Revolutionary War* (New York, Da Capo Press, 1990), 57.
2. Fisher, *Washington's Crossing,* 108-110.
3. Urwin, *The United States Cavalry: An Illustrated History* (Norman, University of Oklahoma Press, 2003), 11; Richard Cannon, *The Historical Record of the Seventeenth Regiment of Light Dragoons–Lancers* (London, John W. Parker, 1841), 18, accessed July 7, 2013, https://play.google.com/books/reader?id=VVykrSD7MG0C&printsec=frontcover&output=reader&authuser=0&hl=en&pg=GBS.PA18; Urwin, *The United States Cavalry: An Illustrated History,* 11.
4. Michael Stephenson, *Patriot Battles: How the War of Independence Was Fought* (New York, Harper, 2008), 248.
5. Johann von Bardeleben, *The Diary of Lieutenant Bardeleben and Other Von Donop Regiment,* ed. Bruce E. Burgoyne (Berwyn Heights, Heritage Books, Inc., 2009), 73.
6. Richard Ketchum, *The Winter Soldiers* (New York, Doubleday & Company, 1973), 158. Fisher, *Washington's Crossing,* 113.
7. Ibid., 242-243.
8. Fisher, David, *Washington's Crossing,* 125-131.
9. Haller, *William Washington,* 16.
10. Haller, *William Washington,* 17.
11. "George Washington to Lund Washington, D.C., December 17, 1776," *The Writings of George Washington from the Original Manuscript Sources 1745-1799,* Vol. VI, ed. John C. Fitzpatrick (Washington, United States Government Printing Office, 1931-1944), accessed July 12, 2013, Electronic Text Center, University of Virginia Library, http://etext.virginia.edu/toc/modeng/public/WasFi06.html.
12. Langguth, *Patriots,* 401.
13. Ketchum, *Winter Soldiers,* 242, 269-270.
14. Ketchum, *Winter Soldiers,* 217; Langguth, *Patriots,* 313. General Howe's mistress was Mrs. Eliziabeth Loring; her husband, Joshua, was a staunch New York Loyalist who encouraged his wife's relationship with Howe. For Mr. Loring's unbridled support of the Crown he was appointed Commissioner of Prisoners and was responsible for the deaths of thousands of American POWs.
15. Fisher, *Washington's Crossing,* 191-198.
16. "Colonel Joseph Reed to George Washington, December 22, 1776," *The George Washington Papers at the Library of Congress 1741-1799,* ed. John C. Fitzgerald, accessed July 12, 2013, http://memory.loc.gov/cgi-bin/query/P?mgw:1:./temp/~ammem_kehZ::.
17. Wood, *Battles of the Revolutionary War,* 60.
18. Fisher, *Washington's Crossing,* 212.
19. Ketchum, *Winter Soldiers,* 295.
20. Ibid.

21. Thomas Paine, *The American Crisis*, December 23, 1776, accessed July 4, 2013, http://www.ushistory.org/paine/crisis/c-01.htm.
22. Stuart Brown, *The Autobiography of James Monroe* (Whitefish, MT, Literary Licensing, LLC, 2011), 25.
23. Fisher, *Washington's Crossing*, 227.
24. Brown, *The Autobiography of James Monroe*, 25.
25. Fisher, *Washington's Crossing*, 231.
26. "George Washington to the President of Congress, December 27, 1776," Fitzpatrick, *The Writings of Washington*, Vol. VI, accessed July 7, 2013, UVA Library, http://etext.virginia.edu/toc/modeng/public/WasFi06.html.
27. Fisher, *Washington's Crossing*, 203-205.
28. Fisher, *Washington's Crossing*, 240.
29. Wood, *Battles of the Revolutionary War*, 66, 68.
30. Douglas Freeman, *George Washington: A Biography*, Vol. 4 (New York, Augustus M. Kelley, 1948), 316.
31. Fisher, *Washington's Crossing*, 237.
32. Brown, *Autobiography of James Monroe*, 25.
33. Ibid., 244; also Ketchum, *The Winter Soldiers*, 308.
34. Richard Ketchum, *The Winter Soldiers*, 309
35. Brown, *Autobiography of James Monroe*, 25.
36. White, *Narrative of Events*, 77.
37. Brown, *Autobiography of James Monroe*, 26.
38. Ketchum, *Winter Soldiers*, 312.
39. James Wilkinson and Abraham Small, *Memoirs of My Own Times* (Philadelphia, Abraham Small, 1816), 130. Bracketed words by the author.

Chapter Four: Creating The Continental Light Dragoons

1. Gregory Urwin, *The United States Cavalry: An Illustrated History 1776-1944* (Norman, University of Oklahoma Press, 2003), 9.
2. Ibid., 11. Douglas Cubbison, "Ambush at Indian Field," *Patriots of the American Revolution*, July/August 2011.
3. "George Washington to Continental Congress, December 11, 1776," Fitzpatick, *Writings of Washington*, Vol. VI, accessed July 12, 2013, UVA Library, http://etext.virginia.edu/toc/modeng/public/WasFi06.html.
4. C. F. William Mauer, *Dragoon Diary: The History of the Third Continental Light Dragoons* (Bloomington, Authorhouse, 2005), 19; Urwin, *The United States Cavalry*, 13-14.
5. Beeler, *Warfare in Feudal Europe 730-1200* (New York, Cornell University Press, 1973), 10, 21-26.
6. Louis DiMarco, *War Horse: A History of the Military Horse and Rider* (Yardley, PA,Westholme Publishing, 2008), 89-91, 94-95.
7. John Ellis, *Cavalry: The History of Mounted Warfare* (Barnsley, Pen and Sword, 2004), 81-84.
8. Ibid., 84.

9. Quote from Frederick the Great in Anthony North, "Seventeenth Century Europe," in *Swords and Hilt Weapons,* ed. Anne Cope (New York, Weidenfeld & Nicolson, 1989), 87.
10. Emanuel Von Warnery, *Remarks on Cavalry* (Nottingham, Cavalier Books, 1997), 1.
11. Louis Nolan, *Cavalry Its History and Tactics* (Yardley, PA, Westholme Publishing, 2007), 38.
12. King Frederick of Prussia, *Frederick the Great on the Art of War,* ed. Jay Luvaas (New York, Da Capo Press, 1966), 80-82; Ellis, *Cavalry: The History of Mounted Warfare,* 92.
13. Anthony North, "Seventeenth Century Europe," in *Swords and Hilt Weapons,* ed. Anne Cope (New York, Weidenfeld & Nicolson, 1989), 76-78; Phillip J. Haythornthwaite, *Napoleonic Cavalry* (London, Casell, 2002), 30. The author's own practical experience in drilling, skill-at-arms displays, and fencing from the saddle for over ten years.
14. Von Warnery, *Remarks on Cavalry,* 34; "Concerning the Review of a Regiment of Hussars and Their Exercise on Horseback," Article 4, "Charge by Divisions," in *Regulations for the Prussian Cavalry, 1757,* trans. Sir William Fawcett (London, J. Haberkorn, 1757), 124, accessed July 7, 2013, https://play.google.com/books/reader?id=yUYIAAAAQAAJ&printsec=frontcover&output=reader&authuser=0&hl=en&pg=GBS.PA124.
15. Rory Muir, *Tactics and the Experience of Battle in the Age of Napoleon* (New Haven, Yale University Press, 2000), 108.
16. Otho Williams, "Battle of Eutaw," in *Documentary History of the American Revolution Consisting of Letters and Papers Relating to the Contest for Liberty, Chiefly in South Carolina,* Vol. II, ed. Robert Gibbs (Bedford, Applewood Books, 1853), 151, Google Books, http://books.google.com/books?id=3GIbrUCmgPUC&pg=PA152&lpg=PA152&dq=.
17. Von Warnery, *Remarks,* 5.
18. Digby Smith, *Charge! Great Cavalry Charges of the Napoleonic Wars.* (Mechanicsburg, Stackpole Books, 1988), 15.
19. Robert Selig, *Hussars in Lebanon!* (Lebanon, Lebanon Historical Society, 2004), 27.
20. Von Warnery, *Remarks on Cavalry,* 5.
21. Daniel Murphy, "Shock and Awe: Mounted Combat in the 18th Century," *American Revolution* (May 2009), 24-27; rpt. in *The Journal of the United States Cavalry* (June 2009), 10-15.
22. Von Warnery, *Remarks on Cavalry,* 19.
23. Daniel Murphy, "Shock and Awe: Mounted Combat in the 18th Century," *American Revolution* (May 2009): 24-27; rpt. in *The Journal of the United States Cavalry* (June 2009), 10-15.
24. Robert Hinde, *The Discipline of the Light Horse* (London, 1778), 150-155.
25. Martin Griffin, *Stephen Moylan, Muster-Master General, Secretary and Aide de Camp to Washington . . .* (Philadelphia, 1909), 5-6.

26. Ibid.,10-15.
27. Ibid., 36-40.
28. Scott Miskimon, "Anthony Walton White: The Trials and Tribulations of a Revolutionary Dragoon," paper submitted for Southern Campaigns of the American Revolution (Cavalry Conference, 2008); "*The Lost Pages of Elmer's Revolutionary Journal*," ed. A. Van Doren. Proceedings of the New Jersey Historical Society New Ser. 10, 412 (October 1925).
29. Scott Miskimon, "Anthony Walton White: A Revolutionary Dragoon," in *Cavalry of the American Revolution,* ed. Jim Piecuch (Yardley, Westholme Publishing, 2012), 109; Arthur Lefkowitz, *Indispensable Men,* (Mechanicsburg, Stackpole Books, 2003), 220-221.
30. "George Washington to George Weedon, March 27, 1777," Fitzpatrick, *The Writings of Washington,* Vol. VII, accessed October 18, 2011, UVA Library, http://etext.virginia.edu/toc/modeng/public/WasFi07.html.
31. "George Washington to Anthony W. White, March 20, 1777," Fitzpatrick, *The Writings of Washington,* Vol. VII, accessed October 18, 2011, UVA Library,
32. Mauer, *Dragoon Diary,* 16, 27; Loescher, *Washington's Eyes,* 98, 100.
33. "George Washington to Continental Congress, May 9, 1777," Fitzpatrick, *The Writings of Washington,* Vol. VIII, accessed October 28, 2011, UVA Library, http://etext.virginia.edu/toc/modeng/public/WasFi08.html.
34. Lee McGee, "European Influences on Cavalry," *Cavalry of the American Revolution,* ed. Jim Piecuch, 38.
35. "George Washington to Stephen Moylan, May 12, 1777," Fitzpatrick, *The Writings of Washington,* Vol. VIII, accessed October 29, 2011, UVA Library, http://etext.virginia.edu/toc/modeng/public/WasFi08.html.
36. Martin, *Stephen Moylan,* 59; Loescher, *Washington's Eyes,* 31.
37. "George Washington to Continental Congress, September 3, 1777," *George Washington Papers LOC,* accessed June 27, 2013, http://memory.loc.gov/cgib-in/query/r?ammem/mgw:@field(DOCID+@lit(gw090178)); Captain Walter Stewart to General Gates, September 2, 1777; Commager and Morris, *The Spirit of 'Seventy-Six,* 610-611.
38. Freeman, *George Washington,* Vol. IV, 471.
39. Wood, *Battles of the Revolutionary War,* 98-105; Gregory J. Urwin, "The Continental Light Dragoons, 1776-1783," *Cavalry of the American Revolution,* ed. Jim Piecuch, 8.
40. Freeman, *George Washington,* Vol. IV, 484.
41. Urwin, *Cavalry of the American Revolution,* ed. Jim Piecuch, 8; AnnMarie Kajencki, *Count Casimir Pulaski* (New York, PowerPlus Books, 2005), 42.
42. "George Washington to Continental Congress, August 28, 1777"; Fitzpatrick, *The Writings of Washington,* accessed October 28, 2011, UVA Library, http://etext.virginia.edu/toc/modeng/public/WasFi09.html.
43. Michael Stephenson, *Patriot Battles: How the War of Independence Was Fought* (New York, HarperCollins, 2007), 279.
44. Urwin, *Cavalry of the American Revolution,* ed. Piecuch, 10.

45. Freeman, *George Washington,* Vol. IV, 508.
46. Ibid., 510
47. "Samuel Hay to William Irvine, Camp White Marsh, November 14, 1777," *William Irvine Papers,* Historical Society of Pennsylvania, Philadelphia, PA.
48. "Casimir Pulaski to George Washington, November 23, 1777," *Washington Papers LOC,* accessed July 12, 2013, http://memory.loc.gov/cgi-bin/query/P?mgw:16:./temp/~ammem_cD7X::; Casimir Pulaski to George Washington, February 28, 1778, *Washington Papers LOC,* accessed July 12, 2013, http://memory.loc.gov/cgi bin/query/P?mgw:17:./temp/~ammem_ cD7X::.
49. "Casimir Pulaski to George Washington, December 29, 1777," *Washington Papers LOC,* accessed July 12, 2013, http://memory.loc.gov/cgi-bin/query/P?mgw:1:./temp/~ammem_s9pl::.
50. An examination of the subscribers list shows that English copies of Frederick the Great's cavalry drill, *Regulations for the Prussian Cavalry,* translated by Sir William Fawcett, were in wide circulation at the time.
51. Freeman, *George Washington: A Biography,* Vol. IV, 537 (see footnote 94).
52. Griffin, *Stephen Moylan,* 63.
53. "George Washington to Continental Congress, March 14, 1778," Fitzpatrick, *The Writings of Washington,* Vol. XI, accessed October 30, 2011, UVA Library, http://etext.virginia.edu/toc/modeng/public/WasFi11.html.
54. Scott Miskimon, "Anthony Walton White: The Trials and Tribulations of a Revolutionary War Dragoon," paper presented at the Southern Campaigns of the American Revolutionary Cavalry Conference, 2007.
55. "Colonel Moylan to General Washington, June 23, 1778," *Washington Papers LOC,* accessed July 12, 2013, http://memory.loc.gov/cgi-bin/query/P?mgw:12:./temp/~ammem_iO8q::; Mauer, *Dragoon Diary,* 100; Griffin, *Stephen Moylan,* 75-76.
56. Testimony of Lieutenant Colonel Richard Harrison at the court-martial of General Lee, in New York Historical Society Collections, *Spirit of 'Seventy-Six,* ed. Commager and Morris, 711-713.
57. Joseph Martin, *Narrative of a Revolutionary Soldier: Some Adventures, Dangers and Sufferings of Joseph Plumb Martin* (Reprint: New York, Signet Classics/Penguin Books, 2001), 91-93.
58. "Colonel Moylan to General Washington, June 29, 1778," *Washington Papers LOC,* accessed July 12, 2013, http://memory.loc.gov/cgi-bin/query/P?mgw:2:./temp/~ammem_iO8q::.
59. Urwin, *The United States Cavalry,* 20-21.
60. Mauer, *Dragoon Diary,* 129-137.

Chapter Five: Field Command

1. Col. Baylor was paroled in February 1779, but didn't get exchanged and take the field until October 1781. Even then he commanded largely in absentia.
2. North, *Swords and Hilt Weapons,* ed. Cope, 84-87; George Neumann, *Swords & Blades of the American Revolution* (Texarkana, Scurlock Publishing, 1995), 56;

Harold Peterson, *The Book of the Continental Soldier* (North Sannich, Promontory Press, 1975), 89-90.
3. Adjutant General, British War Office, *Rules and Regulations for the Sword Exercise of Cavalry 1796* (Reprint: East Sussex, Naval and Military Press, 2009), 46-60; Haythornthwaite, *Napoleonic Cavalry,* 31; Christopher Thompson, *Lannaireachd: Gaelic Swordsmanship* (Charleston, Booksurge Publishing, 2002), 43-66, 67-82.
4. Epaphras Hoyt, *A Treatise on the Military Art* (Brattleborough, 1798), 101, 133. Rpt. in Harold Peterson, *The Book of the Continental Soldier* (Harrisburg, Stackpole Company, 1968), 89.
5. John Keegan, *The Face of Battle: A Study of Agincourt, Waterloo and the Somme* (New York, Penguin Books, 1983), 145-146, 320.
6. Von Warnery, *Remarks on Cavalry,* 46-47.
7. David Wilson, *The Southern Strategy: Britain's Conquest of the South* (Columbia, University of South Carolina Press, 2008), 60-63.
8. Buchanan, *Road to Guilford,* 26.
9. "George Washington to William Washington, February 9, 1779," Fitzpatrick, *The Writings of Washington,* accessed, October 31, 2011, UVA Library, http://etext.virginia.edu/toc/modeng/public/WasFi14.html.
10. "George Washington to Lieutenant Colonel William Washington, May 21, 1779," Fitzpatrick, *The Writings of Washington,* Vol. XV, accessed July 12, 2013, UVA Library, http://etext.virginia.edu/toc/modeng/public/WasFi15.html; "Continental Congress, May 7, 1779, Resolutions on Southern Army," *The George Washington Papers at the Library of Congress, 1741-1799,* accessed July 7, 2013, http://memory.loc.gov/cgi-bin/query/P?mgw:11:./temp/~ammem _bfit::.
11. "George Washington to the Board of War, June 9, 1779," Fitzpatrick, *The Writings of Washington,* Vol. XV, accessed November 3, 2011, UVA Library, http://etext.virginia.edu/toc/modeng/public/WasFi15.html. Bracketed words are author's.
12. Mauer, *Dragoon Diary,* 217.
13. "John Adams to Benjamin Rush, November 11, 1807," *The Spur of Fame: Dialogues of John Adams and Benjamin Rush, 1805-1813* (Indianapolis, Liberty Fund, 2001), 230.
14. Lee, *Memoirs,* 588. Pension application of Lawrence Everhart, S25068.
15. "John Eager Howard to unkown individual," Bayard Papers, MS 109, Box 1, Folder 18, Maryland Historical Society (MHS); Pension application of Henry Wells S11712.
16. Wilson, *The Southern Strategy,* 148-175.
17. Mauer, *Dragoon Diary,* 228.
18. Hill, *Gentleman of Fortune,* Vol. III, 29.

Chapter Six: Into the Low Country

1. Buchannan, *Road to Guilford,* 21.
2. Ibid., 13.

3. Carl Borick, *A Gallant Defense: The Siege of Charleston 1780* (Columbia, University of South Carolina Press, 2012), 27.
4. Wilson, *The Southern Strategy,* 205.
5. Borick, *A G.allant Defense,* 55.
6. "Theodoric Bland to George Washington, December 19, 1779," *Washington Papers LOC,* accessed July 12, 2013, http://memory.loc.gov/cgi-bin/query/P?mgw:2:./temp/~ammem_7n7a::.
7. Lumpkin, *From Savannah to Yorktown,* 39.
8. Muir, *Tactics and the Experience of Battle,* 111.
9. Haythornthwaite, *Napoleonic Cavalry,* 48.
10. Letters of Lieutenant General Thomas Dyneley, Haythornthwaite, *Napoleonic Cavalry,* 45.
11. "Casimir Pulaski to George Washington, December 29, 1777," *Washington Papers LOC,* accessed July 12, 2013, http://memory.loc.gov/cgi-bin/query/P?mgw:1:./temp/~ammem_s9pl::.
12. Haythornthwaite, *Napoleonic Cavalry,* 43.
13. Ibid., 34.
14. Thompson, *Lannaireachd: Gaelic Swordsmanship,* 70-71.
15. Von Warnery, *Remarks on Cavalry,* 17.
16. Borick, *A Gallant Defense,* 56.
17. Baylor Hill, *A Gentleman of Fortune: The Diary of Baylor Hill First Continental Light Dragoons 1777-1781,* Vol. III, ed. John Hayes (Fort Lauderdale, Saddlebag Press, 1995), 38.
18. Holley Calmes, *Banastre Tarleton: A Biography,* accessed June 21, 2013, http://home.golden.net/~marg/bansite/btbiog.html.
19. Robert Bass, *The Green Dragoon: The Lives of Banastre Tarleton and Mary Robinson* (Orangeburg, Sandlapper Publishing Company, 2003), 15.
20. Anthony Scotti, Jr. *Brutal Virtue: The Myth and Reality of Banastre Tarleton* (Berwyn Heights, Heritage Books, 2002), 34.
21. Don Troiani, *Soldiers of the American Revolution* (Mechanicsburg, Stackpole Books, 2007), 34-35; Richard Cannon, *Historical Record of the Seventeenth Regiment of Light Dragoons–Lancers* (London, John W. Parker, 1841), 13, accessed June 23, 2013, https://play.google.com/books/reader?id=VVykrSD7MG0C&printsec=frontcover&output=reader&authuser=0&hl=en&pg=GBS.RA1-PR1.
22. Scott Miskimon, "Anthony Walton White, a Revolutionary Dragoon," *Cavalry of the American Revolution,* ed. Piecuch, 117; Stephen Jarvis, "The King's Loyal Horsemen," *Connecticut Yankees,* ed. John T. Hayes (Fort Lauderdale, Saddlebag Press, 1999), 55-56.
23. "William Washington to Benjamin Lincoln, March 15, 1780," *The Benjamin Lincoln Papers, 1635-1964,* Massachusetts Historical Society.
24. Johann Ewald, *Diary of the American War: A Hessian Journal: Captain Johann Ewald,* Vol. III, ed. Joseph P. Tustin
25. Hill, *A Gentleman of Fortune,* Vol. III, ed. Hayes, 52.

26. Hill, *A Gentleman of Fortune,* Vol. III, ed. Hayes, 54
27. Ibid., 56
28. Anthony Allaire, "Diary of Lieutenant Anthony Allaire of Furguson's Corps, Monday the 27th," *Memorandum of Occurances During the Campaign of 1780,* accessed 7/7/2013.
29. Pension application of Lawrence Everhart, S25068.
30. Haller, *William Washington,* 56.
31. After the war Jane donated the flag to the Washington Light Infantry of Charleston, South Carolina, and it survives in their care to this day.
32. Borrick, *Gallant Defense,* 129.
33. Charles Baxley, "The Battle of Biggin Bridge, April 14, 1780: Tarleton's Cavalry Charge," *Southern Campaigns of the American Revolution* (May, 2005), 3.
34. Ibid., 4.
35. Banastre Tarleton, *A History of the Campaigns of 1780 and 1781 in the Southern Provinces of North America* (Dublin, Colles, Exshaw, White, et al., 1787), 15.
36. Tarleton, *Campaigns,* 17.
37. Baxley, "The Battle of Biggin Bridge," *S.C.A.R.,* 4-5.
38. Charles Stedman, *The History of the Origin, Progress, and Termination of the American War,* Vol. II (Reprint, New York, New York Times and Arno Press, 1969), 183.
39. Isaac Huger to Thomas Rutledge, April 12, 1780," *Lincoln Papers.*
40. Allaire, "Thursday, 13th," accessed July 7, 2013, http://www.tngenweb.org/revwar/kingsmountain/allaire.html.
41. "Lebrun de Bellacore to Benjamin Lincoln, March 24, 1780," *Emmet Collection,* New York Public Library.
42. Tarleton was absent and Major Charles Cochrane led the British Legion in this action. McSkinnon, "Antony Walton White," *Cavalry of the American Revolution,* ed. Piecuch, 114.
43. Ibid.
44. "George Washington to William Heath, August 9, 1779," *The Writings of Washington LOC,* accessed July 12, 2013, http://etext.virginia.edu/toc/modeng/public/WasFi16.html.
45. "John Lewis Gervais to Henry Laurens, May 13, 1780," *The Papers of Henry Laurens, Dec. 11, 1778–Aug. 31, 1781,* ed. David Chestnut (Columbia, University of South Carolina Press, 1988), 291-292.
46. Ibid.
47. Pension application of John Gore, W160.
48. Pension application of Lawrence Everhart, S25068.
49. Ibid.
50. Hill, *Gentleman of Fortune,* Vol. III, 87.
51. Tarleton, *Campaigns,* 42; "Abraham Buford to George Washington, May 6, 1780," Library of Congress, accessed November 11, 2011. Pension application of John Gore, W160.

52. William Washington to unknown recipient, May 5, 1780, *State Records of North Carolina,* Vol. IVX, Walter Clark, ed. (Goldsboro, Nash Bros. 1886), 807.
53. Tarleton, *Campaigns,* 28-29.
54. "Concerning the Review of a Regiment of Hussars, and Their Exercise on Horseback," Article 14, Chapter III, *Regulations for the Prussian Cavalry,* trans. Fawcett, 128.
55. Tarleton, *Campaigns,* 31.
56. Ibid., 31.
57. Ibid., 32.

Chapter Seven: Courts, Campaigns, and Backcountry

1. "June 6, 1780, Resolution of the Virginia General Assembly" and "June 19, 1780, Committee of the Continental Congress," Mauer, *Dragoon Diary,* 259-260.
2. Miskimon, "Anthony Walton White," *Cavalry of the American Revolution, ed.,* Piecuch, 116.
3. William Smallwood Orderly Book, September 24, 1781, *Peter Force Collection, LOC.*
4. "Anthony White to Nathanael Greene, December 28, 1780," *The Papers of General Nathanael Greene,* Vol. VII, ed. Richard Showman and Dennis Conrad (Chapel Hill, University of North Carolina Press, 1994), 15.
5. "William Smallwood Orderly Book, September 26, 1780," *Peter Force Collection, LOC*; Scott A. Miskimom, *Cavalry of the American Revolution,* ed., Pieucuch, 136.
6. "Anthony White to Nathanael Greene, December 28, 1780," Showman and Conrad, *Greene Papers,* Vol. VII, 15.
7. "Nathanael Greene to Henry Lee, January 26, 1781," Showman and Conrad, *Greene Papers,* Vol. VII, 202.
8. "Nathanael Green to Anthony White, January 30, 1781," Showman and Conrad, *Greene Papers,* Vol. VII, 221.
9. "Thornton to von Steuben, February 14, 1781," Steuben Microfilm, Showman and Conrad, *Greene Papers,* Vol. VII, 15.
10. "William Washington to Horatio Gates, October 4, 1780," *Horatio Gates Papers, 1760-1804,* New York Public Library.
11. "Inspection return of 1st & 3rd Continental Regiments of Dragoons with part of the Virginia State Regiments . . . ," inspected by Brigadier General Isaac Huger. October 18, 1780. *Horatio Gates Papers, 1760-1804,* New York Public Library.
12. "Cornwallis to Germain, April 18, 1781," *The Cornwallis Papers: The Campaigns of 1780 and 1781 in the Southern Theatre of the American Revolutionary War,* Vol. IV, ed. Ian Saberton (East Essex, Naval and Military Press, 2010), 105-106; John S. Pancake, *This Destructive War: The British Campaign in the Carolinas, 1780-1782* (Tuscaloosa, University of Alabama Press, 1985), 79-83; Dan Morrill, *Southern Campaigns of the American Revolution*

(Mount Pleasant, Nautical & Aviation Publishing Company of America, 1993), 75-76.
13. Ray Raphael, *A People's History of the American Revolution* (New York, Harper Perennial, 2002), 185.
14. Buchanan, *Road to Guilford,* 150.
15. Ibid., 163-168; Stephenson, *Patriot Battles,* 321; Morrill, *Southern Campaigns,* 93.
16. Morrill, *Southern Campaigns,* 94.
17. Buchanan, *Road to Guilford,* 173-193.
18. Michael Scoggins, "South Carolina's Backcountry Rangers," *Cavalry of the American Revolution,* ed. Piecuch, 146; Buchanan, *Road to Guilford,* 239; Wood, *Battles of the Revolutionary War,* 205.
19. Wood, *Battles,* 200-204, 205.
20. Buchanan, *Road to Guilford,* 276-279.
21. Lawrence Babits, *Devil of a Whipping* (Chapel Hill, University of North Carolina Press, 1998), 24.
22. Ibid., 285-286.
23. Lee McGee, "The Battle of Rugeley's Fort," *Southern Campaigns of the American Revolution* (June 2005), 11, accessed July 7, 2013, http://southern-campaign.org/newsletter/v2n6.pdf.
24. William Seymour, "Journal of the Southern Expedition 1780-1783, by William Seymour, Sergeant-Major of the Delaware Regiment," *Pennsylvania Magazine of History and Biography,* January 1883, 291.
25. "Friedrich Wilhelm von Steuben to George Washington, October 23, 1780," *Washington Papers LOC,* accessed June 6, 2013, http://memory.loc.gov/cgi-bin/query/P?mgw:14:./temp/~ammem_tnAD::..
26. Buchanan, *Road to Guilford,* 297-298.
27. Lee, *Memoirs,* 221; "William Smallwood to Nathanael Greene, December 6, 1780," *The Papers of General Nathanael Greene,* Vol. VI, ed. Richard Showman (Chapel Hill, University of North Carolina Press, 1991), 538-539.
28. Lee McGee, "The Battle of Rugeley's Fort," *Southern Campaigns of the American Revolution,* June 2005, 12.
29. Abatis were essentially man-made hedges bristling with sharpened sticks that would impale men and horses.
30. "William Smallwood to Nathanael Greene, December 6, 1780," Showman, *Green Papers,*Vol. VI, 538-539.
31. Pension application of Jourdan Gilliam, R4037.
32. Lee McGee, "The Battle of Rugeley's Fort," *Southern Campaigns of the American Revolution,* June 2005, 13. A *feu de joie* was a martial celebration wherein a number of guns or muskets were arranged in line or ranks and fired in rapid succession, as opposed to a volley.
33. Seymour, *Journal,* 292.
34. Buchanan, *Road to Guilford,* 260, 264, 274.
35. Richard Showman, ed. *The Papers of General Nathanael Greene,* Vol. I (Chapel Hill, University of North Carolina Press, 1976), 69-70.

36. "George Washington to Continental Congress, October 22, 1780," *Washington Papers LOC*, accessed March 26, 2012, http://memory.loc.gov/cgi-bin/query/P?mgw:1:./temp/~ammem_xdHD::.
37. "Nathanael Greene to George Washington, December 7, 1780," *Washington Papers LOC*, accessed July 8, 2013, http://memory.loc.gov/cgibin/ampage?collId=mgw4&fileName=gwpage073.db&recNum=232&tempFile=./temp/~ammem_K9db&filecode=mgw&next_filecode=mgw&prev_filecode=mgw&itemnum=7&ndocs=100; Lee, *Memoirs*, 233-234.
38. Babits, *Devil of a Whipping*, 6.
39. Edwin C. Bearss, *The Battle of Cowpens: A Documented Narrative* (Johnson City, Overmountain Press, 1967), 2.
40. William Johnson, *Sketches of the Life and Correspondence of Nathanael Greene*, Vol. I (Reprint: Whitefish, Kessinger Publishing, 2007), 350-352.
41. Pancake, *This Destructive War*, 73; "Greene to the President of Congress, December 28, 1780," Showman, *Greene Papers*, Vol. VI, 583.
42. Lee McGee " '. . . The Better Order of Men . . .': Hammond's Store and Ft. Williams," *Southern Campaigns of the American Revolution* (December 2005), 14-21, accessed July 8, 2013, http://southerncampaign.org/newsletter/v2n12.pdf.
43. Seymour, *Journal*, 292; Showman, *Greene Papers*, Vol. VI, 573.
44. Seymour, *Journal*.
45. Buchanan, *Road to Guilford*, 299-302; Pancake, *This Destructive War*, 53, 69.
46. Daniel Murphy and Ron Crawley, "The Real Life Exploits of an Unknown Patriot: Lt. Col. James McCall" in *Southern Campaigns of the American Revolution* (December 2006), 19-23, accessed July 8, 2013, http://southerncampaign.org/newsletter/v3n12.pdf; David P. Reuwer, "Sam Fore on Lt. Col. James McCall," *Southern Campaigns of the American Revolution* (January 2006), 11-13, accessed July 8, 2013, http://southerncampaign.org/newsletter/v3n1.pdf.
47. Robert Davis, "Colonel Thomas Waters: Georgia Loyalist," *Southern Campaigns of the American Revolution* (September 2006), 21-24, accessed July 8, 2013, http://southerncampaign.org/newsletter/v3n9.pdf.
48. "William Washington to Nathanael Greene, December 24, 1780," Showman, *Greene Papers*, Vol. VI, 611.
49. "Daniel Morgan to Nathanael Greene, December 31, 1780," Showman and Conrad, *Greene Papers*, Vol. VII, 30.
50. Thomas Young, *Memoir*; Pension request of Samuel Hammond, October 31, 1832, M804, Roll 1176; Pension request of Manuel McConnell, September 18, 1832, M804, Roll 941.
51. Young, *Memoir*.
52. "Daniel Morgan to Nathanael Greene, December 31, 1780," Showman and Conrad, *Greene Papers*, Vol. VII, 30.
53. Young, *Memoir*, "Daniel Morgan to Nathanael Greene, December 31, 1780," Showman and Conrad, *Greene Papers*, Vol. VII, 30.
54. Young, *Memoir*.

Chapter Eight: Battle at the Cowpens

1. Buchanan, *Road to Guilford,* 73-76.
2. Tarleton, *Campaigns,* 181-183.
3. John Eager Howard to William Johnson, ca. 1822.
4. Babits, *Devil of a Whipping,* 5, 8.
5. Buchanan, *Road to Guilford,* 253-257; Lumpkin, *From Savannah to Yorktown,* 111-115.
6. Tarleton, *Campaigns,* 178-179.
7. Babits, *Devil of a Whipping,* 44-47.
8. Ibid. 25-41.
9. Ibid., 42, 54-56.
10. Bearss, *Battle of Cowpens,* 19, 22.
11. Young, *Memoir*; Bearss, *Battle of Cowpens,* 16, 19.
12. Young, *Memoir.*
13. Murphy and Crawley, "Exploits of an Unknown Patriot," *Southern Campaigns of the American Revolution* (December 2006), 19-23; Pension Application of Samuel Hammond, S21807; Babits, *Devil of a Whipping,* 42.
14. Young, *Memoir*; Pension application of Samuel Hammond, S21807.
15. Young, *Memoir.*
16. Pension application of Samuel Hammond, S21807. See Samuel Hammond, "Account of the Battle of Cowpens," Joseph Johnson, *Traditions and Reminiscences, Chiefly of the American Revolution in the South* (Charleston, Walker and James, 1851), 526-530.
17. Pension Application of Lawrence Everhart.
18. See Samuel Hammond, "Account of the Battle of Cowpens," Johnson, *Traditions and Reminiscences,* 526-530.
19. Ibid.
20. Babits, *Devil of a Whipping,* 82-83.
21. Tarleton, *Campaigns,* 216.
22. Babits, *Devil of a Whipping,* 86. Dr. Babits's groundbreaking book best describes this attack, and goes into much greater detail than any author before or since.
23. Tarleton, *Campaigns,* 216.
24. Pension application of Robert Long, S7157; James Collins, *Autobiography of a Revolutionary Soldier* (North Stratford, Ayer Company Publishing, 1979), 22.
25. Collins, *Autobiography of a Revolutionary Soldier,* 22.
26. Ibid.
27. James Simmons to William Washington, in support of Lawrence Everhart's pension request.
28. Ibid.
29. Daniel Murphy, "Thinking Inside the Box: The Cavalry at Cowpens," *Southern Campaigns of the American Revolution* (February 2006), 23-27.
30. "Concerning the Review of a Regiment of Hussars, and Their Exercise on Horseback," Article 14, Chap. III, *Regulations for the Prussian Cavalry,* trans. Fawcett, 128.

31. Hill, *Gentleman of Fortune,* Vol. III, 54.
32. Murphy, "Thinking Inside the Box: The Cavalry at Cowpens," 23-27.
33. Tarleton, *Campaigns,* 217.
34. McKenzie, *Strictures,* 98; Pension application of Henry Connelly, W8188.
35. Murphy, "Thinking Inside the Box: The Cavalry at Cowpens," 23-27.
36. Young, *Memoir.*
37. Roderick McKenzie, *Strictures on Lt. Col Tarleton's History of the Campaigns of 1780 and 1781, in the Southern Provinces of North America* (London, Jameson, Strand, Faulder, et al., 1787), 98, accessed April 4, 2013, http://books.google.com/books?id=nXNbAAAAQAAJ&printsec=frontcover&source=gbs_ge_summary_r&cad=0#v=onepage&q&f=false.
38. Babits, *Devil of a Whipping,* 112; Buchannan, *Road to Gilford,* 324.
39. "John Eager Howard to William Johnson, ca. 1822"; "John Eager Howard to unknown individual," ca. 1782, Bayard Papers, MHS. The exact date of this letter may be 1804 and the recipient may have been John Marshall.
40. Johnson, *Sketches of Greene,* Vol. I, 381.
41. James Simmons to William Washington, in support of Lawrence Everhart's pension request.
42. Young, *Memoir.*
43. Tarleton, *Campaigns,* 218. Bracketed words by the author.
44. Ibid.
45. Pension application of Henry Wells, S11712.
46. "John Eager Howard to unknown individual," MHS; Margin note; McKenzie, *Strictures,* 99.
47. Lloyd, *Historical Record of the Seventeenth Light Dragoons–Lancers,* 34.
48. John Eager Howard to William Johnson, ca. 1822; Lloyd, *Historical Record of the Seventeenth Light Dragoons,* 34.
49. Some historians have claimed that this young waiter was of African descent. Sadly, there is at this time no documentation to firmly support the waiter's identity or ethnicity. Howard's account, the best to date, refers to him only as a waiter–a young man too small to wield a sword–and doesn't even give a name. Officers typically had waiters or hand servants to tend to their horses, generally of either European or African descent. Whatever this young man's ethnicity, his actions were extraordinary!
50. Pension application of James Kelly, S1544.
51. John Eager Howard to William Johnson, ca. 1822.
52. Ibid. Howard's letter to author William Johnson is a corrective critique of Johnson's two-volume series on Nathanael Greene.
53. Ibid.
54. Pension application of James Kelly, S1544.
55. Johnson, *Sketches of Greene,* Vol. I, footnote, 382, 383.
56. McKenzie, *Strictures,* 3-4.
57. John Eager Howard to unkown individual; Margin note, MHS.
58. McKenzie, *Strictures,* 99.

59. John Eager Howard to William Johnson, ca. 1822.
60. Pension application of Lawrence Everhart, S25068; Cornet James Simmons' statement in support of Lawrence Everhart's pension application.
61. "John Eager Howard to unknown individual," MHS.
62. Ibid.
63. Babits, *Devil of a Whipping,* 142.
64. Murphy, "Thinking Inside the Box," *S.C.A.R.* (February 2006), 23-27.
65. Morrill, *S.C.A.R.* (February 2006), 132; Commager and Morris, *Spirit of 'Seventy-Six,* 1159.

Chapter Nine: Flight and Fight

1. "Cornwallis to Germain, March 17, 1781," *The Cornwallis Papers,* Vol. IV; *The Campaigns of 1780 and 1781 in the Southern Theatre of the American Revolutionary War,* ed. Ian Saberton (East Sussex, Naval and Military Press, 2010), 12-13.
2. Babits, *Devil of a Whipping,* 144.
3. Lawrence Babits and Joshua Howard, *Long, Obstinate, and Bloody: The Battle of Guilford Courthouse* (Chapel Hill, University of North Carolina Press, 2009), 17.
4. Pancake, *This Destructive War,* 160-161; Morrill, *Southern Campaigns of the American Revolution,* 136, 140.
5. Babits and Howard, *Long, Obstinate, and Bloody,* 30; Buchanan, *Road to Guilford,* 288-289.
6. Buchanan, *Road to Guilford,* 352-353.
7. Babits and Howard, *Long, Obstinate, and Bloody,* 29.
8. Buchanan, *Road to Guilford,* 351, 161; Morrill, *Southern Campaigns of the American Revolution,* 143.
9. "Cornwallis to Germain, March 17, 1781," Saberton, *The Cornwallis Papers,* Vol. IV, 13.
10. Babits and Howard, *Long, Obstinate, and Bloody,* 15; Pancake, *This Destructive War,* 161; Morrill, *Southern Campaigns of the American Revolution,* 138-140.
11. Spring, *With Zeal and Bayonets,* 57-62. Grenadiers were given tall helmets to make them appear even larger to the enemy across the field, and light infantry were typically issued lightweight caps while the regular companies retained the standard-issue cocked black hats of the British Army.
12. John W. Hall, "Petite Guerre in Retreat," *Patriots of the American Revolution,* September/October 2011, 14-19.
13. Buchanan, *Road to Guilford,* 359-360; Pancake, *This Destructive War,* 172.
14. "Thomas Jefferson to Nathanael Greene, February 19, 1781." Showman and Conrad, *Greene Papers,* Vol. VII, 313.
15. Henry Lee, *Memoirs of the War in the Southern Department of the United States* (New York, University Publishing Company, 1869), 258, accessed April 1, 2012, Internet Archive: Digital Library of Free Books, http://archive.org/

stream/memoirswarinsou04leegoog; Cornwallis to Germain, March 17, 1781, Saberton, *The Cornwallis Papers,* Vol. IV, 15.
16. Morrill, *Southern Campaigns of the American Revolution,* 149; Showman and Conrad, *Greene Papers,* Vol. VII, 371; Buchanan, *Road to Guilford,* 365.
17. Spring, *With Zeal and Bayonets,* 55; *The Annual Register, or View of the History, Politics, and Literature for the Year 1781* (London, J. Dodsley, 1782).
18. William Graham, *General Joseph Graham and his Papers on North Carolina Revolutionary History* (Raleigh, Edwards & Broughton, 1904), 342.
19. Ibid., 343.
20. Buchanan, *Road to Guilford,* 366-367.
21. Lee, *Memoirs,* 266.
22. Graham, *General Joseph Graham,* 343; Lee, *Memoirs,* 266; "Conwallis to Germain, March 17, 1781," Saberton, *The Cornwallis Papers,* Vol. IV, 16.
23. Graham, *General Joseph Graham,* 343.
24. A period unit of length equal to 5 1/2 yards.
25. Graham, *General Joseph Graham,* 345. Bracketed words by author.
26. "Gen. Nathanael Greene to Lt. Col. Henry Lee," March 9, 1781, Showman and Conrad, *Greene Papers,* Vol. VII, 415.
27. "Nathanael Greene to Lord Cornwallis," March 7, 1781, Showman and Conrad, *Greene Papers,* Vol. VII, 410.
28. "Nathanael Greene to William Washington," March 9, 1781, Showman and Conrad, *Greene Papers,* Vol. VII, 416, notes 417-418.
29. "Otho Williams to Nathanael Greene to George Washington," March 7, 1781, Showman and Conrad, *Greene Papers,* Vol. VII, 409.
30. "Nathanael Greene to William Washington," March 9, 1781, Showman and Conrad, *Greene Papers,* Vol. VII, 416.
31. "Nathanael Greene to George Washington, March 10, 1781," Showman and Conrad, *Greene Papers,* Vol. VII, 422.
32. Babits and Howard, *Long, Obstinate, and Bloody,* 49.
33. William Henry Foote, *Sketches of Virginia Historical and Biographical* (Philadelphia, J. B. Lippincott & Co., 1856), 403; Pension Application of Philemon Holcombe, S4399, supporting statement made by John Lee Holcombe.

Chapter Ten: Guilford Courthouse

1. Buchanan, *Road to Guilford,* 372-373.
2. "Nathanael Greene to Henry Lee," March 9, 1781, Showman and Conrad, *Greene Papers,* Vol. VII, 415.
3. "Nathanael Greene to Colonel Henry Lee, March 10, 1781," Showman and Conrad, *Greene Papers,* Vol. VII, 421.
4. "Nathanael Greene to Samuel Huntington, March 16, 1781," Showman and Conrad, *Greene Papers,* Vol. VII, 434.
5. Babits and Howard, *Long, Obstinate, and Bloody,* 103.
6. Roger Lamb, *An Original and Authentic Journal of Occurrences During the*

Late American War (Dublin, Wilkinson and Courtney, 1809), 350, 361; Spring, *With Zeal and Bayonets,* 226-227.
7. "Cornwallis to Germain, March 17, 1781," Saberton, *The Cornwallis Papers,* Vol. IV, 18. Bracketed words by the author.
8. Seymour, *Journal,* 379.
9. Babits and Howard, *Long, Obstinate, and Bloody,* 123.
10. "Nathanael Greene to Samuel Huntington, March 16, 1781," Showman and Conrad, *Greene Papers,* Vol. VII, 435.
11. "Cornwallis to Germain, March 17, 1781," Saberton, *Cornwallis Papers,* Vol. IV, 18.
12. Seymour, *Journal,* 379.
13. Ibid.
14. Babits and Howard, *Long, Obstinate, and Bloody,* 124, 123.
15. Babits and Howard, *Long, Obstinate, and Bloody,* 145.
16. Spring, *With Zeal and Bayonets,* 214-215.
17. John Eager Howard, *"Notes on the Battle of Hobkirk's Hill and Guilford Courthouse"* ca 1782, Bayard Papers, MHS. The exact date of these notes is currently undetermined but in the author's opinion they appear to be a continuation of Howard's letter to William Johnson ca. 1822.
18. Ibid.
19. Babits and Howard, *Long, Obstinate, and, Bloody,* 147.
20. Ibid., 90.
21. Buchanan, *Road to Guilford,* 378.
22. Babits and Howard, *Long, Obstinate, and Bloody,* 92.
23. "Cornwallis to Germain, March 17, 1781," Saberton, *Cornwallis Papers,* Vol. IV, 18. Bracketing by author.
24. Lee, *Memoirs,* 347.
25. Babits and Howard, *Long, Obstinate, and Bloody,* 148.
26. Ibid., 149.
27. Andrew Gunby, *Colonel John Gunby of the American Line: Being Some Account of His Contribution to American Liberty* (Cincinnati, Clark, 1902), 57, accessed June 26, 2013, https://play.google.com/books/reader?id=6JlBAAAAYAAJ&printsec=frontcover&output=reader&authuser=0&hl=en&pg=GBS.PA57.
28. Andrew Gunby, *Colonel John Gunby,* 56-57.
29. Buchanan, *Road to Guilford,* 378.
30. "Cornwallis to Germain, March 17, 1781," Saberton, The *Cornwallis Papers,* Vol. IV, 18.
31. Howard, "Notes on the Battle . . . ." MHS.
32. "Nathanael Greene to Henry Lee," March 9, 1781, Showman and Conrad, *Greene Papers,* Vol. VII, 415.
33. Jim Piecuch, "The Evolving Tactician," *General Nathanael Greene and the American Revolution in the South,* ed. Gregory Massey and Jim Piecuch (Columbia, University of South Carolina Press, 2012), 220.

34. Rev. W.H. Foote, *Sketches of Virginia, Historical and Biographical, Book 1*, 403. Rockwood, TN: EagleRidge Technologies. Original work published 1850 found online December 31, 2010, from http://www.roanetnhistory.org/foote-virginia.php?loc=Foote-Sketches-Virginia-First&pgid=41.
35. Washington's column of fours was 600 feet long. A three-rank line was 60 feet deep. Washington's tail rank of fours would have to travel 540 feet to reach the 3rd rank. Washington was still moving at a canter of approximately 15mph/22 feet per second, while the tail ranks would be at a hand gallop of 27mph/39 feet per second (feet = mph x 1.46). So *A* (Washington's head rank) is moving 17 feet per second slower than *B* (the tail rank). How long will it take *B* to catch *A*, if *B* starts out 540 feet behind *A*? 540/17 = 31.76 seconds. 31 seconds x 22 feet per second (Washington's continuing speed) = 682 feet or 227 yards.
36. "Baron von Steuben to George Washington, October 23, 1780." *Washington Papers LOC,* accessed July 12, 2013, http://memory.loc.gov/cgi-bin/query/P?mgw:1:./temp/~ammem_FEvQ::.
37. Seymour, *Journal,* 378. Bracketing by author.
38. "Samuel Mathis to General William Davie, 1819," as edited by Rev. Millard H. Osborne, 1963, with additional editing by Charles B. Baxley (republished by the Kershaw County Historical Society), accessed April 12, 2012, http://southerncampaign.org/hobkirk/ps.html#alet.
39. Tarleton described the hat bands of the troops defending the guns in the 2d Maryland's line in detail. If he witnessed the Guards sweeping over Singleton's battery, it follows that he was in time to witness Washington's charge. See Babits and Howard, *Long Obstinate, and Bloody,* 151.
40. Tarleton, *Campaigns,* 274.
41. "Cornwallis to Germain, March 17, 1781," Saberton, *Cornwallis Papers,* Vol. IV, 18.
42. Tarleton's *Campaigns* was published six years after the battle.
43. "John Smith to Nathanael Greene, April 30, 1781," *The Papers of General Nathanael Greene,* Vol. VIII, ed. Dennis Conrad (Chapel Hill, University of North Carolina Press, 1995), 180.
44. "Major John Doyle to Nathanael Greene, April 29, 1781," Conrad, *Greene Papers,* Vol. VIII, 174.
45. "Howard to unknown individual," MHS.
46. Ibid.
47. "Letter from Peter Francisco to the Virginia General Assembly, November 11, 1820," accessed July 4, 2013, *The William and Mary Quarterly,* http://www.jstor.org/stable/1916145.
48. "Howard to unknown individual," MHS.
49. "Cornwallis to Germain, March 17, 1781," Saberton, *Cornwallis Papers,* Vol. IV, 18.
50. "Nathaniel Pendleton to William Washington, March 17, 1781," Showman and Conrad, *Greene Papers,* Vol. VII, 445.

51. "Cornwallis to Germain, March 17, 1781," Saberton, *The Cornwallis Papers,* Vol. IV, 18.
52. "Nathanael Greene to Samuel Huntington, March 16, 1781," Showman and Conrad, *Greene Papers,* Vol. VII, 433.
53. Babbits and Howard, *Long, Obstinate, and Bloody,* 175.
54. "Returns of Troops, etc. and Care of Wounded," Saberton, *The Cornwallis Papers,* Vol. IV, 64-65.
"Cornwallis to Germain, March 17, 1781," Saberton, *The Cornwallis Papers,* Vol. IV, 19.
55. The National Park Service, *Other Judgments, Public and Private,* accessed July 4, 2013, http://www.nps.gov/nr/twhp/wwwlps/lessons/32guilford/32facts3.htm.

Chapter Eleven: Hobkirk's Hill

1. Lee, *Memoirs,* 320-325.
2. Ibid., 322.
3. "Nathanael Greene to Joseph Reed, March 18, 1781," *Life and Correspondence of Joseph Reed,* Vol. II, 350; Hugh Rankin, *The North Carolina Continentals* (Chapel Hill, University of North Carolina Press, 2005), 311.
4. "Richard Call to Thomas Jefferson, March 29, 1781," *The Papers of Thomas Jefferson, Digital Edition,* University of Virginia, ed. Barbara Oberg and J. Looney, accessed July 12, 2013, http://rotunda.upress.virginia.edu/founders/default.xqy?keys=TSJN-print-01-05-02&mode=TOC.
5. "October 24, 1777–Headquarters," General Orders, Mauer, *Dragoon Diary,* 42, accessed July 12, 2013; *The Writings of Washington LOC,* UVA Library, http://etext.virginia.edu/toc/modeng/public/WasFi09.html.
6. Pension application of Henry Wells, S11712.
7. "Governor Thomas Jefferson to General Nathanael Greene, March 24, 1781," Conrad, *Greene Papers,* Vol. VII, 467.
8. "General Nathanael Greene to Governor Thomas Jefferson, April 6, 1781"; also "Greene to Jefferson, April 28, 1781," Showman and Conrad, *Greene Papers,* Vol. VIII, 58.
9. Daniel Murphy, "Greene's Gamble at Hobkirk's Hill," *Military Heritage* (February 2012), 40-47.
10. Pancake, *This Destructive War,* 190.
11. Lee, *Memoirs,* 320.
12. "Nathanael Greene to Samuel Huntington, March 23, 1781," Showman and Conrad, *Greene Papers,* Vol. VII, 464.
13. "John Eager Howard to William Johnson," 1822.
14. Lee, *Memoirs,* 322.
15. "Nathanael Greene to George Washington, March 29, 1781," Showman and Conrad, *Greene Papers,* Vol. VII, 481.
16. Pancake, *This Destructive War,* 193.
17. Buchanan, *Road to Guilford,* 130.

18. Pancake, *This Destructive War,* 192-193.
19. Buchanan, *Road to Guilford,* 80.
20. Murphy, "Greene's Gamble at Hobkirk's Hill," 40-47.
21. "Lord Rawdon to Lord Balfour, April 12, 1781," Saberton, *Cornwallis Papers,* Vol. IV, 173.
22. *Journal of Robert Kirkwood,* 254, accessed June 28, 2013, http://www.archive.org/stream/journalorderbook00kirk/journalorderbook00kirk_djvu.txt.
23. "Lord Rawdon to Lord Balfour, April 13, 1781"; also "Lord Rawdon to Lord Balfour, April 15, 1781," Saberton, *The Cornwallis Papers,* Vol. IV, 174-175.
24. "Lord Rawdon to Lord Cornwallis, April 26, 1781," Saberton, *The Cornwallis Papers,* Vol. IV, 181-182.
25. Ibid.
26. Lumpkin, *From Savannah to Yorktown,* 180.
27. Murphy, *Greene's Gamble at Hobkirk's Hill,* 40-47.
28. "John Eager Howard to unknown individual," MHS.
29. Kirkwood, *Journal,* 254.
30. Pancake, *This Destructive War,* 196.
31. Ibid.
32. Pension application of Guilford Dudley, W8681.
33. "General Greene to Samuel Huntington, April 27, 1781," Showman and Conrad, *Greene Papers,* Vol. VII, 155-157.
34. Ibid.; also "Major William Pierce to General Butler, May 2, 1781," *Rediscovering Hobkirk's Hill,* The Kershaw County Historical Society, accessed July 12, 2013, http://www.hobkirkhill.org/hobkirk/primary.aspx; "Otho Williams to Eli Williams, April 27, 1781," *Battle of Hobkirk's Hill, Southern Campaigns of the American Revolution,* accessed July 12, 2013, http://southern-campaign.org/hobkirk/ps.html#alet.
35. Ian Saberton, "Rawdon to Cornwallis, April 26, 1781," *The Cornwallis Papers,* Vol. IV, 180-182.
36. "John Eager Howard to unknown individual," MHS.
37. Howard, *"Notes on the Battle…"*, margin note, MHS.
38. "Major William Pierce to General John Butler, May 2, 1781."
39. Howard, *"Notes on the Battle…"*, margin note, MHS; "Rawdon to Cornwallis, April 26, 1781," Saberton, *Cornwallis Papers,* Vol. IV, 180-182. Pension application of Richard Porterfield, W2341, mentions having a horse killed from under him and, tactically, this would have been more likely to have occurred while charging the armed teamsters and infantry in the British rear than while charging Coffin's troopers.
40. Howard, *"Notes on the Battle…"*, margin note, MHS; "Greene to Huntington, April 27, 1781," Conrad, *Greene Papers,* Vol. VIII, 159.
41. "Lord Rawdon to Lord Cornwallis, April 26, 1781," Saberton, *The Cornwallis Papers,* Vol. IV, 181-182.
42. Gunby, *Colonel John Gunby,* 87-89. See G. W. Greene, *Life of Nathanael Greene,* Vol. III (Boston, Houghton, Mifflin, and Company, 1884), 247,

American Libraries Internet Archive, accessed July 12, 2013, http://archive.org/details/lifeofnathanaelg003gree.
43. Lee, *Memoirs of the War in the Southern Dept.*, 338, accessed November 17, 2012, http://www.archive.org/stream/memoirswarinsou04leegoog#page/n360/mode/2up. Lt. Col. Ford later died of this wound.
44. Tiffany Osmond, *A Sketch of the Life and Services of Gen. Otho Holland Williams* (Baltimore, John Murphy, 1851), 10, accessed July 14, 2013, Project Guttenberg, http://www.gutenberg.org/catalog/world/readfile?fk_files=1547782.
45. "Samuel Mathis to William Davie," 1819.
46. Pension Application of Guilford Dudley, W8681.
47. "Samuel Mathis to William Davie, 1819," *The Papers of Andrew Jackson,* Vol. I, 1770–1803, ed. Sam B. Smith (Knoxville, University of Tennessee Press, 1980), 6.
48. "Rawdon to Cornwallis, April 25, 1781," Saberton, *The Cornwallis Papers,* Vol. IV, 179; Conrad, *Greene Papers,* Vol. VIII, 159. Joseph Johnson claims Washington and his dragoons arrived to rescue the Continental guns "at the critical moment." Capt. Smith was defending them against Coffin's Dragoons, but there is no firsthand account to fully verify this claim. See Joseph Johnson, *Traditions and Reminiscences,* 464.
49. Pension application of Guilford Dudley, W8681.
50. "Otho Williams to Elie Williams, April 27, 1781," Osmond, *Sketch of the Life of Otho Williams,* 12; Lee, *Memoirs,* 224.
51. "Rawdon to Cornwallis, April 26, 1781," Saberton, *The Cornwallis Papers,* Vol. IV, 181-182.
52. "Nathanael Greene to Samuel Huntington, April 27, 1781," Conrad, *Greene Papers,* Vol. VIII, 155.
53. Lee, *Memoirs,* 339; "Nathanael Greene to Samuel Huntington, April 27, 1781"; also "Otho Williams to Elie Williams, April 27, 1781," Osmond, *Sketch of the Life and Services of Otho Williams,* 12. There is little firsthand evidence to clearly document these post-battle activities and the number of charges made by Washington's Light Dragoons. Colonel Williams describes Washington making a charge on the British van, and General Greene describes a charge supported by infantry on the evening of the battle several hours after the main combat had worn down. Lord Rawdon wrote on April 25 that Washington's cavalry prevented the British from taking prisoners. Rawdon was almost certainly referring to the period of Greene's retreat. With the evidence currently available, it is possible that these were separate events. General Greene also described Washington as making several charges through the course of the day, and therefore the exact number is hard to determine in such a fluid and chaotic environment. It is this author's hope that continued scholarship will eventually discover more clear and definitive evidence of these events.
54. David Ramsay, *Ramsay's History of South Carolina: From Its First Settlement in 1670 to 1808* (Newberry, W. J. Duffie, 1858), 240.

Chapter Twelve: Rebels Resurgent

1. "Otho Williams to Elie Williams, April 27, 1781," Osmond, *A Sketch of the Life of Otho Holland Williams,* 12.
2. "Nathanael Greene to Samuel Huntington, April 27, 1781," Conrad, *Greene Papers,* Vol. VIII, 155. Bracketed words by the author.
3. "Nathanael Greene to Henry Lee, April 27, 1781," Conrad, *Greene Papers,* Vol. VIII, 162. Bracketed words by the author.
4. "Major William Pierce to General Butler, May 2, 1781," accessed July 12, 2013, http://www.hobkirkhill.org/hobkirk/primary.aspx.
5. "General Greene to Joseph Reed, August 6, 1781," John Scharf, *The History of Maryland from the Earliest Period to the Present Day* (Baltimore, John B. Piet, 1879), 420, accessed July 14, 2013, Google Books, https://play.google.com/books/reader?id=9IEjAAAAMAAJ&printsec=frontcover&output=reader&authuser=0&hl=en&pg=GBS.PR3.
6. Court of inquiry record, May 2, 1781; Ibid., 419; Gunby, "The Court of Inquiry," *Colonel John Gunby,* 109-124.
7. "Nathanael Greene to Samuel Huntington, April 27, 1781," Conrad, *Greene Papers,* Vol. VIII, 155.
8. Lee, *Memoirs,* 226. Bracketed words by the author.
9. See Massey and Piecuch, *General Nathanael Greene,* 133-134, 220; Pancake, *This Destructive War,* 198-199.
10. Conrad, *Greene Papers,* Vol. VIII, 159*n.*
11. Howard, *"Notes on the Battle…"* margin note.
12. "Rawdon to Cornwallis, April 26, 1781," Saberton, *The Cornwallis Papers,* Vol. IV, 181.
13. "Cornwallis to Germain, April 18, 1781," Saberton, *The Cornwallis Papers,* Vol. IV, 104-105.
14. "Cornwallis to Germain, April 18, 1781," Saberton, *The Cornwallis Papers,* Vol. IV, 105-106.
15. "Cornwallis to Craig, May 12, 1781," Saberton, *The Cornwallis Papers,* Vol. IV, 168.
16. Lee, *Memoirs,* 414; Tarleton, *Campaigns,* 291.
17. Seymour, *Journal,* 382.
18. John Eager Howard to William Johnson, 1822.
19. Lee, *Memoirs,* 344; Seymour, *Journal,* 383.
20. Pension application of Guilford Dudley, W8681.
21. Lee, *Memoirs,* 344.
22. Pancake, *This Destructive War,* 200-201.
23. Lumpkin, *From Savannah to Yorktown,* 192; Lee, *Memoirs,* 358.
24. Seymour, *Journal,* 383.
25. Lumpkin, *From Savannah to Yorktown,* 194-195.
26. "Baron von Steuben to General Greene, May 26, 1781"; also "Marquis de Lafayette to General Greene, June 3, 1781"; also "General Greene to Marquis de Lafayette, June 9, 1781," Conrad, *Greene Papers,* Vol. VIII, 315, 343, 366-368.
27. Lee, *Memoirs,* 371.

28. "General Greene to Samuel Huntington, June 9 1781"; also "General Greene to Marquis de Lafayette, June 9, 1781," Conrad, *Greene Papers,* Vol. VIII, 363-364, 366-368.
29. "Captain William Pierce Jr. to General Thomas Sumter, June 13, 1781," Conrad, *Greene Papers,* 385-386.
30. "General Greene to Colonel William Washington, June 14, 1781," Conrad, *Greene Papers,* Vol. VIII, 389.
31. "Nathanael Greene to Thomas Sumter, June 17, 1781," Conrad, *Greene Papers,* Vol. VIII, 404.
32. "General Thomas Sumter to General Greene, June 18, 1781"; also "General Thomas Sumter to General Greene, June 19, 1781, 'Dutch Settlement' "; also "General Thomas Sumter to General Greene, 'Wright's,' June 19, 1781," Conrad, *Greene Papers,* Vol. VIII, 412, 416, 418.
33. "General Thomas Sumter to General Greene, June 16, 1781"; also "General Thomas Sumter to General Greene, June 17, 1781," Conrad, *Greene Papers,* Vol. VIII, 403, 408.
34. "Thomas Sumter to General Greene, June 18, 1781," Conrad, *Greene Papers,* Vol. VIII, 412.
35. This Hessian detachment was comprised of troops on loan to Rawdon from Lieutenant General von Bose for the Ninety-Six expedition. Conrad, *Greene Papers,* Vol. VIII, 482.
36. Conrad, *Greene Papers,* Vol. VIII, 417.
37. "General Thomas Sumter to General Greene, June 19, 1781," Conrad, *Greene Papers,* Vol. VIII, 416-417.
38. Pension Application of John Chaney, S32177.
39. "General Thomas Sumter to General Greene, June 19, 1781," Conrad, *Greene Papers,* Vol. VIII, 418.
40. "General Greene's Orders, June 19, 1781," Conrad, *Greene Papers,* Vol. VIII, 413.
41. "General Greene to Colonel Henry Lee, June 24, 1781," Conrad, *Greene Papers,* Vol. VIII, 452.
42. "Rawdon to Cornwallis, August 2, 1781," Conrad, *Greene Papers,* 453.
43. "General Greene to Colonel Henry Lee, June 25, 1781," Conrad, *Greene Papers,* Vol. VIII, 455.
44. "Nathanael Greene to Henry Lee, June 25, 1781," Conrad, *Greene Papers,* Vol. VIII, 456.
45. "Francis Marion to Nathanael Greene, June 25, 1781," Conrad, *Greene Papers,* Vol. VIII, 459.
46. Pancake, *This Destructive War,* 215; Lee, *Memoirs,* 384.
47. "General Greene to Colonel Washington, June 29, 1781"; also "General Greene to Colonel Henry Lee, June 29, 1781," Conrad, *Greene Papers,* Vol. VIII, 475, 473.
48. "Colonel Henry Lee to General Greene, June 26, 1781," Conrad, *Greene Papers,* Vol. VIII, 462; "Colonel Henry Lee to General Greene, June 30, 1781," Ibid., 477.

49. "Henry Lee to Nathanael Greene, June 29, 1781," Conrad, *Greene Papers,* Vol. VIII, 476.
50. "Henry Lee to Nathanael Greene, June 30, 1781," Ibid., 477.
51. Ibid.
52. "William Pierce to Nathanael Greene, Sept. 14, 1782," Conrad, *Greene Papers,* Vol. XII, 660.
53. "Nathanael Greene to William Washington, June 29, 1781," Conrad, *Greene Papers,* Vol. VIII, 475.
54. "Nathanael Greene to Henry Lee, June 29, 1781," Ibid., 473; also "Nathanael Greene to Charles Myddelton, June 29, 1781," Ibid.
55. "Thomas Sumter to Nathanael Greene, July 2, 1781," Ibid., 482.
56. "Francis Marion to Nathanael Greene, June 28, 1781," Ibid., 472
57. "General Greene to Colonel Hezekiah Maham, June 21, 1781," Ibid., 433.
58. "Nathanael Greene to William Washington, July 3, 1781," Conrad, *Greene Papers,* Vol. VIII, 486.
59. "Henry Lee to Nathanael Greene, July 3, 1781," Ibid., 486, 487.
60. Ibid., 488.
61. Lee, *Memoirs,* 383. Regarding the state of Rawdon's forces, see "Henry Lee to Nathanael Greene, June 22, 1781"; also "Nathanael Greene to Henry Lee, June 24, 1781"; also "Henry Lee to Nathanael Greene, July 2, 1781," Conrad, *Greene Papers,* Vol. VIII, 442, 452, 481.
62. "Henry Lee to Nathanael Greene, June 30, 1781," Conrad, *Greene Papers,* Vol. VIII, 477.
63. Lee, *Memoirs,* 383.
64. "General Francis Marion to General Greene, July 8, 1781, 'Whiteman's,' " Conrad, *Greene Papers,* Vol. VIII, 509.
65. "Nathanael Greene to Thomas McKean, July 17, 1781," Conrad, *Greene Papers,* Vol. IX, 27.
66. Ibid.
67. Kirkwood, *Journal and Orderly Book,* 19; Lee, *Memoirs,* 386.
68. Lee, *Memoirs,* 387; Lumpkin, *From Savannah to Yorktown,* 212.
69. Pancake, *This Destructive War,* 215.
70. Lumpkin, *From Savannah to Yorktown,* 227; Pancake, *This Destructive War,* 224.
71. "Nathanael Greene to Thomas Burke, August 2, 1781," Conrad, *Greene Papers,* Vol. IX, 126.
72. "Nathanael Greene to Thomas McKean, August 25, 1781," Conrad, *Greene Papers,* Vol. IX, 241.
73. Lee, *Memoirs,* 453; Rankin, *North Carolina Continentals,* 349.
74. "Isaac Hayne, American Patriot Hanged by the British," *John Adams Bennett, Kith and Kin,* John Stuart Adams, accessed July 11, 2013, http://www.milliganfamily.org/isaac_hayne.htm.
75. Conrad, *Greene Papers,* Vol. IX, 251-252.
76. "William Washington to Nathanael Greene, August 22, 1781," Conrad, *Greene Papers,* Vol. IX, 226.

77. "William Henderson to Nathanael Greene, August 25, 1781," Conrad, *Greene Papers,* Vol. IX, 245; "Officers of the Southern Army, August 20, 1781," Ibid., 217.
78. Lee, *Memoirs,* 456.
79. "Nathanael Greene to Lord Cornwallis, August 26, 1781," Conrad, *Greene Papers,* Vol. IX, 253.
80. Pancake, *This Destructive War,* 216.
81. "Nathanael Greene to Henry Knox, July 18, 1781," *The Cambridge Illustrated History of Warfare,* ed. Geoffery Parker (Cambridge, Cambridge University Press, 2008), 190, accessed July 10, 2013, Google Books, http://books.google.com/books?id=yqNj5BlEMtcC&pg=PA 190&lpg=PA190 &dq=.

Chapter Thirteen: Eutaw Springs

1. "William Pierce to St. George Tucker, July 23, 1781," Rankin, *The North Carolina Continentals,* 347.
2. "General Greene to Thomas McKean, September 11, 1781," *Greene Papers,* Vol. IX, 328-333; James Piecuch, "One of the Most Important and Bloody Battles that Ever Was Fought in America: The Battle of Eutaw Springs, September 8, 1781," Jim Piecuch, *Southern Campaigns of the American Revolution* (September 2006), 28, accessed July 7, 2013, http://southerncampaign.org/newsletter/v3n9.pdf.
3. "General Greene to Thomas McKean, September 11, 1781," *Greene Papers,* Vol. IX, 328-333.
4. Rankin, *The North Carolina Continentals,* 351.
5. "Stewart to Cornwallis, September 9, 1781." *Documents of the American Revolution,* Vol. 20, ed. K.G. Davis (Dublin, Irish University Press, 1979), 226-229.
6. Massey and Piecuch, *General Nathanael Greene,* 228.
7. Lee, *Memoirs,* 466.
8. Lee, *Memoirs,* 466; Conrad, *Greene Papers,* Vol. IX, 328-333.
9. Conrad, *Greene Papers,* Vol. IX, 328-333.
10. Lee McGee, "Most Astonishing Efforts," *Southern Campaigns of the American Revolution* (March 2006), 16, accessed July 7, 2013, http://southern-campaign.org/newsletter/v3n3.pdf.
11. Joshua Howard, "NC Continentals at Eutaw Springs," *Southern Campaigns of the American Revolution* (September 2006), 22-24, accessed July 11, 2013, http://southerncampaign.org/newsletter/v3n9.pdf.
12. Rankin, *The North Carolina Continentals,* 356.
13. Gibbes, *Documentary History of the American Revolution,* 149.
14. "General Greene to Thomas McKean, September 11, 1781," *Greene Papers,* Vol. IX, 328-333.
15. Gibbes, *Documentary History of the American Revolution,* 150.
16. Howard, "NC Continentals at Eutaw Springs," *Southern Campaigns of the American Revolution.*
17. Gibbes, *Documentary History of the American Revolution,* 151.

18. Both Henry Lee and Otho Williams stated that Greene ordered Washington to make the charge; see Lee, *Memoirs,* 469, for Williams's account; see also Robert Gibbes, *Documentary History of the American Revolution Consisting of Letters and Papers Relating to the Contest for Liberty, Chiefly in South Carolina,* Vol. II (Bedford, Applewood Books, 1853), 152, "Battle of Eutaw," Colonel Otho Williams, "Gen Greene now saw that Marjoribanks must be dislodged, . . . Therefore, orders were dispatched to Washington."
19. Lee McGee, "Most Astonishing Efforts," *Southern Campaigns of the American Revolution,* 15-33.
20. Lee, *Memoirs,* 469.
21. Pension application of George Hood [Va2].
22. Quote of Otho Williams in Gibbs, *Documentary History of the American Revolution,* 152.
23. Pension application of George Hood [Va2].
24. The exact layout of the thicket in relation to Marjoribanks's infantry is not known and to date no blackjack is to be found on this portion of the battlefield.
25. Pension application of George Hood [Va2].
26. Otho Williams's description, shown later in the text, describes the aftermath of the charge as seen from a distance implying that the woods were quite open and may have allowed such a formation.
27. John Marshall and Bushrod Johnson, *The Life of George Washington: Commander in Chief of the American Forces,* Vol. IV (Philadelphia, C. P. Wayne, 1805), 495, accessed March 31, 2012, http://books.google.com/books?id=1qkOAAAAQAAJ&pg=PA495&dq=. Marshall's biography is mostly anecdotal, but Marshall is known to have corresponded with John Eager Howard and William Washington.
28. Pension application of George Hood [Va2].
29. Pension application of John Chaney, S32177; Pension application of George Hood [Va2].
30. "William Washington to Nathanael Greene, September 8, 1781," Conrad, *Greene Papers,* Vol. IX, 306.
31. Johnson, *Sketches of Greene,* Vol. II, 228, 229.
32. Pension application of George Hood [Va2].
33. Pension application of Lorentz Miller, S31257. Trumpeter Miller was the head trumpeter of the 3d Light Dragoons and, along with Sgt. Major Perry, formed part of Washington's field staff.
34. Pension application of John Chaney, S32177. This was the same John Cheney who had nearly been killed by the Hessian Dragoon at Juniper Springs but was now healed and back for another go.
35. Johnson, *Sketches of Greene,* Vol. II, 228. Bracketed words by the author.
36. Joseph Johnson, *Traditions and Reminiscences: Chiefly of the American Revolution in the South* (Charleston, Walker and James, 1851), 300-305.
37. Johnson, *Sketches of Greene,* Vol. II, 229; Ward, *Delaware Continentals,* 462.

38. *The State Records of North Carolina,* Vol. XV, ed. Walter Clark (Goldsboro, Nash Brothers, 1898), 637.
39. Pension application of John Chaney, S32177.
40. Massey and Piecuch, *General Nathanael Greene,* 226.
41. Warnery, *Remarks on Cavalry,* 85-86.
42. Marjoribanks's command was involved in heavy fighting throughout the day.
43. Clark, *NC Records,* Vol. XV, 637.
44. Exact percentages are difficult to determine. Clark, *NC Records,* Vol. XV, 637.
45. "Nathanael Greene to Thomas McKean, September 11, 1781," *Greene Papers,* Vol. IX, 328-333.
46. Gibbes, *Documentary History of the American Revolution,* 151; Lumpkin, *From Savannah to Yorktown,* 219.
47. "General Greene to Thomas McKean, September 11, 1781," *Greene Papers,* Vol. IX, 328-333; Lee, *Memoirs,* 471.
48. Lee, *Memoirs,* 471, 473.
49. Pension application of George Hood [Va2].
50. Lee, *Memoirs,* 471.
51. Statement of Samuel Hammond, *Charleston Gazette,* January 30, 1826, rpt. in *Charleston Daily Gazette,* July 21, 1858.
52. John Eager Howard to William Johnson, 1822.
53. Gibbes, *Documentary History of the American Revolution,* 155. Bracketed words by the author. Samuel Hammond, later expanded on General Greene's sentiments and recalled a dinner Greene held for his officers a few days after the battle. The fight at Eutaw was of course the primary topic of conversation and Hammond claimed Lt. Col. Lee "confidently" aired his views on keeping at hand a ready reserve to help explain his own actions and lapses during the recent battle and stated "that every battle he [Lee] went into," had convinced Lee of the "usefulness and even the necessity of keeping up a respectable corps of reserve." To which General Greene replied, "dryly" in Hammond's opinion, "that he [Greene] had always understood the propriety and necessity" of a ready and waiting reserve, but "no officer ought to take upon himself that duty who was not specifically charged with it." See statement of Sarmuel Hammond, *Charleston Gazette,* January 30, 1826, rpt. in *Charleston Daily Gazette,* July 21, 1858.
54. Gibbes, *Documentary History of the American Revolution,* 154.
55. Gibbes, *Documentary History of the American Revolution,* 154; Stewart to Cornwallis Sept. 9, 1781," in James Piecuch, "The Battle of Eutaw Springs, Southern Campaigns of the American Revolution (September 2006): 25-37.
56. "Stewart to Cornwallis, Sept. 9, 1781," 25-37.
57. "General Greene to Thomas McKean, September 11, 1781," Conrad, *Greene Papers,* Vol. IX, 328-333; Lumpkin, *From Savannah to Yorktown,* 220.
58. John Eager Howard to William Marshall, 1822.
59. Johnson, *Life Of Greene,* Vol. II, 231.

60. Massey and Piecuch, *General Nathanael Greene and the American Revolution in the South,* 231.
61. Gibbes, *Documentary History of the American Revolution,* 155.
62. Quote from William Polk in Gibbs, *Documentary History of the American Revolution,* 155.
63. Lee, *Memoirs,* 479; John Eager Howard to William Johnson, ca. 1822; Otho Williams, *"Battle of Eutaw."*
64. "General Greene to Thomas McKean, September 11, 1781," Conrad *Greene Papers,* Vol. IX, 328-333.
65. Mauer, *Dragoon Diary,* 351; Lee, *Memoirs,* 478.
66. "William Washington to Nathanael Greene, September 8, 1781," Conrad, *Greene Papers,* Vol. IX, 306.

Chapter Fourteen: The War Winds Down

1. Haller, *William Washington,* 150; Mauer, *Dragoon Diary,* 341.
2. "Nathaniel Pendleton to Nathanael Greene, September 2, 1782," Conrad, *Greene Papers,* Vol. XI, 682.
3. Wilson, *Southern Strategy,* 63; Borick, *A Gallant Defense,* 5.
4. John Irving, *The South Carolina Jockey Club* (Charleston, Russell and Jones, 1857), 164, accessed July 22, 2013, Open Library.com, http://archive.org/stream/southcarolinajoc00irvi#page/n5/mode/2up.
5. Felix Warley, "In the Senate, December 16, 1794. The committee, to whom were referred the several petitions [for reform of representation; gives committee's report, amendedversion and votes] By order of the Senate," Felix Warley, C. S., *South Carolina Digital Collections, University Libraries,* accessed July 22, 2013, http://digital.tcl.sc.edu/cdm/singleitem/collection/bro/id/162/rec/16.
6. Haller, *William Washington,* 160.
7. Lee, *Memoirs,* 588.
8. Charles Royster, *Light Horse Harry Lee and the Legacy of the American Revolution* (New York, Alfred A. Knopf, 1981), 176-177.
9. "William Jackson to Major Alexander Garden at Philadelphia, September 1822 or 1823," *Williams-Chesnut-Manning Families Papers,* South Carolina Library, accessed August 24, 2013, http://lib.jrshelby.com/wmwashington.htm.

BIBLIOGRAPHY

Manuscript Sources

Bayard Papers, Maryland Historical Society
Thomas Addis Emmet Collection, New York Public Library
Peter Force Collection, Library of Congress
The Horatio Gates Papers, New York Public Library
Nathaniel Greene Papers, William L. Clements Library, University of Michigan
William Irvine Papers, Historical Society of Pennsylvania
The Papers of Henry Laurens, Historical Society of Pennsylvania
Charles Carter Lee Collection, Library of Virginia
Benjamin Lincoln Papers, Massachusetts Historical Society
Thomas Jefferson Papers, University of Virginia
George Washington Papers, Library of Congress

Newspapers

Charleston Gazette

Primary Sources

Allaire, Anthony. "Diary of Loyalist Lieutenant Anthony Allaire of Furguson's Corps." *Memorandum of Occurrences During the Campaign of 1780.* http://www.tngenweb.org/revwar/kingsmountain/allaire.html.

Brown, Stuart. *The Autobiography of James Monroe.* Whitefish, MT: Literary Licensing, LLC, 2011.

Burgoyne, Bruce, ed. *The Diary of Lieutenant Von Bardeleben and Other Von Donop Regiment.* Bowie, MD: Heritage, 2009.

Cannon, John. "Historical Record of the Seventeenth Regiment of Light Dragoons, Lancers: Containing an Account . . ." *Internet Archive: Digital Library of Free Books, Movies, Music & Wayback Machine.* John W. Parker. http://archive.org/stream/historicalrecor01canngoog.

Clark, Walter, ed. *The State Records of North Carolina,* Vol. 14. Goldsboro, NC: Nash Bros., Printers, 1886.

Collins, James Potter, and John M. Roberts. *Autobiography of a Revolutionary Soldier.* New York: Arno, 1979.

Commager, Henry Steele, and Richard Morris, eds. *The Spirit of 'Seventy-Six: The Story of the American Revolution as Told by Participants.* New York: Da Capo, 1995.

Cornwallis, Lord, and Ian Saberton. *The Cornwallis Papers: The Campaigns of 1780 and 1781 in the Southern Theatre of the American Revolutionary War,* Vol. IV. Tuscaloosa: University of Alabama Press, 1985.

"Documenting the American South: Colonial and State Records of North Carolina." University of North Carolina. http://docsouth.unc.edu/csr/index.html/document/csr14-0767.

Fawcett, William, Sir, trans. *Regulations for the Prussian Cavalry . . . 1757.* London: J. Haberkorn, 1757. Google Books. https://play.google.com/books/reader?id=yUYIAAAAQAAJ.

Fitzpatrick, John C., ed. "The Writings of George Washington from the Original Manuscript Sources, 1745-1799." *Washington Resources at the Virginia Library.* http://etext.virginia.edu/washington/fitzpatrick/.

Frederick, William. "Regulations for the Prussian Cavalry, 1757." *Google Books.* Trans. Sir William Fawcett. http://books.google.com/books?id=rC1EAAAAYAAJ.

Graham, William A. *General Joseph Graham and His Papers on North Carolina Revolutionary History; with Appendix: An Epitome of North Carolina's Military Services in the Revolutionary War and of the Laws Enacted for Raising Troops.* Raleigh: Edwards & Broughton, 1904.

Greene, Nathanael. *The Papers of General Nathanael Greene.* Edited by Richard K. Showman, Dennis Michael Conrad, and Roger N. Parks. Chapel Hill: Published for the Rhode Island Historical Society by the University of North Carolina, 1976.

Hayes, John T. *A Gentleman of Fortune: The Diary of Baylor Hill First Continental Light Dragoons 1777-1781, Volume Three.* Ft. Lauderdale, Florida: Saddlebag, 1995.

Hinde, Robert. *The Discipline of the Light-horse.* London: W. Owen, 1778.

Kirkwood, Robert. "Full Text of 'The Journal and Order Book of Captain Robert Kirkwood of the Delaware Regiment of the Continental Line . . .' " *Internet Archive: Digital Library of Free Books, Movies, Music & Wayback Machine.* http://archive.org/stream/journalorderbook00kirk/journalorderbook00kirk_djvu.txt.

Lee, Henry. "Memoirs of the War in the Southern Department of the United States." *Internet Archive: Digital Library of Free Books, Movies, Music & Wayback Machine.* http://archive.org/stream/memoirswarinsou04leegoog.

McKenzie, Roderick. *Strictures on Lt. Col Tarleton's History "Of the Campaigns of 1780 and 1781, in the Southern Provinces of North America."* London: Jameson, Strand, Faulder, et al., 1787. Google Books. http://books.google.com/books?id=nXNbAAAAQAAJ.

Seymour, William. "Seymour, William, Sgt. Maj., DE Rgt., Journal: 1780-'83." *Index Page. Documentary History of the Battle of Camden, August 16, 1780. (Also called Battle Near Camden and Battle of Gum Swamp.)* http://battleofcamden.org/seymour.htm.

Southern Campaigns of the American Revolution database at http://revwarapps.org/. The following pension applications of Revolutionary War veterans were accessed:
Pension Application of Alvin Mountjoy: W8471, Mary Fn50VA
Pension Application of George Hood [Va2]
Pension Application of GOARE (GORE), John (Elizabeth). W. 160
Pension Application of Guilford Dudley: W8681, Fn145NC
Pension Application of Henry Wells (Wales): S11712, Fn42DE
Pension Application of James Kelly: S1544
Pension Application of John Chaney: S32177, Fn42SC/NC
Pension Application of Jourdan Gilliam: R4037
Pension Application of Lawrence Everhart, S25068, with supporting statement of Cornet James Simmons, 3d Light Dragoons, in support of Sergeant Lawrence Everhart's Pension Application in 1805
Pension Application of Lawrence (Lorentz) Miller: S31257, Fn24VA
Pension Application of Richard Porterfield: W2341

Tarleton, Banastre. "Banastre Tarleton: 'The Campaigns of 1780 and 1781,' Index." *Welcome to Raptor.golden.net.* http://home.golden.net/~marg/bansite/campaigns/campaigns.html.

Tustin, Joseph. *Diary of the American War: A Hessian Journal: Captain Johann Ewald,* Vol. III. New Haven: Yale University Press, 1979. http://www.jaegerkorps.org/reference/Ewalds%20DIARY%20OF%20THE%20AMERICAN%20WAR.pdf.

Warnery, Emanuel Von. *Remarks on Cavalry.* London: Constable, 1997.

Washington, George, and Donald Jackson. *The Diaries of George Washington, Vol. II: 1766-1770.* Charlottesville: University of Virginia Press, 1976.

Washington, George, and John C. Fitzgerald. *The George Washington Papers at the Library of Congress, 1741-1799.* Library of Congress.

White, Joseph. *An Narrative of Events, as They Occurred from Time to Time, in the Revolutionary War: With an Account of the Battles, of Trenton, Trenton-bridge, and Princeton.* Charlestown, MA: 1833.

Wilkinson, James, and Abraham Small. *Memoirs of My Own Times.* Philadelphia: Printed by Abraham Small, 1816.

Young, Thomas. "Memoir of Major Thomas Young." *Orion,* November 1843. http://sc_tories.tripod.com/thomas_young.htm.

Young, Thomas. "Memoir of Major Thomas Young: 1764-1848." *SC Backcountry Loyalists and Rebels.* http://sc_tories.tripod.com/thomas_young.htm.

Secondary Sources

Adams, John, and Benjamin Rush. *The Spur of Fame: Dialogues of John Adams and Benjamin Rush, 1805-1813.* Indianapolis: Liberty Fund, 2001.

Addyson, Joseph. "Act II Scene IV," from *Cato: A Tragedy.*

Babits, Lawrence Edward. *A Devil of a Whipping: The Battle of Cowpens.* Chapel Hill: University of North Carolina Press, 1998.

Babits, Lawrence Edward, and Joshua B. Howard. *Long, Obstinate, and Bloody: The Battle of Guilford Courthouse.* Chapel Hill: University of North Carolina Press, 2009.

Baskin, Marg. "Lord Rawdon." *Archeological Reconnaisance & Computerization of Hobkirk's Hill.* Kershaw County Historical Society.

Bass, Robert. *The Green Dragoon: The Lives of Banastre Tarleton and Mary Robinson.* Orangeburg: Sandlapper Publishing, 2003.

Baxley, Charles B. "The Battle of Biggin Bridge." *Southern Campaigns of the American Revolution.* May 2005.

Bearss, Edwin C. *The Battle of Cowpens: A Documented Narrative and Troop Movement Maps.* Johnson City, TN: Overmountain, 1996.

Beeler, John. *Warfare in Feudal Europe, 730-1200.* Ithaca: Cornell University Press, 1971.

Borick, Carl P. *A Gallant Defense: The Siege of Charleston, 1780.* Columbia: University of South Carolina Press, 2003.

Buchanan, John. *The Road to Guilford Courthouse: The American Revolution in the Carolinas.* New York: Wiley, 1997.

Calmes, Holly. "Banastre Tarleton: A Biography." *Oatmeal for the Foxhounds: Banastre Tarleton and the British Legion.* http://home.golden.net/~marg/bansite/_entry.html.

Cochrane, Willard Wesley. *The Development of American Agriculture: A Historical Analysis.* Minneapolis: University of Minnesota Press, 1993.

Cope, Anne D., ed. *Swords and Hilt Weapons.* New York: Weidenfeld & Nicolson, 1989.

Cubbison, Douglas. "Ambush at Indian Field." *American Revolution.* July/August 2011.

Davis, Robert S. "Colonel Thomas Waters: Georgia Loyalist." *Southern Campaigns of the American Revolution.* September 2006.

DiMarco, Louis A. *War Horse: A History of the Military Horse and Rider.* Yardley, PA: Westholme, 2008.

Durant, John. "Virginia's Finest Horseman." *Sports Illustrated.* July 1956. http://sportsillustrated.cnn.com/vault/article/magazine/MAG1132077/1/index.htm.

Edwards, Elwyn Hartley. *The New Encyclopedia of the Horse.* New York: Dorling Kindersley, 1994.

Ellis, John. *Cavalry: The History of Mounted Warfare.* Newton Abbot: Westbridge, 1978.

Emmet, Thomas Addis. *The Battle of Harlem Heights.* New York: T. A. Emmet, 1907. *Columbia University Digital Collections.* http://www.columbia.edu/cu/lweb/digital/collections/cul/texts/ldpd_6219521_000/pages/ldpd_6219521_000_00000015.html?tog.

Fischer, David Hackett. *Washington's Crossing.* New York: Oxford University Press, 2005.

Foote, William Henry. *Sketches of Virginia: Historical and Biographical.* Philadelphia: William S. Martien, 1850.

Freeman, Douglas. *George Washington: A Biography,* Vol. IV. New York: August Kelley, 1948.

Galvin, John. *The Minute Men.* Washington, D.C.: Brassey's/AUSA, 1989.

Gibbes, Robert, ed. *Documentary History of the American Revolution Consisting of Letters and Papers Relating to the Contest for Liberty, Chiefly in South Carolina,* Vol. II. Bedford: Applewood, 1853. Google Books. http://books.google.com/books?id=3GIbrUCmgPUC.

Graves, Robert. *Sergeant Lamb's America.* New York: Random House, 1940.

Griffin, Martin I. J. *Stephen Moylan, Muster-master General, Secretary and Aide-de-camp to Washington, Quartermaster-general, Colonel of Fourth Pennsylvania Light Dragoons and Brigadier-general of the War for American Independence, the First and the Last President of the Friendly Sons of St. Patrick of Philadelphia.* Philadelphia, 1909.

Hall, John W. "Petit Geurre in Retreat." *Patriots of the American Revolution.* September/October 2011.

Haller, Stephen E. *William Washington: Cavalryman of the Revolution.* Bowie, MD: Heritage, 2001.

Haythornthwaite, Philip J. *Napoleonic Cavalry.* London: Cassell, 2001.

Howard, Joshua B. "Fortitude and Forebearance: North Carolina Continentals at Eutaw Springs." *Southern Campaigns of the American Revolution.* September 2006.

Irving, John. *The South Carolina Jockey Club.* Charleston: Russell and Jones, 1857. *Open Library.com.* http://archive.org/stream/south-carolinajoc00irvi#page/n5/mode/2up.

Jensen, Merrill. *The Founding of a Nation: A History of the American Revolution, 1763-1776.* New York: Oxford University Press, 1968.

Johnson, Joseph. *Traditions and Reminiscences, Chiefly of the American Revolution in the South,* Charleston: Walker & James, 1851.

Johnson, William. "Sketches of the Life and Correspondence of Nathanael Greene: Volumes 1 & 2." Google Books. http://books.google.com/books?id=m1VXYdFfeR8C.

Johnston, Henry P. "The Battle of Harlem Heights, September 16, 1776." Google Books. http://books.google.com/books?id=MTdCAAAAIAAJ.

Johnston, Henry Phelps. *The Battle of Harlem Heights, September 16, 1776: With a Review of the Events of the Campaign.* New York: Pub. for the Columbia University Press, 1897. Google Books. http://books.google.com/ books?id=MTdCAAAAIAAJ.

Jones, Caroline. "American Heritage." *Fox Hunting in America.* http://www.americanheritage.com/content/fox-hunting-america.

Kajencki, AnnMarie Francis. *Count Casimir Pulaski: From Poland to America, a Hero's Fight for Liberty.* New York: PowerPlus, 2005.

Keegan, John. *The Face of Battle: A Study of Agincourt, Waterloo, and the Somme.* New York: Penguin, 1983.

Ketchum, Richard. *The Winter Soldiers.* New York: Doubleday & Company, 1973.

Langguth, A. J. *Patriots: The Men Who Started the American Revolution.* New York: Simon and Schuster, 1988.

Lefkowitz, Arthur S. *George Washington's Indispensable Men: The 32 Aides-de-camp Who Helped Win American Independence.* Mechanicsburg, PA: Stackpole, 2003.

Loescher, Burt Garfield. *Washington's Eyes: The Continental Light Dragoons.* Fort Collins, CO: Old Army, 1977.

Lumpkin, Henry. *From Savannah to Yorktown: The American Revolution in the South.* Columbia: University of South Carolina Press, 1981.

Luvass, Jay. *Frederick the Great on the Art of War.* New York: Da Capo Press, 1966.

Marshall, John. *The Life of George Washington,* Vol. 4. Google Books. Edited by Bushrod Washington. http://books.google.com/books?id=1qkOAAAAQAAJ.

Massey, Gregory, D., and Jim Piecuch. *General Nathanael Greene and the American Revolution in the South.* Columbia: University of South Carolina Press, 2012.

Maurer, C. F. William. *Dragoon Diary: The History of the Third Continental Light Dragoons.* Bloomington, IN: AuthorHouse, 2005.

McGee, Lee F. "Battle of Rugeley's Fort." *Southern Campaigns of the American Revolution.* June 2005.

McGee, Lee F. "Greene's Cavalry at Hobkirk's Hill." *Southern Campaigns of the American Revolution.* June 2005.

McGee, Lee F. "Most Astonishing Efforts: The Continental Light Dragoons at the Battle of Eutaw Springs." *Southern Campaigns of the American Revolution.* March 2006.

Miller, Lillian B. *The Die Is Now Cast: The Road to American Independence, 1774-1776.* Washington, D.C.: Smithsonian Institution, 1975.

Miskimon, Scott. "Anthony Walton White: The Trials and Tribulations of a Revolutionary Dragoon." *Southern Campaigns of the American Revolution Cavalry Conference,* 2008.

Morrill, Dan L. *Southern Campaigns of the American Revolution.* Baltimore, MD: Nautical & Aviation Pub. of America, 1993.

Muir, Rory. *Tactics and the Experience of Battle in the Age of Napoleon.* New Haven, CT: Yale University Press, 1998.

Murphy, Daniel. "The Cavalry at Cowpens." *Southern Campaigns in the American Revolution* February 2006.

Murphy, Daniel. "Greene's Gamble at Hobkirk's Hill." *Military Heritage.* February 2012.

Murphy, Daniel. "Shock and Awe: Mounted Combat in the 18th Century." *American Revolution.* May 2009. Rpt. in *The Journal of the United States Cavalry.* June 2009.

Murphy, Daniel, and Ron Crawley. "Unknown Patriot: The Real Life Exploits of Lt. Col. James McCall." *Southern Campaigns of the American Revolution.* December 2006.

Neumann, George. *Swords and Blades of the American Revolution.* Texarkana: Scurlock Publishing, 1995.

Nolan, Louis Edward. *Cavalry: Its History and Tactics.* Columbia, SC: Evans and Cogswell, 1864.

Paine, Thomas. "The American Crisis." Independence Hall Association. *USHistory.org.* July 4, 1995. http://www.ushistory.org/paine/crisis/c-01.htm.

Pancake, John S. *This Destructive War: The British Campaign in the Carolinas, 1780-1782.* Tuscaloosa: University of Alabama Press, 2003.

Parker, Geoffery. *The Cambridge Illustrated History of Warfare.* Cambridge: Cambridge University Press, 2008. Google Books. http://books.google.com/books?id=yqNj5BlEMtcC.

Peterson, Harold L. *The Book of the Continental Soldier: Being a Compleat Account of the Uniforms, Weapons, and Equipment with Which He Lived and Fought.* Harrisburg, PA: Stackpole, 1968.

Piecuch, James. "The Battle of Eutaw Springs, September 8th, 1781." *Southern Campaigns of the American Revolution.* September 2006.

Piecuch, James. *Cavalry of the American Revolution.* Yardley, PA: Westholme, 2012.

Rankin, Edward S. "Lost Pages of Elmer's Revolutionary Journal." *Digital Antiquaria.* New Jersey Historical Society. http://www.digitalantiquaria.com/NJHS/All.html.

Rankin, Hugh F. *The North Carolina Continentals.* Chapel Hill: University of North Carolina Press, 1971.

Raphael, Ray. *A People's History of the American Revolution: How Common People Shaped the Fight for Independence.* New York: New, 2001.

"Rediscovering Hobkirk's Hill." The Kershaw County Historical Society. http://www.hobkirkhill.org/hobkirk/primary.aspx.

Renatus, Flavius Vegetius. "The Military Institutions of the Romans." *The Regimental Rogue.* Translated by John Clark, Lt. http://regimentalrogue.com/quotes/quotes_morale3.htm.

Royster, Charles. *Light-Horse Harry Lee and the Legacy of the American Revolution.* New York: Knopf, 1981.

Scotti, Anthony J. *Brutal Virtue: The Myth and Reality of Banastre Tarleton.* Bowie, MD: Heritage, 2002.

Selig, Robert A. *Hussars in Lebanon!: A Connecticut Town and Lauzun's Legion During the American Revolution.* Lebanon, CT: Lebanon Historical Society, 2004.

Smith, Digby George. *Charge!: Great Cavalry Charges of the Napoleonic Wars.* London: Greenhill, 2003.

Spring, Matthew H. *With Zeal and with Bayonets Only: The British Army on Campaign in North America, 1775-1783.* Norman: University of Oklahoma Press, 2008.

Stedman, Charles, *The History of the Origin, Progress, and Termination of the American War,* Vol. II. Rpt. in New York: New York Times and Arno Press, 1969.

Stephenson, Michael. *Patriot Battles: How the War of Independence Was Fought.* New York: Harper, 2008.

Thompson, Christopher. *Lannaireachd: Gaelic Swordsmanship.* Charleston: Booksurge Publishing, 2002.

Tiffany, Osmond. *A Sketch of the Life and Services of Gen. Otho Holland Williams, Read before the Maryland Historical Society.* Baltimore: Printed by J. Murphy, 1851.

Troiani, Don, Earl J. Coates, and James L. Kochan. *Soldiers in America 1754-1865.* Mechanicsburg: Stackpole Books, 1998.

Twohig, Dorothy, Peter Henriques, and Don Higginbotham. *George Washington and the Legacy of Character.* Fathom. Columbia University. http://www.fathom.com/course/10701018/session2.html.

Urwin, Gregory J. W. *The United States Cavalry: An Illustrated History, 1776-1944.* Norman: University of Oklahoma Press, 2003.

Van Doren, A., ed. "The Lost Pages of Elmer's Revolutionary Journal." *Proceedings of the New Jersey Historical Society* (October 1925): 412.

Wilson, David K. *The Southern Strategy: Britain's Conquest of South Carolina and Georgia, 1775-1780.* Columbia: University of South Carolina Press, 2005.

Wood, W. J. *Battles of the Revolutionary War: 1775-1781.* New York: Da Capo, 1995.

Wright, Louis B. *Everyday Life in Colonial America.* New York: Putnam, 1966.

ACKNOWLEDGMENTS

This work would not have been possible without the help of others. First and foremost is my wife Jennifer for her fantastic support throughout. Second, are my reenacting "pards" that I ride with in the modern day 3d Light Dragoons. It was only after riding with them for a number of years that I was able to form my opinions of what was and wasn't possible on an eighteenth-century battlefield. By no means is this book meant to be the end all on the subjects within. There are scores of qualified historians interested in the history of cavalry, William Washington, and the American Revolution, and I look forward to reading future works.

On the writing front the list is extensive. Bruce H. Franklin and his team at Westholme Publishing were terrific. Friend and author Charles Price was an unwavering supporter. Dr. Lawrence Babits was extremely generous and shared a number of letters from his private collection and continued to support me even when we reached different conclusions. William C. Mauer was always on hand with a quick answer, and I am also in debt to Sam Fore and Lee McGee. Charles Baxley and his Corps of Discovery, along with all the folks at *Southern Campaigns of the American Revolution* were instrumental, and Michael Scoggins at the *Southern Revolutionary War Institute* was a great help as well.

Also, special thanks go to Burt Cook who taught me how to fence with epee and sabre in period "D'Angelo" style, cavalry re-enactor Mike Kyle, who first put me on a horse at an event, and finally, my horse, "Call Me Jet Man," known to his closest friends simply as, Mick. I couldn't have done it without you, pal.

INDEX